Network+

Scott Reeves
Kalinda Reeves

Network+ Exam Cram
© 1999 The Coriolis Group. All Rights Reserved.

This book may not be duplicated in any way without the express written consent of the publisher, except in the form of brief excerpts or quotations for the purposes of review. The information contained herein is for the personal use of the reader and may not be incorporated in any commercial programs, other books, databases, or any kind of software without written consent of the publisher. Making copies of this book or any portion for any purpose other than your own is a violation of United States copyright laws.

Limits Of Liability And Disclaimer Of Warranty

The author and publisher of this book have used their best efforts in preparing the book and the programs contained in it. These efforts include the development, research, and testing of the theories and programs to determine their effectiveness. The author and publisher make no warranty of any kind, expressed or implied, with regard to these programs or the documentation contained in this book.

The author and publisher shall not be liable in the event of incidental or consequential damages in connection with, or arising out of, the furnishing, performance, or use of the programs, associated instructions, and/or claims of productivity gains.

Trademarks

Trademarked names appear throughout this book. Rather than list the names and entities that own the trademarks or insert a trademark symbol with each mention of the trademarked name, the publisher states that it is using the names for editorial purposes only and to the benefit of the trademark owner, with no intention of infringing upon that trademark.

The Coriolis Group, LLC
14455 N. Hayden Road, Suite 220
Scottsdale, Arizona 85260

480/483-0192
FAX 480/483-0193
http://www.coriolis.com

Library of Congress Cataloging-in-Publication Data
Reeves, Scott.
   Network+ exam cram / by Scott and Kalinda Reeves
     p. cm.
   Includes index.
   ISBN 1-57610-405-2
   1. Electronic data processing personnel--Certification. 2. Computer networks--Examinations Study guides. I. Reeves, Kalinda. II. Title.
QA76.3.R44   1999
004.6--dc21   99-25789
                                                      CIP

Printed in the United States of America
10 9 8 7 6 5 4 3 2

Publisher
Keith Weiskamp

Acquisitions Editor
Shari Jo Hehr

Marketing Specialist
Cynthia Caldwell

Project Editor
Toni Zuccarini

Production Coordinator
Kim Eoff

Cover Design
Jody Winkler
Jesse Dunn

Layout Design
April Nielsen

The Coriolis Group, LLC • 14455 North Hayden Road, Suite 220 • Scottsdale, Arizona 85260

ExamCram.com Connects You to the Ultimate Study Center!

Our goal has always been to provide you with the best study tools on the planet to help you achieve your certification in record time. Time is so valuable these days that none of us can afford to waste a second of it, especially when it comes to exam preparation.

Over the past few years, we've created an extensive line of *Exam Cram* and *Exam Prep* study guides, practice exams, audio training, and interactive training. To help you study even better, we have now created an e-learning and certification destination called **ExamCram.com**. (You can access the site at www.examcram.com.) Now, with every study product you purchase from us, you'll be connected to a large community of people like yourself who are actively studying for their certifications, developing their careers, seeking advice, and sharing their insights and stories.

I believe that the future is all about collaborative learning. Our **ExamCram.com** destination is our approach to creating a highly interactive, easily accessible collaborative environment, where you can take practice exams and discuss your experiences with others, sign up for features like "Questions of the Day," plan your certifications using our interactive planners, create your own personal study pages, and keep up with all of the latest study tips and techniques.

I hope that whatever study products you purchase from us—*Exam Cram* or *Exam Prep* study guides, *Practice Tests, Flash Cards, Personal Trainers,* or one of our interactive Web courses—will make your studying fun and productive. Our commitment is to build the kind of learning tools that will allow you to study the way you want to, whenever you want to.

Help us continue to provide the very best certification study materials possible. Write us or email us at **learn@examcram.com** and let us know how our study products have helped you study. Tell us about new features that you'd like us to add. Send us a story about how we've helped you. We're listening!

Visit ExamCram.com now to enhance your study program.

Good luck with your certification exam and your career. Thank you for allowing us to help you achieve your goals.

Keith Weiskamp
President and CEO

About The Authors

Scott Reeves is a Master Certified Novell Engineer (MCNE), Microsoft Certified Professional (MCP) in Windows NT, and Compaq Accredited Systems Engineer (ASE), who has worked in the networking field for over ten years. He is the Vice President of Operations at MicroAge Computer Center in York, PA. His department is responsible for hardware repair, LAN integration using Windows NT and NetWare, WAN connectivity to remote locations and the Internet, and wireless WAN networking.

Scott's personal interests include amateur radio (N3JGI), with an emphasis in the packet radio area using the GPS satellites to transmit moving position reports. He also has a rekindled interest in amateur astronomy.

Kalinda Reeves has fifteen years of experience writing research, business, technical, and engineering documentation for government, military, and civilian customers. Her focus is hardware and software writing. She has been a freelance writer for five years. Together, she and Scott wrote and published the book *NetWare 5 CNE: Integrating Windows NT*.

When she is not writing, Kalinda home schools her children and has a diversity of hobbies, which include amateur (ham) radio, gardening, all manner of crafts, and drama writing and directing.

Acknowledgments

We would like to extend our sincere thanks to the team at Coriolis for the hard work and guidance provided during this project. It takes a team effort to put a book into production, and we would like to recognize a few members of the team with whom we had close interaction. Thanks to Shari Jo Hehr for getting the project off the ground and to Toni Zuccarini for keeping us on track, coordinating the on-going circus, and providing us with motivation when we needed it. Thanks also to Bruce Owens for hammering out our sometimes questionable grammar practices. In addition, we need to thank Kim Eoff, who coordinated the production of this book; April Nielsen, the layout designer; and Jody Winkler and Jesse Dunn, who created the cover.

In addition, a heartfelt thanks to our children, Stephen, Jacqueline, Kathrine, and James, for their patience and understanding, without which we could never have accomplished this task. Most importantly, humble thanks to our Heavenly Father for anointing us with the understanding and knowledge that we needed to write this book.

Contents At A Glance

Chapter 1	The Network+ Certification Exam
Chapter 2	Network Structure
Chapter 3	Operating Systems
Chapter 4	Protocols
Chapter 5	Fault Tolerance
Chapter 6	Remote Connectivity
Chapter 7	Security
Chapter 8	ISO Open Systems Interconnect (OSI) Model
Chapter 9	Designing The Network
Chapter 10	Installing The Network
Chapter 11	Standard Operating Procedures
Chapter 12	Change Control System
Chapter 13	Network Support And Preventive Maintenance
Chapter 14	Troubleshooting And Corrective Maintenance
Chapter 15	Sample Test
Chapter 16	Answer Key

Table Of Contents

Introduction xv

Self-Assessment xxi

Chapter 1
The Network+ Certification Exam 1
    The Exam Situation 2
    Exam Layout And Design 3
    Using CompTIA's Exam Software Effectively 5
    Exam-Taking Basics 6
    Question-Handling Strategies 6
    Mastering The Inner Game 7
    Additional Resources 8

Chapter 2
Network Structure 11
    Network Structure 12
    The Network Medium 13
    Network Interface Cards (NICs) 20
    Routers 20
    Gateways 20
    Networking Models 21
    Topologies 22
    Duplexing 26
    Broadband And Baseband 27
    Practice Questions 28
    Need To Know More? 33

Chapter 3
Operating Systems 35
    Microsoft Windows NT Server 36
    Novell NetWare 40
    Unix 45
    Directory Services 47
    Network Clients 49
    Practice Questions 51
    Need To Know More? 54

Chapter 4
Protocols 55
    Internetwork Packet Exchange 56
    NetBEUI 59
    Internet Protocol 59
    TCP/IP 63
    Practice Questions 74
    Need To Know More? 84

Chapter 5
Fault Tolerance 85
    Disk-Level Fault Tolerance 86
    Server Fault Tolerance 89
    Tape Backup 89
    Removable Media 93
    Practice Questions 94
    Need To Know More? 98

Chapter 6
Remote Connectivity 99
    Encapsulation Protocols 100
    Point-To-Point Tunneling Protocol 103
    Integrated Services Digital Network 106
    Plain Old Telephone Service 108
    Modem Configuration 108
    Requirements For Remote Connectivity 110
    Practice Questions 111
    Need To Know More? 115

Table Of Contents xi

Chapter 7
Security 117
Security Model 118
Password Policy 122
Data Encryption 123
Viruses 124
Nonviral Destructive Programs 128
Preventing Virus Infections 129
Firewalls 130
Practice Questions 132
Need To Know More? 136

Chapter 8
ISO Open Systems Interconnect (OSI) Model 137
Layer 1: Physical Layer 139
Layer 2: Data Link Layer 142
Layer 3: Network Layer 148
Layer 4: Transport Layer 150
Layer 5: Session Layer 152
Layer 6: Presentation Layer 152
Layer 7: Application Layer 152
How The OSI Layers Work 152
DoD Network Model 153
Practice Questions 155
Need To Know More? 164

Chapter 9
Designing The Network 165
Evaluating Business Requirements 166
Determining Equipment Compatibility 166
Costing Out The System 167
Identifying Equipment Availability 169
Developing An Installation Plan 170
Developing A Migration Plan 173
Coordinating With Vendors 173
Practice Questions 175
Need To Know More? 181

Chapter 10
Installing The Network 183
    Getting Prepared   184
    Identifying And Configuring Network Components   185
    Staging The System   194
    Cabling Scenarios   195
    Implementing The Network   196
    Practice Questions   197
    Need To Know More?   204

Chapter 11
Standard Operating Procedures 205
    Cabling Configuration   206
    Client Configuration   206
    Server Configuration   207
    Peripherals Setup   207
    Network Setup   208
    Emergency Response   212
    System Change And Upgrade Approvals   216
    Practice Questions   218
    Need To Know More?   222

Chapter 12
Change Control System 223
    Document Network Baseline   224
    Contingency Plan   224
    Network Changes   225
    Housekeeping   228
    Practice Questions   230
    Need To Know More?   236

Chapter 13
Network Support And
Preventive Maintenance 237
    Developing A Maintenance Schedule   238
    Preventive Maintenance   238
    Monitoring Network And Server Health   243

Scheduled Testing   244
Upgrades   246
Practice Questions   248
Need To Know More?   252

Chapter 14
Troubleshooting And Corrective Maintenance 253

Preparation   254
Trouble Calls   256
Duplicating The Error   259
Troubleshooting   259
Network Troubleshooting   264
Diagnostics   272
Corrective Maintenance   280
Test The Solution   280
CM Follow-Up   281
Practice Questions   282
Need To Know More?   287

Chapter 15
Sample Test 289

Questions, Questions, Questions   290
Picking Proper Answers   290
Decoding Ambiguity   291
Working Within The Framework   292
Deciding What To Memorize   293
Preparing For The Test   293
Taking The Test   294
Practice Test   295

Chapter 16
Answer Key 317

Glossary 333

Index 345

Introduction

Welcome to the *Network+ Exam Cram*! This book aims to help you get ready to take—and pass—the CompTIA Network+ Certification Exam. This Introduction explains CompTIA's Network+ exam in general and talks about how the Exam Cram series can help you prepare for the exam.

Exam Cram books help you understand and appreciate the subjects and materials you need to pass CompTIA's Network+ Certification Exam. Exam Crams are aimed strictly at test preparation and review. They do not teach you everything you need to know about a topic (such as configuring network hardware and software). Instead, we (the authors) present and explain the questions and problems we've found that you're likely to encounter on a test. Our aim is to bring together as much information as possible about the Network+ exam.

Nevertheless, to completely prepare yourself for any CompTIA test, we recommend that you begin your studies with some classroom training, or that you pick up and read one of the many available study guides, including The Coriolis Group's Exam Prep series. We also strongly recommend that you exercise your knowledge of basic networking principles by putting together a few small networks. Try a hub network or a switched network using VLAN, and use a router to connect two locations, because nothing beats hands-on experience and familiarity when it comes to understanding the questions you're likely to encounter on a certification test. Book learning is essential, but hands-on experience is the best teacher of all!

The New Network+ Certification Exam

The Network+ Certification Exam is designed to certify the knowledge of networking technicians with 18 to 24 months of experience in the information technology industry. Ideally, you will have an A+ certification or equivalent knowledge before you pursue this certification. However, it is not mandatory.

The Network+ exam will test your skills and knowledge as they relate to the IT industry. The subject area is separated into two groups: your knowledge of networking technology, and your knowledge of networking practices. Although you will be tested in two areas, there is only one comprehensive test.

Taking A Certification Exam

Unfortunately, testing is not free. Each computer-based exam costs $185 ($135 if you are a CompTIA member), and if you do not pass, you must pay an additional $185 for a retest. In the U.S. and Canada, the Network+ Certification Exam is administered by Sylvan Prometric. Sylvan Prometric can be reached at 888-895-6116, any time from 7:00 A.M. to 6:00 P.M., Central Time, Monday through Friday.

To schedule an exam, call at least one day in advance. To cancel or reschedule an exam, you must call at least 12 hours before the scheduled test time (or you may be charged regardless). When calling Sylvan Prometric, please have the following information ready for the telesales staffer who handles your call:

➤ Your name, organization, and mailing address.

➤ Your Social Security number. Citizens of other nations can use their taxpayer IDs or make other arrangements with the order taker.

➤ The name of the exam you wish to take. (For this book, the exam name is "Network+ Certification Exam.")

➤ A method of payment. (The most convenient approach is to supply a valid credit card number with sufficient available credit. Otherwise, payments by check, money order, or purchase order must be received before a test can be scheduled. If the latter methods are required, ask your order taker for more details.)

When you show up to take a test, try to arrive at least 15 minutes before the scheduled time slot. You must bring and supply two forms of identification, one of which must be a photo ID.

All exams are completely closed-book. In fact, you will not be permitted to take anything with you into the testing area, but you will be furnished with a marker board and an erasable marker after you enter. We suggest that you immediately write down all the information you've memorized for the test.

In Exam Cram books, this information appears on a tear-out sheet inside the front cover of each book. You will have some time to compose yourself, to record this information, and even to take a sample orientation exam before you must begin the real thing. We suggest you take the orientation test before taking your first exam, but because they're all more or less identical in layout, behavior, and controls, you probably won't need to do this more than once.

When you complete a CompTIA certification exam, the software will tell you whether you've passed or failed. All tests are scored on a basis of 1,000 points, and results are broken into several topic areas. Even if you fail, we suggest you ask for—and keep—the detailed report that the test administrator should print for you. You can use this report to help you prepare for another go-round, if needed.

How To Prepare For An Exam

Preparing for the Network+ exam requires that you obtain and study materials designed to provide comprehensive information about networking technologies and practices. The following list of materials will help you study and prepare:

- **Study Guides** Several publishers—including Certification Insider Press—offer CompTIA study guides. We've reviewed them and found the Certification Insider Press, Sybex, and IDG Books Worldwide titles to be informative and helpful for learning the materials necessary to pass the tests. The Certification Insider Press series includes:

    - **The Exam Cram series** These books give you information about the material you need to know to pass the tests.

    - **The Exam Prep series** These books provide a greater level of detail than the Exam Crams.

    - **The Practice Tests** These books provide you with extra practice tests to help you prepare for the exam.

- **Classroom Training** Third-party training companies such as Wave Technologies and American Research Group (now called Global Knowledge Network) now offer, or will soon be offering, classroom training on Network+ and networking technologies. These companies aim to help prepare networking professionals to perform all phases of network skills and pass the Network+ Certification Exam. While such training runs upwards of $350 per day in class, most individuals find them to be quite worthwhile.

- **Other Publications** You'll find direct references to other publications and resources in this text, but there's no shortage of materials available on general networking practices. To help you sift through some of the publications out there, we end each chapter with a "Need To Know More?" section that provides pointers to more complete and exhaustive resources covering the chapter's information. This should give you an idea of where we think you should look for further discussion.

By far, this set of recommended materials represents some excellent resources for learning network technologies and general skills. We anticipate that you'll find that this book belongs in their company. In the section that follows, we explain how this book works, and we give you some good reasons why this book counts as a member of the recommended materials list.

About This Book

Each topical Exam Cram chapter follows a regular structure, along with graphical cues about important or useful information. Here's the structure of a typical chapter:

> ➤ **Opening Hotlists** Each chapter begins with a list of the terms and techniques that you must learn and understand before you can be fully conversant with that chapter's subject matter. We follow the hotlists with one or two introductory paragraphs to set the stage for the rest of the chapter.

> ➤ **Topical Coverage** After the opening hotlists, each chapter covers a series of at least four topics related to the chapter's subject title. Throughout this section, we highlight topics or concepts likely to appear on a test using a special Exam Alert layout, like this:

> This is what an Exam Alert looks like. Normally, an Exam Alert stresses concepts, terms, software, or activities that are likely to relate to one or more certification test questions. For that reason, we think any information found offset in Exam Alert format is worthy of unusual attentiveness on your part. Indeed, most of the information that appears on The Cram Sheet appears as Exam Alerts within the text.

Pay close attention to material flagged as an Exam Alert; although all the information in this book pertains to what you need to know to pass the exam, we flag certain items that are really important. You'll find the information that appears in the body of each chapter to be worth knowing, too, when preparing for the test. Because this book's material is very condensed, we recommend that you use this book along with other resources to achieve the maximum benefit.

In addition to the Exam Alerts, we have provided tips that will help build a better foundation for networking knowledge. Although the information may not be on the exam, it is certainly related and will help you become a better test taker.

Introduction **xix**

> This is how tips are formatted. Keep your eyes open for these, and you'll become a networking guru in no time!

➤ **Practice Questions** Although we talk about test questions and topics throughout each chapter, this section presents a series of mock test questions and explanations of both correct and incorrect answers. We also try to point out especially tricky questions by using a special icon, like this:

Ordinarily, this icon flags the presence of a particularly devious inquiry, if not an outright trick question. Trick questions are calculated to be answered incorrectly if not read more than once, and carefully, at that. Although they're not ubiquitous, such questions make regular appearances on the Network+ exam. That's why we say exam questions are as much about reading comprehension as they are about knowing your material inside out and backwards.

➤ **Details And Resources** Every chapter ends with a section titled "Need To Know More?", which provides direct pointers to CompTIA and third-party resources offering more details on the chapter's subject. If you find a resource you like in this collection, use it, but don't feel compelled to use all the resources. On the other hand, we only recommend resources we use on a regular basis, so none of our recommendations will be a waste of your time or money (but purchasing them all at once probably represents an expense that many network administrators and would-be network professionals might find hard to justify).

The bulk of the book follows this chapter structure slavishly, but there are a few other elements that we'd like to point out. Chapter 15 is a sample test that provides a good review of the material presented throughout the book to ensure you're ready for the exam. Chapter 16 is an answer key to the sample test that appears in Chapter 15. Additionally, you'll find a Glossary that explains terms and an index that you can use to track down terms as they appear in the text.

Finally, the tear-out Cram Sheet attached next to the inside front cover of this Exam Cram represents a condensed and compiled collection of facts, figures, and tips that we think you should memorize before taking the test. Because you can dump this information out of your head onto a piece of paper before answering any exam questions, you can master this information by brute force—you only need to remember it long enough to write it down when you walk into the test room. You might even want to look at it in the car or in the lobby of the testing center just before you walk in to take the test.

How To Use This Book

If you're prepping for a first-time test, we've structured the topics in this book to build on one another. Therefore, some topics in later chapters make more sense after you've read earlier chapters. That's why we suggest you read this book from front to back for your initial test preparation. If you need to brush up on a topic or you have to bone up for a second try, use the index or table of contents to go straight to the topics and questions that you need to study. Beyond the tests, we think you'll find this book useful as a tightly focused reference to some of the most important aspects of networking practices and skills.

Given all the book's elements and its specialized focus, we've tried to create a tool that will help you prepare for—and pass—the CompTIA Network+ Certification Exam. Please share your feedback on the book with us, especially if you have ideas about how we can improve it for future test-takers. We'll consider everything you say carefully, and we'll respond to all suggestions.

Please send your questions or comments to us at **cipq@coriolis.com**. Please remember to include the title of the book in your message; otherwise, we'll be forced to guess which book you're writing about. Also, be sure to check out the Web pages at **www.certificationinsider.com**, where you'll find information updates, commentary, and clarifications on documents for each book that you can either read online or download for use later on.

Thanks, and enjoy the book!

Self-Assessment

We included a self-assessment in this Exam Cram is to help you evaluate your readiness to tackle Network+ certification. It should also help you understand what you need to master the topic of this book—namely the CompTIA Network+ Certification Exam. But before you tackle this self-assessment, let's talk about concerns you may face when pursuing the Network+ certification, and what an ideal Network+ candidate might look like.

Network+ Engineers In The Real World

In the next section, we describe an ideal Network+ candidate, knowing full well that not all candidates will meet this ideal. In fact, our description of that ideal candidate might seem downright scary. But take heart: More than 90,000 CompTIA A+ technicians are already certified, so CompTIA certification is obviously an attainable goal. You can get all the real-world motivation you need from knowing that many others have gone before, so you will be able to follow in their footsteps. If you're willing to tackle the process seriously and do what it takes to obtain the necessary experience and knowledge, you can take—and pass—the certification test involved in obtaining a Network+ certification. In fact, we've designed this Exam Cram and the companion Exam Prep and Practice Test Exam Cram to make it as easy on you as possible to prepare for the exam. But prepare you must!

The same, of course, is true for other CompTIA certifications, including:

➤ A+ certification is a testing program that certifies the competency of entry-level service technicians in the computer industry. It consists of a Core exam and a DOS/Windows exam. It is targeted at computer technicians with six months of experience.

➤ Certified Document Imaging Architech is a testing program that is divided into sections that correspond to an imaging professional's areas of responsibility. The technologies include: Input/Capture, Display, Storage, Communications, Output, Standard Computing Environment,

Integration, and Management Applications, as well as areas such as pre-processing and paper handling.

The Ideal Network+ Candidate

Just to give you some idea of what an ideal Network+ candidate is like, here are some relevant statistics about the background and experience such an individual might have. Don't worry if you don't meet these qualifications, or don't come that close—this is a far from ideal world, and where you fall short is simply where you'll have more work to do.

➤ Academic or professional training in network theory, concepts, and operations. This includes everything from networking media and transmission techniques through network operating systems, services, and applications.

➤ Between 18 and 24 months of professional networking experience, including experience with Ethernet, token ring, modems, the OSI model, and other networking media. This must include installation, configuration, upgrade, and troubleshooting experience.

➤ Two-plus years in a networked environment that includes hands-on experience with Windows NT Server, Windows NT Workstation, Windows 95 or Windows 98, and NetWare. A solid understanding of each system's architecture, installation, configuration, maintenance, and troubleshooting is also essential.

➤ A thorough understanding of key networking protocols, addressing, and name resolution, including TCP/IP, IPX/SPX, and NetBEUI.

➤ A thorough understanding of NetBIOS naming, browsing services, and file and print services.

➤ Familiarity with key Windows NT-based TCP/IP-based services, including HTTP (Web servers), DHCP, WINS, and DNS, plus familiarity with one or both of the following: Internet Information Server (IIS) and Proxy Server.

➤ Working knowledge of NetWare 3.x and 4.x, including IPX/SPX frame formats; NetWare file, print, and directory services; and both Novell and Microsoft client software. Understanding the NetWare Client for Windows (NT, 95, and 98) is essential.

Fundamentally, this boils down to 18 to 24 months of work experience in a technical position involving network design, installation, configuration, and maintenance. We believe that well under half of all certification candidates meet these requirements, and that, in fact, most meet less than half of these requirements—at least, when they begin the certification process. But because others who already have been certified have survived this ordeal, you can survive it, too—especially if you heed what our self-assessment can tell you about what you already know and what you need to learn.

Put Yourself To The Test

The following series of questions and observations is designed to help you figure out how much work you must do to pursue CompTIA Network+ certification and what kinds of resources you may consult on your quest. Be absolutely honest in your answers, or you'll end up wasting money on an exam you're not yet ready to take. There are no right or wrong answers, only steps along the path to certification. Only you can decide where you really belong in the broad spectrum of aspiring candidates.

Two things should be clear from the outset, however:

➤ Even a modest background in computer science will be helpful.

➤ Hands-on experience in networking technologies is an essential ingredient to certification success.

Educational Background

1. Have you ever taken any Windows NT Administration or NetWare Administration training classes? [Yes or No]

    If Yes, proceed to question 2; if No, consider taking classroom training for these areas, or at the very least reading up on them. Microsoft provides a self-study system entitled *Microsoft Windows NT Network Administration Training: Hands-On, Self-Paced Training for Administering Version 4.0*, or you can read *Essential Windows NT System Administration*, by Aeleen Frisch (O'Reilly & Associates, 1998, ISBN 1565922743). For NetWare administration, you might try *NetWare 5 CNA/CNE: Administration and Design Study Guide*, by Michael G. Moncur, et al (Sybex, 1999, ISBN 0782123872).

2. Have you taken any networking concepts or technologies classes? [Yes or No]

    If Yes, you will probably be able to handle CompTIA's Knowledge of Networking Technology components. If you're rusty, brush up on basic networking concepts and terminology, especially networking media, the OSI Reference model, network security, TCP/IP fundamentals, and remote connectivity. Then, proceed to Question 3.

If No, you might want to read one or two books in this topic area. The two best books that we know of are *Computer Networks, 3rd Edition*, by Andrew S. Tanenbaum (Prentice-Hall, 1996, ISBN 0-13-349945-6) and *Computer Networks and Internets*, by Douglas E. Comer (Prentice-Hall, 1997, ISBN 0-13-239070-1).

3. Do you have practical networking experience? [Yes or No]

If Yes, you will probably be able to handle CompTIA's Knowledge of Networking Practices components. If you're rusty, brush up on basic networking practices by actually putting together a small network.

If No, consider some basic reading in this area. We strongly recommend a good general networking book, such as *Encyclopedia of Networking: Electronic Edition* by Tom Sheldon (Osborne McGraw-Hill, 1998, ISBN 0-07-882333-1). If this title doesn't appeal to you, check out reviews for other, similar titles at your favorite online bookstore.

Hands-On Experience

The most important key to success on the CompTIA Network+ test is hands-on experience, especially with Novell and Microsoft, plus a working knowledge of network devices. If we leave you with only one realization after taking this self-assessment, it should be that there's no substitute for time spent installing, configuring, and using the various networking products upon which you'll be tested repeatedly and in depth. If you have never worked with any of the networking products or operating systems mentioned earlier, you would be well advised to visit the CompTIA Web site (**www.comptia.org**) and find the nearest authorized training center and try to attend their classes.

Testing Your Exam-Readiness

Whether you attend a formal class on a specific topic to get ready for an exam or use written materials to study on your own, some preparation for the CompTIA certification exam is essential. At $185 a try ($135 for CompTIA members), pass or fail, you want to do everything you can to pass on your first try. That's where studying comes in.

For any given subject, consider taking a class if you've tackled self-study materials, taken the test, and failed anyway. The opportunity to interact with an instructor and fellow students can make all the difference in the world, if you can afford that privilege. For information about Network+ classes, visit **www.comptia.org/networkplus/index.htm** and click on the Training Resources link.

If you can't afford to take a class, visit the Training Resources page anyway for any pointers to free practice exams. And even if you can't afford to spend much at all, you should still invest in some low-cost practice exams from commercial vendors, because they can help you assess your readiness to pass a test better than any other tool.

We have included practice questions at the end of each chapter, plus a practice exam in Chapter 15 of this book, so if you don't score that well on the chapter tests, you can study more and then tackle the test in Chapter 15. If you want to take more practice tests, consider purchasing the *Network+ Practice Test Exam Cram* by Robert Gradante (Certification Insider Press, 1999, 1-57610-484-2).

Have you taken a practice exam? If you have, and you scored 68 percent or better, you're probably ready to tackle the real thing. If your score isn't above that crucial threshold, obtain all the free and low-budget practice tests you can find (this is a new certification so practice tests may be hard to find) and get to work. Keep at it until you can break the passing threshold comfortably.

When it comes to assessing your test readiness, there is no better way than to take a good-quality practice exam and pass with a score of 68 percent or better. When we're preparing ourselves, we shoot for 80-plus percent, just to leave room for the "weirdness factor" that sometimes shows up on CompTIA exams.

You should also cruise the Web looking for "braindumps" (recollections of test topics and experiences recorded by others) to help you anticipate topics you're likely to encounter on the test.

When using any braindump, it's OK to pay attention to information about questions. But you can't always be sure that a braindump's author will also be able to provide correct answers. Thus, use the questions to guide your studies, but don't rely on the answers in a braindump to lead you to the truth. Double-check everything you find in any braindump.

It is recommended to check the Microsoft Knowledge Base (available on its own CD as part of the TechNet collection, or on the Microsoft Web site at **support.microsoft.com/support/**) for meaningful issues that relate to the Network+ exam topics. We also recommend that you check the Novell Knowledge

Base (available on its own CD as part of the Support Connection collection, or on the Novell Web site at **support.novell.com/servlet/knowledgebase**) for issues that relate to the Network+ exam topics.

You should also check out the Cisco Web site at **www.cisco.com** and the Bay Networks Web site at **www.baynetworks.com** to familiarize yourself with the latest hub, switch, and router features. These sites contain many white papers on how to integrate these products.

One last note: It might seem counterintuitive to talk about hands-on experience in the context of the Network+ exam. But as you review the material for that exam, you'll realize that hands-on experience with networking media and technologies will be invaluable. Surprisingly, you'll also benefit from hands-on experience with Windows NT, NetWare, and network hardware.

Onward, Through The Fog!

Once you've assessed your readiness, undertaken the right background studies, obtained the hands-on experience that will help you understand the technologies at work, and reviewed the many sources of information to help you prepare for a test, you'll be ready to take a round of practice tests. When your scores come back positive enough to get you through the exam, you're ready to go after the real thing. If you follow our assessment regime, you'll not only know what you need to study, but when you're ready to make a test date at Sylvan. Good luck!

The Network+ Certification Exam

Terms you'll need to understand:
- √ Radio button
- √ Checkbox
- √ Exhibit
- √ Multiple-choice question formats
- √ Careful reading
- √ Process of elimination

Techniques you'll need to master:
- √ Preparing to take a certification exam
- √ Practicing (to make perfect)
- √ Making the best use of the testing software
- √ Budgeting your time
- √ Saving the hardest questions until last
- √ Guessing (as a last resort)

Exam taking is not something that most people anticipate eagerly, no matter how well prepared they may be. In most cases, familiarity helps ameliorate test anxiety. In plain English, this means you probably won't be as nervous when you take your fourth or fifth certification exam as you'll be when you take your first one.

Whether it's your first exam or your tenth, understanding the details of exam taking (how much time to spend on questions, the environment you'll be in, and so on) and the exam software will help you concentrate on the material rather than on the setting. Likewise, mastering a few basic exam-taking skills should help you recognize—and perhaps even outfox—some of the tricks and gotchas you're bound to find in some of the exam questions.

This chapter, besides explaining the exam environment and software, describes some proven exam-taking strategies that you should be able to use to your advantage.

The Exam Situation

When you arrive at the testing center where you scheduled your exam, you'll need to sign in with an exam coordinator. He or she will ask you to show two forms of identification, one of which must be a photo ID. After you've signed in and your time slot arrives, you'll be asked to deposit any books, bags, or other items you brought with you. Then, you'll be escorted into a closed room. Typically, the room will be furnished with anywhere from one to half a dozen computers, and each workstation will be separated from the others by dividers designed to keep you from seeing what's happening on someone else's computer.

You'll be furnished with a pen or pencil and a blank sheet of paper, or, in some cases, an erasable plastic sheet and an erasable felt-tip pen. You're allowed to write down any information you want on both sides of this sheet. Before the exam, you should memorize as much of the material that appears on The Cram Sheet (inside the front cover of this book) as you can, so you can write that information on the blank sheet as soon as you are seated in front of the computer. You can refer to your rendition of The Cram Sheet anytime you like during the test, but you'll have to surrender the sheet when you leave the room.

Most test rooms feature a wall with a large picture window. This permits the exam coordinator standing behind it to monitor the room, to prevent exam takers from talking to one another, and to observe anything out of the ordinary that might go on. The exam coordinator will have preloaded the appropriate CompTIA certification exam—for this book, that's the Network+ Certification Exam—and you'll be permitted to start as soon as you're seated in front of the computer.

All CompTIA certification exams allow a certain maximum amount of time in which to complete your work (this time is indicated on the exam by an onscreen counter/clock, so you can check the time remaining whenever you like). The Network+ exam consists of 65 randomly selected questions. You may take up to 90 minutes to complete the exam.

The CompTIA Network+ Certification Exam is computer generated and uses a multiple-choice format along with picking graphics from an exhibit. Although this may sound quite simple, the questions are constructed not only to check your mastery of basic facts and figures about networking essentials, but they also require you to evaluate one or more sets of circumstances or requirements. Often, you'll be asked to give more than one answer to a question. Likewise, you might be asked to select the best or most effective solution to a problem from a range of choices, all of which technically are correct. Taking the exam is quite an adventure, and it involves real thinking. This book shows you what to expect and how to deal with the potential problems, puzzles, and predicaments.

Exam Layout And Design

Some exam questions require you to select a single answer, whereas others ask you to select multiple correct answers. The following multiple-choice question requires you to select a single correct answer. Following the question is a brief summary of each potential answer and why it is either right or wrong.

Question 1

What layer is routing performed at in the OSI model?
- ○ a. Application
- ○ b. Network
- ○ c. Data Link
- ○ d. Transport

The correct answer is b. Routing is performed at the Network layer in the OSI model. The Application layer is where programs such as FTP and Telnet operate. Therefore, answer a is incorrect. The Data Link layer is responsible for taking information from the Network layer, generating packets, and sending them via the Physical layer across the network to the address of the destination device. Therefore, answer c is incorrect. The Transport layer manages the end-to-end control and error checking by providing an end-to-end connection between the source and destination nodes to ensure reliable delivery of data. Therefore, answer d is incorrect.

This sample question format corresponds closely to the CompTIA Network+ Certification Exam format—the only difference on the exam is that questions are not followed by answer keys. To select an answer, position the cursor over the radio button next to the answer. Then, click the mouse button to select the answer.

Let's examine a question that requires choosing multiple answers. This type of question provides checkboxes rather than radio buttons for marking all appropriate selections.

Question 2

A brouter works at which layers of the OSI model? [Choose the two best answers]

❏ a. Network
❏ b. Transport
❏ c. Data Link
❏ d. Application

The correct answers are a and c. A brouter does bridging, which is a Data Link layer function, and it does routing, which is a Network layer function. The Transport layer manages the end-to-end control and error checking by providing an end-to-end connection between the source and destination nodes to ensure reliable delivery of data. Therefore, answer b is incorrect. The Application layer is where programs such as FTP and Telnet operate. Therefore, answer d is incorrect.

For this type of question, more than one answer is required. Such questions are scored as wrong unless all the required selections are chosen. In other words, a partially correct answer does not result in partial credit when the test is scored. If you are required to provide multiple answers and you do not provide the number of answers that the question asks for, it will mark the question for you and indicate at the end of the test that you did not complete that question. For Question 2, you have to check the boxes next to items a and c to obtain credit for a correct answer. Notice that picking the right answers also means knowing why the other answers are wrong!

Although these two basic types of questions can appear in many forms, they constitute the foundation on which all the Network+ Certification Exam questions rest. More complex questions include exhibits, which are usually screenshots of network topologies. For some of these questions, you'll be asked to make a selection by clicking on the portion of the exhibit that answers the question.

Other questions involving exhibits use charts or network diagrams to help document a workplace scenario that you'll be asked to troubleshoot or configure. Careful attention to such exhibits is the key to success.

Using CompTIA's Exam Software Effectively

A well-known principle when taking exams is to first read over the entire exam from start to finish while answering only those questions you feel absolutely sure of. On subsequent passes, you can dive into more complex questions more deeply, knowing how many such questions you have left.

Fortunately, CompTIA exam software makes this approach easy to implement. At the top of each question is a checkbox that permits you to mark that question for a later visit. (Note: Marking questions makes review easier, but you can return to any question if you are willing to click the Forward or Back button repeatedly.) As you read each question, if you answer only those you're sure of and mark for review those that you're not sure of, you can keep working through a decreasing list of questions as you answer the easier ones first.

There's at least one potential benefit to reading the exam over completely before answering the trickier questions: Sometimes, information supplied in later questions will shed more light on earlier questions. Other times, information you read in later questions might jog your memory about networking facts, figures, or behavior that also will help with earlier questions. Either way, you'll come out ahead if you defer those questions about which you're not absolutely sure.

Keep working on the questions until you're certain of all your answers or until you know you'll run out of time. If questions remain unanswered, you'll want to zip through them and guess. Not answering a question guarantees you won't receive credit for it, and a guess has at least a chance of being correct.

At the very end of your exam period, you're better off guessing than leaving questions unanswered.

Exam-Taking Basics

The most important advice about taking any exam is this: Read each question carefully. Some questions are deliberately ambiguous, some use double negatives, and others use terminology in incredibly precise ways. The authors have taken numerous exams—both practice and live—and in nearly every one have missed at least one question because they didn't read it closely or carefully enough.

Here are some suggestions on how to deal with the tendency to jump to an answer too quickly:

➤ Make sure you read every word in the question. If you find yourself jumping ahead impatiently, go back and start over.

➤ As you read, try to restate the question in your own terms. If you can do this, you should be able to pick the correct answer(s) much more easily.

➤ When returning to a question after your initial read-through, read every word again—otherwise, your mind can fall quickly into a rut. Sometimes, revisiting a question after turning your attention elsewhere lets you see something you missed, but the strong tendency is to see what you've seen before. Try to avoid that tendency at all costs.

➤ If you return to a question more than twice, try to articulate to yourself what you don't understand about the question, why the answers don't appear to make sense, or what appears to be missing. If you chew on the subject for awhile, your subconscious might provide the details that are lacking or you might notice a "trick" that will point to the right answer.

Above all, try to deal with each question by thinking through what you know about networking essentials—the characteristics, behaviors, facts, and figures involved. By reviewing what you know (and what you've written down on your information sheet), you'll often recall or understand things sufficiently to determine the answer to the question.

Question-Handling Strategies

Based on exams the authors have taken, some interesting trends have become apparent. For those questions that take only a single answer, usually two or three of the answers will be obviously incorrect, and two of the answers will be plausible—of course, only one can be correct. Unless the answer leaps out at you (if it does, reread the question to look for a trick; sometimes those are the ones you're most likely to get wrong), begin the process of answering by eliminating those answers that are most obviously wrong.

Things to look for in obviously wrong answers include nonexistent commands, incorrect utility names, inconsistent conditions, and terminology you've never seen. If you've done your homework for an exam, no valid information should be completely new to you. In that case, unfamiliar or bizarre terminology probably indicates a totally bogus answer.

Numerous questions assume that you understand the network topologies and TCP/IP utilities inside and out. If your knowledge in these areas is well grounded, it will help you cut through many otherwise confusing questions.

As you work your way through the exam, budget your time by making sure that you've completed one-quarter of the questions one-quarter of the way through the exam period (or the first 16 or 17 questions in the first 22 or 23 minutes) and three-quarters of them three-quarters of the way through (48 or 49 questions in the first 66 to 68 minutes).

If you're not finished when 85 minutes have elapsed, use the last 5 minutes to guess your way through the remaining questions. Remember, guessing is potentially more valuable than not answering, because blank answers are always wrong, but a guess may turn out to be right. If you don't have a clue about any of the remaining questions, pick answers at random, or choose all a's, b's, and so on. The important thing is to submit an exam for scoring that has an answer for every question.

Mastering The Inner Game

In the final analysis, knowledge breeds confidence, and confidence breeds success. If you study the materials in this book carefully and review all the practice questions at the end of each chapter, you should become aware of those areas where additional learning and study are required.

Next, follow up by reading some or all of the materials recommended in the "Need To Know More?" section at the end of each chapter. The idea is to become familiar enough with the concepts and situations you find in the sample questions that you can reason your way through similar situations on a real exam. If you know the material, you have every right to be confident that you can pass the exam.

After you've worked your way through the book, take the sample test in Chapter 15. This will provide a reality check and help you identify areas you need to study further. Make sure you follow up and review materials related to the questions you miss on the sample test before scheduling a real exam. Only when you've covered all the ground and feel comfortable with the whole scope of the sample test should you take a real one.

TIP: If you take the sample test and don't score at least 68 percent correct, you'll want to practice further. If you need more practice, you might want to purchase the *Network+ Practice Test Exam Cram* (ISBN 1-57610-484-2), which contains additional tests.

Armed with the information in this book and with the determination to augment your knowledge, you should be able to pass the certification exam. However, you need to work at it, or you'll have to pay for the exam more than once before you finally pass. If you prepare seriously, you should do well. Good luck!

Additional Resources

A good source of information about CompTIA certification exams comes from CompTIA itself; and the best place to go for exam-related information is online. If you haven't already visited the CompTIA Web site, do so right now. The CompTIA Network+ home page resides at **www.comptia.org/networkplus/ index.htm** (see Figure 1.1).

Note: This page might not be there by the time you read this, or it might have been replaced by something new and different. Should this happen, please read the sidebar titled "Coping With Change On The Web."

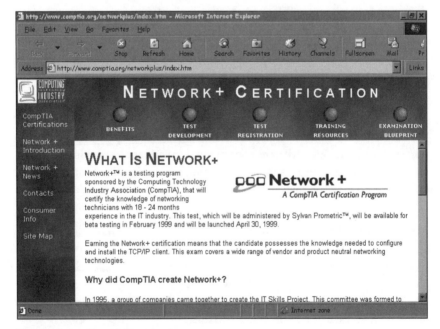

Figure 1.1 The Network+ home page.

The menu options at the top of the Network+ home page point to the most important sources of information in the CompTIA Network+ pages. Here's what to check out:

- **Examination Blueprint** Use this menu entry to review the skills and knowledge that will be tested on the Network+ exam, as well as the weighted percentile average of each area of questioning.
- **Benefits** This area discusses the benefits to the professional of taking (and passing) the Network+ Certification Exam.
- **Training Resources** This page lists the computer-based training materials that are endorsed by CompTIA, as well as some of the more frequently asked questions.

These are just the high points of what's available in the CompTIA Network+ pages. As you browse through them—and we strongly recommend that you do—you'll probably find other informational tidbits mentioned that are every bit as interesting.

Coping With Change On The Web

Sooner or later, all the information we've shared with you about the CompTIA Network+ pages and the other Web-based resources mentioned throughout the rest of this book will go stale or be replaced by newer information. In some cases, the URLs you find here might lead you to their replacements; in other cases, the URLs will go nowhere, leaving you with the dreaded "404 File not found" error message. When that happens, don't give up.

There's always a way to find what you want on the Web if you're willing to invest some time and energy. CompTIA's site has a site map to help you find your way around. Most large or complex Web sites offer a search engine. Finally, feel free to use general search tools—such as www.search.com, www.altavista.com, and www.excite.com—to search for related information. Although CompTIA offers the best information about its certification exams online, there are plenty of third-party sources of information, training, and assistance in this area. The bottom line is this: If you can't find something where the book says it lives, start looking around. If worse comes to worst, you can always email us. We just might have a clue.

Network Structure

Terms you'll need to understand:

- Coaxial, category 3, and category 5 cable
- Fiber-optics
- Unshielded twisted pair (UTP)
- Shielded twisted pair (STP)
- Full- and half-duplexing
- Gateway
- Local area network (LAN)
- Wide area network (WAN)
- Network medium
- Network interface card (NIC)
- Router

Techniques you'll need to master:

- Describing the appropriate conditions and advantages and disadvantages of coaxial, category 3, category 5, fiber-optic, UTP, and STP cable
- Understanding broadband and baseband communications
- Understanding how gateways work as default IP routers and as a method to connect dissimilar systems or protocols
- Identifying the characteristics of star, bus, mesh, and ring topologies
- Understanding both server-based and peer-to-peer networking
- Identifying the characteristics of segments and backbones
- Knowing the advantages, disadvantages, lengths, and speeds of 10Base2, 10Base5, 10BaseT, 100VGAnyLan, 100BaseT, and 100BaseTX

To understand how a network functions, you need to understand its physical components and how they interact and interconnect. Because all networks are not completely composed of new equipment, you might run across networks that are composed entirely of old equipment or are older networks that are integrated with new equipment. With this in mind, we discuss networks from their basic beginnings.

Network Structure

The structure of your network depends on the age of the network and associated equipment, the topology of both the network and the equipment associated with that topology, and the size of the network and the total number of segments. The network structure comprises the medium, the networking model, and the network topology.

Older networks were mainly 10Base2 (Thinnet), 10Base5 (Thicknet), category 3 (CAT 3), unshielded twisted pair (UTP), shielded twisted pair (STP), IBM Type 1 cable, or a combination of these, and were usually either Ethernet or token ring. As the networks grew, they were segmented into smaller sections and bridges connected those segments. Bridges have several types of ports that allow you to connect older, unstructured network media to newer network media.

Modern *local area networks (LANs)* follow a structured cabling scheme that allows for dynamic change. These LANs use mainly CAT 5 UTP cable that is terminated in an intermediate distribution facility (IDF), with multiple IDFs connecting to a main distribution facility (MDF). The connection from the IDF to the MDF is usually a fiber-optic cable connected to a layer 3 routing switch that distributes packets for the entire network.

The size of your network determines the best topology to use. Small business networks usually terminate in a centrally located closet where a shared media hub acts as the backbone. Medium business networks might have one or several IDFs connected to an MDF. In addition, one or several *wide area network (WAN)* connections will terminate in the MDF, which need not always require a layer 3 switch. Large business networks use the same scenario as medium business networks but add enterprise-level equipment to the scheme. Enterprise-level equipment has many ports and can transfer gigabytes of information.

Local Area Network

The LAN provides a means of communication between network nodes. Network nodes can consist of workstations with network interface cards (NICs), hubs, bridges, switches, routers, and servers. Category 5 and fiber-optic cable usually constitute the physical media on a LAN.

The category 5 cable (horizontal cable) is installed point to point between the workstation and the electronics that make up the network, such as a hub or a switch. The category 5 cable terminates to an IDF that must be within 100 meters of the workstation.

The fiber-optic cable connects all the electronic devices throughout the campus to an MDF. The MDF houses the enterprise category network equipment, such as switches capable of switching packets at a rate of 10 or more gigabits per second and routers with multiple ports connecting the enterprise together.

Wide Area Network

A WAN provides a means of communicating between geographically separated locations. The WAN consists of routers, channel service unit/data service units (CSU/DSUs), and leased lines. The router connects the LAN to the WAN, acting as a gateway between the LAN and WAN topologies. The LAN port on the router has to match the LAN topology and signaling characteristics, such as Ethernet. The WAN port is generally a serial connection to a CSU/DSU. The CSU/DSU connects to a T1 or FT1 that the local telephone company normally provides. The connection can be a dedicated point-to-point circuit between two locations, or it can terminate into a frame relay cloud. The *frame relay cloud* is a shared packet switch network, and all major telephone companies offer this service. Frame relay is distance insensitive and is the most cost-effective method of connecting multiple locations over a large geographic area.

The Network Medium

The *network medium* is the cabling medium—the "data packet highway" on which all information travels to get to a specific destination. The destination is usually a file server, a Web server, a database server, or the Internet. The network medium has certain characteristics that allow the packets to travel at a high rate of speed between the source and the destination. The medium is the foundation of all networks and is one of the most critical components of the network. An analogy of its importance is the difference between traveling on a country road and an interstate highway. The better the road, the faster you can safely travel.

A cable tester that can test all types of network media installed in an organization is a necessary piece of equipment. Cable testers are programmed with the specifications of the different types of media and can test either a range of parameters or specific parameters. During the installation of a cable plant, it is imperative that you test and certify all the cable runs. If a workstation is having a problem connecting to the network and it is localized to that workstation, use a cable tester to ensure the cable does not have any faults.

 Pay close attention to Table 2.1 and make sure that you learn the cable types and their respective lengths and speeds, specifically, 10Base2, 10Base5, 10BaseT, 100BaseTX, and 100VGAnyLan coaxial.

Coaxial cable, normally called *coax*, has a solid copper core surrounded by insulating material, a shield that doubles as a ground wire, a polymer casing for outer protection, and 50-ohm terminators at each end of the cable. This type of cable was deployed in the early days of networking. The two main types of networking are Thicknet and Thinnet, so called because of the size of the coaxial cable. The proper nomenclature for these types of networks is 10Base5 and 10Base2, respectively.

Table 2.1 Cable tolerances and specifications.

Cable Name	Cable Type	Maximum Length	Data Rate
10Base5	Coaxial	500 m per segment	10Mbps
10Base2	Coaxial	185 m per segment	10Mbps
10BaseT	UTP	100 m per segment	10Mbps
10BaseF	Fiber-optic	2 km	10Mbps
100BaseT	UTP	100 m per segment	100Mbps
100VG-AnyLan	UTP	100 m per segment	100Mbps Fast Ethernet
100BaseT4	4 pairs category 3, 4, or 5 UTP	100 m per segment	100Mbps
100BaseTX	2 pairs category 5 UTP or category 1 STP	100 m between the hub and the network node	100Mbps Fast Ethernet
100BaseFX	Fiber-optic	2 km	100Mbps Fast Ethernet
Category 3	UTP	100 m, including patch panel and patch cables	10Mbps Ethernet, 4 and 16Mbps token ring and VGAnyLan at 16MHz
Category 5	UTP	90 m (100 m, including patch panels and patch cables)	100Mbps Fast Ethernet at 100MHz

The advantage of coax cable over UTP is the greater length of the segments between repeaters and the greater total network length (see Table 2.1). The disadvantage is that you can stop the entire network by disconnecting the cable at any point in the network. Because of this, current technology is focusing on twisted-pair and fiber-optic rather than coax cable.

10Base5 (Thicknet)

Thicknet has a communication speed of 10 megabits per second (Mbps), uses baseband signaling, and is limited to a length of 500 meters per segment. 10Base5 is one of the original wiring types but is becoming less popular. Thicknet uses RG58 U cable, which has a solid copper core that accounts for the size and, therefore, the name of the cable. The transceivers for 10Base5 are fitted with connectors, or nonintrusive taps called *vampire taps*, which pierce the cable to allow you to attach devices to the network. However, you can place vampire taps at intervals no closer than 2.5 meters along the segment. In addition, you can place a maximum of only four repeaters between any two nodes on the network. You can have up to 100 nodes on any one segment, but are limited to only 3 Ethernet segments between any 2 end nodes.

10Base2 (Thinnet)

Thinnet has a communication speed of 10Mbps, uses baseband signaling, and is limited to a length of 185 meters per segment, for a total length of no more than 900 meters. Thinnet cable uses 50-ohm, RG58 A/U coaxial cable. Thin Ethernet networks consist of the following components: RG58 A/U cable, BNC connectors, BNC T-connectors, BNC barrel connectors, BNC 50-ohm terminators, and Ethernet repeaters. RG58 A/U cable size differs from Thicknet because it uses stranded copper. The difference in construction between the two makes it prohibitory to mix RG58 A with RG58 A/U.

With 10Base2 you can have a maximum of five segments but can populate only three of those segments. Each of those three segments can have a maximum of 30 nodes, with the repeater counting as one node. The shortest acceptable cable length between two nodes is .5 meters, and each end of the cable must have a terminator that matches the ohm value of the cable. T-connectors connect nodes to the Ethernet segment. You can disconnect the node from the network, but if you disconnect the T-connector from the cable, you will break the path to the terminator, and the entire network will stop functioning.

Twisted-Pair Cable

The telephone industry has used twisted-pair cable as the transmission medium for voice-grade networks for many years, but it is now becoming one of the preferred cable types for modern LANs.

The most common cable type is UTP, which has four individually twisted pairs of wires in a common sheath. The lay length of the twists is different for each pair to reduce cross talk. Lay length is the distance between the individual twists of wire. UTP may have a plenum-insulating jacket if the building in which it is installed has an open air-return system.

The first cable type that was designed specifically for structured cabling is STP. It has two individually shielded twisted pairs in a common outer sheath. The shielding minimizes cross talk and protects the cable from outside interference.

Twisted-pair cable is grouped into five categories, and a sixth category is under review for inclusion as a standard. These categories are detailed in Table 2.2.

Remember that although data rate (measured in Mbps) and frequency (measured in MHz) may look the same, they are two different transmission characteristics. *Frequency* measures the signal frequency whereas *data rate* measures how fast the signal can be sent down the line.

The standard wiring for twisted-pair cable installations follows the TIA/EIA-568-A or TIA/EIA-568-B structured cabling standards. Chapter 8 discusses CSMA/CD (carrier sense multiple access/collision detection) arbitration in detail.

10BaseT

10BaseT performs half-duplex transmissions through category 3, category 4, or category 5 UTP cable but uses only two of the four pairs. It uses RJ-45 connectors, with pins 1 and 2 receiving data and pins 3 and 6 transmitting data. Each pair is crossed over so that the transmitter at one end connects to

Table 2.2 UTP categories.

Category	Usage	Data Rate
1	Voice frequencies	Voice Only
2	100 ohm UTP, 4MHz transmissions	4Mbps
3	100 ohm UTP, 16MHz transmissions	16Mbps
4	100 ohm UTP, 20MHz transmissions	20Mbps
5	100 ohm UTP, 100MHz transmissions	100Mbps
Enhanced Category 5	100 ohm UTP, 200MHz transmissions	200Mbps

the receiver at the other. In addition, 10BaseT uses CSMA/CD. The maximum distance from the hub to a network node is 100 meters (328 feet).

100BaseX

100BaseX consists of two basic types of cabling schemes for twisted-pair wire—100BaseTX and 100BaseT4:

- ➤ **100BaseTX**   This cabling scheme is for Fast Ethernet CSMA/CD arbitration. 100BaseTX uses two of the four twisted pairs in a category 5 UTP cable in half-duplex operation. The maximum distance from the hub to a network node is 100 meters.

- ➤ **100BaseT4**   This cabling scheme uses all four pairs of category 3, category 4, or category 5 UTP cable for Fast Ethernet transmissions. The signal is transmitted and received across all four pairs, reducing the signal frequency and allowing you to use a lower category of twisted-pair cable. 100BaseT4 works in half-duplex operation and uses CSMA/CD.

Class I hubs accept 100BaseTX and 100BaseT4 signals and retransmit them, but Class II hubs will retransmit only 100BaseTX signals.

100VGAnyLan

This is an alternative to the Fast Ethernet standard and adheres to the IEEE 802.12 standard. It is based on a demand-priority access scheme that provides higher performance than the CSMA/CD associated with Ethernet. However, it does support both Ethernet and token ring frame formats. It uses two or four pairs of category 3, category 4, or category 5 UTP.

Category 3 Unshielded Twisted Pair Cable (CAT 3 UTP)

Category 3 UTP cable is rated for signals of 16MHz or less. It has four pairs of wires with a lay length of three to four twists per foot. It supports 10Mbps Ethernet, 4Mbps and 16Mbps token ring, and 100VGAnyLAN networks. Individual cable runs should not exceed 100 meters, including the patch panel and patch cables.

Category 5 Unshielded Twisted Pair Cable (CAT 5 UTP)

Category 5 UTP cable has four pairs of wires with a lay length of eight twists per foot. It is rated for signals of 100MHz or less and supports 100Mbps Fast Ethernet. Individual cable runs should not exceed 100 meters, including the patch panel and patch cables. All components, such as the patch panels, connectors, wall plates, and patch cables in the network, must be rated for category 5 compliance.

Fiber-Optic Cable

Fiber-optic cable is composed of a chemically formed glass and is slightly thicker than a human hair. Because fiber-optic cable uses reflected photon (light) energy instead of an electromagnetic charge to transmit its signal, it is resistant to electromagnetic interference. Fiber-optic cable does not radiate an electromagnetic field, so tapping into the fiber-optic strand is difficult because it will bring down everything that is on that cable run. This makes fiber-optic appropriate for deployment in high-security environments. Signals transmitted over fiber-optic cable can travel greater distances, with less signal degradation, than can signals transmitted over copper wire. An "F" or "FX" suffix represents a fiber-optic cable suitable for Ethernet. The two types of fiber-optic cable are single mode and multimode.

Single-Mode Fiber-Optic Cable

Single-mode fiber-optic cable uses laser for signal transmission. Signals transmitted by laser travel much farther than signals transmitted by diodes over multimode fiber. Telephone companies and industries that provide communications over large geographical areas commonly deploy laser transmitters.

Multimode Fiber-Optic Cable

Multimode fiber-optic cable uses diode transmitters and is used mainly in LAN and campus environments, up to a distance of 2 kilometers. Multimode fiber uses two types of transmitters, most of which are diodes. The most common multimode fiber-optic cable is 62.5/125—the core alone is 62.5 microns, but is 125 microns with its cladding.

Other Media

In addition to the cabling plant, you must also take into account the patch panels, patch cables, and crossover cables when estimating the total length of the cable runs and segment lengths. These elements are described in the following subsections.

 Remember that you must include the length of the patch cables when you are calculating the overall cable length.

Patch Cables

Patch cables can connect computers to UTP faceplates, or connect a patch panel to a network device, such as a hub or switch. Patch cables are constructed from stranded copper to allow flexibility in use. Because the high-frequency characteristics of flexible patching cables are worse than those

Network Structure

of solid conductor cables used for fixed installation, you should keep them as short as possible. Patch cables should also be of the same overall construction as the floor wiring that they serve, and cable types should not be mixed, such as an unshielded patch cable serving a shielded cable drop. To make a patch cable, follow these steps:

1. Cut the UTP cable to the desired length.
2. Strip the outer sheathing of the cable and order the wires (pins) in this sequence: orange/white (1), orange (2), green/white (3), blue (4), blue/white (5), green (6), brown/white (7), and brown (8).
3. Crimp two RJ-45 connectors onto each end.

Patch Panels

Patch panels allow flexibility within the structured cabling system and are used for either horizontal patching, which reroutes service between desks, or vertical patching, which reroutes service between floors. Although patch panels are grouped into four categories, we are only concerned with two: cable patching and fiber patching. Cable patching is more common in a structured cabling environment. Fiber patching performs linking by fiber-patching cables.

Crossover Cables

Crossover cables connect two network devices together, such as two hubs, two computers without a hub, two switches, or a hub and a switch. A crossover cable is the same as a patch cable, except that you switch (cross) two pairs of wires before you crimp on the RJ-45 connector. To construct a crossover cable, follow the steps outlined in making a patch cable, except switch pins 1 and 3 and pins 2 and 6 on one end of the cable and then crimp on the RJ-45 connector.

It is a good idea to always have a crossover cable available. There will be times when it is necessary to connect two network devices together or two computers together without using a hub. In this case, a crossover cable is invaluable.

Know how to make a crossover cable, what the pin-out is, and what the function of a crossover cable is. The pin-out (the order that the colored strands of wire are in) is: green/white (3), green (6), orange/white (1), blue (4), blue/white (5), orange (2), brown/white(7), and brown (8) on one end of the cable. The other end of the cable should be made according to the instructions in this chapter under the Patch Cables heading.

Network Interface Cards (NICs)

A network interface card (NIC) is the only layer 1 (Physical layer) device that is actually inside a computer. NICs provide the connection between the computer and the network hardware. They are especially designed for the different network types, such as Ethernet and token ring, and have different connectors for specific medium types. The NIC comes from the manufacturer with a preinstalled media access control (MAC) address.

Remember that the MAC address is preinstalled by the manufacturer onto the NIC.

Routers

Routers connect similar and heterogeneous network segments into internetworks, allowing each interconnected network to retain its subnetwork address and broadcast characteristics while allowing the networks to communicate through the router connections to other networks. Routers will be covered in detail in Chapter 8.

Gateways

A gateway is a network device that acts as a translator between two systems that do not communicate using the same protocols. It is very similar in concept to a translator who hears one side of the communication and translates it into another language. Gateways can provide some security functions, such as acting as routers and firewalls. Most protocol gateways operate at the Application layer of the Open Systems Interconnect (OSI) model. The following sections discuss several types of the most common gateways.

A gateway (not a default IP gateway) connects two separate systems that do not communicate using the same protocol.

Internet Gateway

The IT industry deploys three types of Internet gateways: the standard router, the firewall gateway, and the proxy server.

> ➤ **Standard router** The most common gateway for access to the Internet. Initially, it offered basic connectivity to external networks but eventually had to implement TCP/IP port filtering for network security.

Network Structure

➤ **Firewall gateway** Offers a greater level of security from external intrusion and provides greater protection for trusted networks.

➤ **Proxy server** Acts as an intermediate between trusted and nontrusted networks. It receives all internal requests for Internet access and passes those requests on to the Internet.

All TCP/IP networks that are connected to an external network must have a gateway specified at the host for communication beyond the local subnet to take place.

Simple Mail Transfer Protocol Gateway

The *Simple Mail Transfer Protocol (SMTP)* gateway is the main email transport for Internet email. The SMTP gateway uses Domain Name System (DNS) addressing to deliver the mail to the correct location throughout the Internet. An example of an email address is **webmaster@coriolis.com**. The SMTP gateway forwards the mail to the mail server on the coriolis.com domain. The server transmits mail to a client through POP3 by using the DNS to direct the mail, whereas SMTP transfers the mail to the mail servers on the Internet.

Remember that POP3 transfers mail to the Internet client and that SMTP is the protocol that the client uses to attach to the Internet mail server.

System Network Architecture Gateway

The *System Network Architecture (SNA)* gateway translates LAN protocols—such as TCP/IP, IPX, and NetBEUI—to IBM's SNA protocol. IBM deploys the SNA protocol on its midrange and mainframe computers. Because TCP/IP is fast becoming the industry-standard protocol, IBM and other third-party vendors have developed applications that use TCP/IP to communicate to the midrange and mainframe computers.

Networking Models

The resources that employees need to access determine the type of network that a company needs. In most cases, companies deploy client/server-based networks because they can provide security, disaster recovery, fault tolerance, resource sharing, and many other capabilities in a centrally managed server.

Client/Server-Based Networking

In a client/server network, the data, print queues, data backup, shared modems, and security are stored on a central server, such as Windows NT, Novell, or Unix. The workstations connect to the server and receive a security login prompt. The username and password determine the level of access that the workstations have to the system, according to their user rights and profile restrictions. The advantages of a server-based network are ease of management and central control of critical company data.

Peer-To-Peer Networking

Peer-to-peer networks decentralize all data access and security control, allowing each machine on the network to serve as both server and workstation. Each workstation must locally enforce access control through local security tools. Peer-to-peer networks generally have less security than server-based networks. A peer-to-peer network is acceptable for a small office or department that does not require the checks and balances that a server-based network offers. However, most shared applications require a server-based network, thus requiring small offices and departments to deploy more server-based networks than peer-to-peer networks.

> Peer-to-peer networks can share files and printers like a client/server network does, but they lack the functionality and security of a server.

Topologies

You should design the topology of your network on the basis of the size and use of the network, and always remember to design room for growth into the network. Design the electronics to maximize the speed of the media and to segment the network into smaller workgroups. Larger networks will use several different types of topologies to accomplish different goals.

Star

The star topology is so named because all the devices connect individually to a central hub at the local wiring closet (the IDF or MDF). The simplest type of star topology has workstations connected to a hub and the cable acts as a point-to-point connection between the workstations and the hub. If a break occurs in the cable, the workstation is the only network node affected. Because of its simple, straightforward design, the star topology lets you make equipment changes at one location. The star topology is the basis for structured cabling systems and can be combined with a bus, mesh, ring, or hierarchical star topology to form a

Network Structure   23

LAN or a WAN. It is usually configured so that lines terminate within a multiaccess unit (MAU), hub, or switch. It is also well suited to carrying out polling mechanisms for multiple access from the central location to outlying nodes (see Figure 2.1).

Mesh

Mesh networks are characterized by multiple paths to the same point, connecting one set of routers to other routers. To get an idea of how a mesh network is connected, imagine a net with its many cross-connecting segments. The two types of mesh topologies are the simple mesh and the fully interconnected mesh. Many large organizations employ mesh topologies for their WANs. The largest mesh network is the Internet (see Figure 2.2).

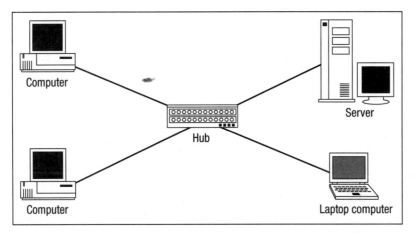

Figure 2.1 Star topology.

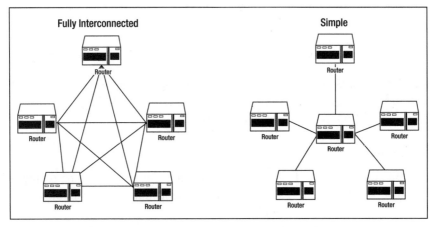

Figure 2.2 Mesh topologies.

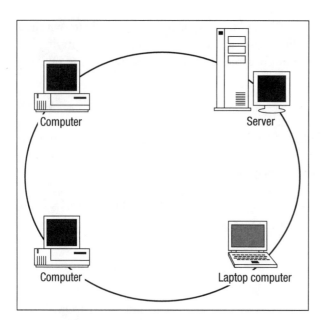

Figure 2.3 Ring topology.

Ring

The most common type of ring topology is the token ring network (see Figure 2.3). In a token ring topology, an electronic token is passed around the network. When a station receives the token, it then has the authorization to transmit and receive data. The network nodes are connected to an MAU device that has a collapsed ring inside it. It also has special circuitry to detect when a device is connected to a port and allows the device into the ring or shuts the device out of the ring. The early token ring networks were 4Mbps, but current token ring networks operate at 16Mbps. The IEEE 802.5 standard defines the token ring topology.

 Remember that the network topologies are named like their configuration. A mesh network has multiple paths to many points, like a screen mesh; a ring network looks like a ring; and a star topology has a central location with "legs" going out from the center like points on a star.

Segment

A segment is a separate LAN broadcast domain. The most common segmentation device is a switch. A switch creates segments that are logically separated from other segments, yet are physically connected to the same network. The two types of segments are basic segments and complex segments.

Backbone

In a hierarchical network structure, a high-speed backbone connects the servers while the workstations connect to shared media in a star configuration. A backbone structure is beneficial when several servers in a campus environment are remotely located and they all need access to the high-speed backbone. If all the servers are in a central location, you should attach them directly to a high-speed switch. Fiber distributed data interface (FDDI) and asynchronous transfer mode (ATM) are the usual choices for high-speed backbones (see Figure 2.4).

Bus

A bus topology is a single backbone cable that interconnects all the workstations on a LAN. The bus structure provides simultaneous access to a central bus by several nodes and is the most commonly used networking structure in office LANs. Tree topologies are also forms of bus structures. This was the main type of network in the early days of Ethernet. In today's network environment, you might implement a bus topology to connect network equipment that would connect workstations in a star topology. Its main drawback is that if a break occurs in the cable, it takes the whole backbone segment down, and all workstations will lose connection with the network (see Figure 2.5).

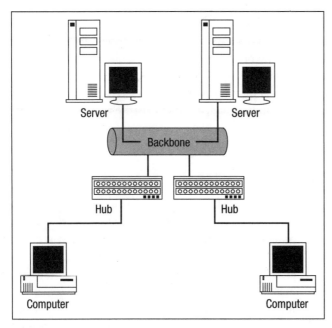

Figure 2.4 Backbone topology.

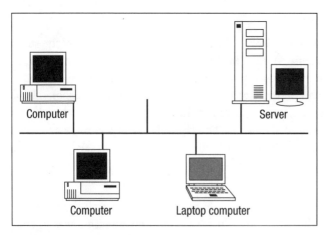

Figure 2.5 Bus topology.

Duplexing

Duplexing refers to the send and receive criteria of the medium, which is like a highway on which communications signals travel. The two types of duplexing are half duplex and full duplex.

Half-Duplex Transmission

Half-duplex transmission allows data to flow in only one direction at a time. UTP network topologies are rated for 100Mbps, which is half-duplex operation. As an analogy, if the medium is a road and your signal is the car, half-duplex operation is like a narrow mountain pass. If one car (the transmit signal) is traveling in one direction on the road, another car (the receive signal) cannot pass in the opposite direction. It must wait for the transmit signal to complete before it can travel on the same road.

Full-Duplex Transmission

Full-duplex transmission is one method of increasing network speed. For full-duplex transmission, the signal must be a point-to-point connection between the two pieces of equipment and cannot be connected to a shared-access medium, such as a hub. In a standard Ethernet and Fast Ethernet network, only two pairs of wires are utilized. Such transmission is based on the CSMA/CD network arbitration scheme. Full duplex uses all four pairs of wires in a category 5 cable. Each piece of equipment uses different wire pairs to transmit and receive data. This allows simultaneous communications between the two pieces of equipment, the design of which must specifically allow full-duplex operation. To continue our previous analogy, full duplex is a two-way road in which two signals can pass in opposite directions at the same time.

Broadband And Baseband

Broadband transmissions are analog transmissions that can handle a large number of frequencies. *Broadband networks* allow multiple, simultaneous transmissions on different frequencies. The most common broadband network is cable television. Broadband networks can span greater distances than baseband networks and can transmit in the gigabit range.

Baseband networks apply direct current to the cable to transmit digital signals. The signal is either a high-voltage or a low-voltage pulse that represents a binary 1 or 0. Signals can travel limited distances over a baseband network before they become degraded beyond use. In addition, baseband networks are susceptible to outside interference from electric fields generated by fluorescent lights or electric motors. The higher the data rate, the more susceptible to interference the baseband network is. Baseband networks have stringent guidelines for distance, cable types, shielding, and other criteria to ensure a successful network implementation. Two examples of baseband networks are Ethernet and token ring.

Practice Questions

Question 1

What type of network methodology allows all the computers to act as both workstations and servers?

- a. Client/server
- b. Hybrid mesh
- c. Peer-to-peer
- d. Switched network

The correct answer is c. A peer-to-peer environment has a protocol installed that allows all the workstations to share files and printers. Because file and print sharing is the basic function of a network operating system, a peer-to-peer network can be viewed as a network in which all the workstations are servers. The NetBEUI protocol from Microsoft allows peer-to-peer and client/server access using the same protocol. It combines transport and broadcast names (NetBIOS) as one entry. Its self-tuning nature makes it ideal for small networks; however, its broadcast nature makes it unsuitable for large networks. Switched networks and hybrid mesh networks are networking topologies; therefore answers b and d are incorrect. In a client/server network, the workstations connect to a central server for file and print sharing. Therefore, answer a is incorrect.

Question 2

What network device is responsible for translating from one protocol to another?

- a. Hub
- b. Switch
- c. Bridge
- d. Router
- e. Gateway

The correct answer is e. A gateway is a network device that translates between two networks that do not use the same protocols or language. The most common type of gateway is the SNA gateway. It translates from such protocols as

IPX and TCP/IP to the SNA protocol. A hub, switch, and bridge are all network devices that retransmit packets without looking at the protocol in the packet. Therefore answers a, b, and c are incorrect. A router is used to connect remote locations to a central location such as a corporate site, frame relay cloud, or the Internet using the same protocol throughout the network. Therefore answer d is incorrect.

Question 3

> What type of coaxial Ethernet media supports a maximum segment length of 185 meters?
>
> ○ a. 10Base5
> ○ b. 10BaseT
> ○ c. 10BaseFX
> ○ d. 10Base2
> ○ e. 10Base185

The correct answer is d. 10Base2, or Thinnet, uses 50-ohm RG58 A/U coaxial cable and has a maximum distance of 185 meters. 10Base5, or Thicknet, is the other type of coaxial cable, and it has a maximum distance of 500 meters. Therefore, answer a is incorrect. 10BaseT uses UTP and 10BaseFX uses fiber-optic cable; therefore answers b and c are incorrect. 10Base185 does not exist; therefore answer e is incorrect.

Question 4

> What type of network has multiple connections to one node and is similar in design to the Internet?
>
> ○ a. Star
> ○ b. Mesh
> ○ c. Bus
> ○ d. Ring

The correct answer is b. A mesh network is designed with redundancy built into it; it has two or more paths to the same point. The Internet is a mesh network, and the major carriers have several paths of redundancy built into it. The redundancy can be configured to provide load balancing and fail-over backup. Star, bus, and ring networks are representations of LAN topologies that are designed for a single connection to a shared medium; therefore answers a, c, and d are incorrect.

Question 5

What is the best media to use when connecting to a remote building that is more than 1 mile away from the main building?

- ○ a. 10Base5
- ○ b. 10Base2
- ○ c. 10Base185
- ○ d. 10BaseFX
- ○ e. 10Base1000

The correct answer is d. Multimode fiber-optic cable can span approximately 2 kilometers. 10Base5 has a distance limitation of 500 meters and 10Base2 has a distance limitation of 185 meters; therefore answers a and b are incorrect. 10Base185 and 10Base1000 do not exist; therefore answers c and e are incorrect.

Question 6

What is a crossover cable?

- ○ a. A cable that has crossed over the maximum length specified by the IEEE group, but is still able to provide a reliable connection.
- ○ b. The same as a UTP patch cable.
- ○ c. A UTP crossover cable that can connect two hubs or two computers without using a hub.
- ○ d. A cable that connects two different types of media, such as UTP and STP.

The correct answer is c. A crossover cable is used to connect two hubs, and can connect two workstations without using a hub. A crossover cable is similar to a patch cable, except that in a crossover cable pins 1 and 3 and pins 2 and 6 are switched on one end of the cable. A network cable outside the specified lengths will provide an unreliable connection; therefore answer a is incorrect. A UTP patch cable does not have any pins crossed over; therefore answer b incorrect. A transceiver connects two different type of media together; therefore answer d is incorrect.

Question 7

What are the characteristics of full-duplex Ethernet or full-duplex Fast Ethernet?

- ○ a. It is automatically implemented when the cable plant is totally category 5 cable.
- ○ b. It requires a category 5 cable plant and a minimum of one hub to work.
- ○ c. It requires category 3 or greater UTP cable, a nonshared link, a switch, and a NIC that supports full duplex.
- ○ d. It requires a totally redundant set of switches that duplex the signals across a mesh network.

The correct answer is c. Full-duplex operation allows simultaneous transmit and receive signals and can theoretically double the speed of the link. Full-duplex operation requires a point-to-point UTP connection between a device, such as a switch, and a NIC that supports full-duplex operation. Full-duplex operation cannot work in a shared collision domain, such as a hub or coaxial Ethernet network. A category 5 cable plant by itself is only cable without any devices; therefore answer a is incorrect. A hub is a shared collision domain and full duplex cannot operate in a shared collision domain; therefore answer b is incorrect. Answer d is not possible and it is not relevant to this question.

Question 8

If you moved a computer that was working seamlessly on a 10Mbps hub-based network to a 100Mbps hub-based network, and you're having intermittent problems staying connected to the network, what is the first thing you should do?

- ○ a. Open the computer and replace the NIC card.
- ○ b. Replace the hub.
- ○ c. Test the cable.
- ○ d. Uninstall and reinstall the NIC driver.

The correct answer is c. The cable could be too close to a fluorescent light, it could be too long, or it could be the wrong category of cable to run at 100Mbps. Replacing the NIC is an option, but it should be tested before arbitrarily being replaced. Therefore answer a is incorrect. Replacing the hub is an option, but not the first option. Therefore answer b is incorrect. Uninstalling and reinstalling the NIC driver is an option, but the computer worked seamlessly on the first network and only experienced problems on the second network; therefore answer d is incorrect.

Need To Know More?

 Mazda, Fraidoon, ed.: *Telecommunications Engineer's Reference Book*. Reed Educational and Professional Publishing Ltd., Woburn, MA, 1998. ISBN 0-240-51491-2. An excellent reference book explaining the intricacies of telecommunications in great detail.

 Sheldon, Tom: *Encyclopedia of Networking, Electronic Edition*. Osborne McGraw-Hill, New York, 1998. ISBN 0-07-882333-1. A good overview of general networking terms and networking characteristics. Covers everything from A to Z.

 www.cisco.com has numerous white papers on switches and full-duplex characteristics.

Operating Systems

Terms you'll need to understand:

- √ Network operating system (NOS)
- √ Pre-emptive multitasking
- √ Primary domain controller (PDC)
- √ Backup domain controller (BDC)
- √ Client
- √ Directory services
- √ Novell Directory Services (NDS)
- √ NetWare and intraNetWare
- √ Lightweight Directory Access Protocol (LDAP)
- √ OS/2
- √ NT Directory Services (NTDS)

Techniques you'll need to master:

- √ Knowing the different network operating systems
- √ Understanding the different directory services
- √ Identifying the NOS utilities
- √ Understanding how clients connect to operating systems

The *network operating system (NOS)* is the operating system software that you load onto your server to provide basic network services to users, such as file, print, and directory services. In addition to the basic services, most operating systems have other common functions that provide many of the same features, including:

► Redundant Array of Inexpensive Disks (RAID), duplexing, and mirroring of hard drives

► Backup services and virus checking

► Security access through login control

► TCP/IP support

► Data security

► Centralized administration

In this chapter, we discuss only the most widely used NOSs, specifically, Windows NT, Novell, Unix, and OS/2, and their components.

 You must have administrator rights and privileges to manage an NOS. In Windows NT, that account is *Administrator,* and in NetWare and intraNetWare it is *Admin*. In Unix, it is the *root* or *su* user, and in OS/2 it is the *administrator*.

Microsoft Windows NT Server

Windows NT Server is Microsoft's network operating system for local area network (LAN) and wide area network (WAN) environments. You can deploy it in a single-server configuration for small-office environments or in a LAN or WAN for multiple-server environments. Windows NT Server is scalable for small, medium, large, or enterprise network environments and is available in Enterprise Edition, Standard Edition, Small Business Server Edition, and Terminal Server Edition.

Windows NT Server 4 is a 32-bit operating system that provides better performance than 16-bit operating systems. It supports symmetric multiprocessing (SMP) servers that use up to 32 processors on Intel, DEC Alpha, and PowerPC platforms. The Standard Windows NT Server 4 licenses you for SMP servers with up to four processors, and the Enterprise Edition 4 licenses you for SMP servers with more than four processors.

Windows NT Server uses *pre-emptive multitasking* to allocate processing time and deter any single application from utilizing the processor to the exclusion of other tasks. In addition, it uses multithreading to execute multiple, simultaneous processes.

You can tailor your Windows NT Server-based network for several different business models. It can be used as a *primary domain controller (PDC)* for network authentication, a *backup domain controller (BDC)* for security database redundancy, or a member server. The PDC and the BDC are the main components of any Windows NT network. Only one PDC is present on a Windows NT network, and it stores the Security Accounts Manager (SAM) database and the user accounts database for the network. The BDCs, more than one of which might be present, are redundant databases that provide for fault tolerance and auxiliary user login and authentication if the PDC goes offline.

Your member server can be an applications server that uses the Microsoft BackOffice suite of products, which includes SQL Server, SMS Server, Exchange Server, and SNA Server. Or, you can set it up as a print server to coordinate traffic to the network printers, a file server to coordinate file sharing, or a modem/fax server to coordinate communications traffic.

You can also tailor Windows NT servers to use TCP/IP, IPX, or NetBEUI as the standard protocol. All these protocols can be configured during installation, but it is best to standardize on one protocol because the network will function much faster if only one is loaded on all the computers. The protocol of choice is TCP/IP, which is becoming widely accepted and has a large installation base.

Windows NT Services

Windows NT 4 has the same desktop interface as the ever-familiar Windows 95/98. However, Windows NT Servers come standard with many features that you can implement individually, depending on the requirements of your current network environment and future network plans.

Remote Access Service

The Remote Access Service (RAS) allows users to dial in to the domain for a shared modem or modem pool and provides remote users with secure access to all network services.

➤ **Dynamic Host Configuration Protocol (DHCP) server** The DHCP server automatically assigns TCP/IP addresses to workstations throughout the network. The IP addresses that the DHCP server can assign include, but are not limited to, the default gateway, the DNS server, and the WINS server.

➤ **Domain Name System (DNS) Server** The DNS server resolves TCP/IP addresses to fully qualified domain names (FQDNs). For example, the basis for the Internet is root DNS servers that resolve DNS names to TCP/IP addresses.

Chapter 3

➤ **Internet Information Server (IIS)** IIS gives you an avenue for publishing Web pages for intranets and the Internet and comes standard as part of the Windows NT 4 server package.

➤ **Windows Internet Name Service (WINS) server** The WINS server resolves NetBEUI names to IP addresses. This is an important feature to implement when TCP/IP is the only protocol used on the network.

 Remember that WINS is the name resolution service for Windows NT.

Windows NT Utilities

Windows NT has several utilities that help you accomplish network administration tasks, which are discussed in the following sections:

Disk Administrator

The Windows NT Disk Administrator is a graphical tool that allows you to set up, configure, format, and manage the system computer's hard disk(s) and hard disk partitions. You can also use Disk Administrator to accomplish these tasks:

➤ Creating and deleting partitions, logical drives with extended partitions, and stripe sets

➤ Formatting, labeling, creating, and deleting volumes

➤ Obtaining disk space and partition size information

➤ Changing drive letter assignments

In addition to these capabilities, Windows NT has several levels of disk fault tolerance built into the operating system that is manageable through the Disk Administrator. It is capable of disk mirroring (RAID 1) and disk striping with parity (RAID 5) from within the operating system. Chapter 5 discusses RAID concepts in more detail.

Network Neighborhood

When you first start up your workstation, you will see the Windows NT Network Neighborhood icon. The Network Neighborhood gives your computer access to available network resources, such as printers and servers. It also lets you connect to other computers on the network, establish drive mappings, and browse the network for resources. The Entire Network icon allows you access to the rest of the network.

User Manager For Domains

In Windows NT, a domain user account contains information that defines a user to a Windows NT Server domain controller. Through User Manager for Domains, you can create, manage, delete, or disable domain user accounts. You can also manage security policies, create and manage groups, and add user accounts to those groups. User Manager for Domains is one of the main utilities used for Windows NT network administration.

In a peer-to-peer environment, a plain-vanilla User Manager does the same tasks as User Manager for Domains, but on a smaller scale. In addition, you can use the Add User Accounts Wizard through the Administrative Wizards utility to do some, but not all, of the same user account management.

Administrative Wizard

The Windows NT Administrative Wizard is a consolidated interface of graphical utilities (wizards) that lets you easily perform administrative functions and assists you in performing the required steps for each task. The wizards help you add new users (Add User Accounts Wizard), create and manage new groups (Group Management Wizard), and manage/share client drives, files, and folders, including security settings (Managing File and Folder Access Wizard). You can also add printers (Add Printer Wizard), add and remove programs (Add/Remove Programs Wizard), and install new modems (Install New Modem Wizard). In addition, you can install or update network client workstations (Network Client Administrator Wizard) and keep track of server and client software licenses (License Wizard).

Server Manager

Server Manager allows you to manage individual servers, local and remote domains, workgroups, and computers. It also lets you view lists of connected users and manage shared resources, directories, and properties on individual servers. In addition, you can send messages to connected users and manage the communication between domain controllers within a domain. Server Manager also allows you to promote a BDC to a PDC, synchronize servers with PDCs, control directory replication, and add or remove computers from the domain.

Event Viewer

Events are significant incidents in the system or in an application that require the system to notify users or initiate a log entry. Logging allows administrators to anticipate and identify sources of system problems and security issues. You initiate event logging automatically when you boot the system, at which time all services and applications on the network generate log entries, called *events*, according to your system's Audit Policy. The Event Log Service records the event information in the event logs, which contain a record of login errors, security audits, and other significant system events. Through the Event Viewer, you can view and manage the event logs and set event-logging policies. Windows NT records three types of events in the Event logs:

- **System logs** Contain information, errors, or warnings that the system components generate to indicate their condition. The Windows NT operating system preselects the events during installation.

- **Application logs** Contain errors, warnings, or other information generated by installed applications and services.

- **Security logs** Show events generated by security subsystem components, such as login attempts and events related to resource use. The auditing policies determine the selection of events in the Security log.

System Policy Editor

Policies are the rules (rights and permissions) that control any user's networking environment in a Windows NT network; you implement those rules through the System Policy Editor. The desktop settings for user profiles, user login requirements, and network access settings are stored in the computer's Registry database. The system policy for users overwrites settings in the current user area of the Registry, and the system policy for computers overwrites the settings in the current local machine area of the Registry. This way, you can control user actions (user profiles) as well as computer actions for users and groups.

User Profiles

User profiles are the work environment settings for a given user that the system loads during user login. These settings include all the user-specific settings of a user's Windows environment, such as screen colors, network connections, printer connections, mouse settings, shortcuts, and window size and position. The username identifies the appropriate user profile to the system. Profiles can be local user profiles, roaming user profiles, and mandatory user profiles.

Novell NetWare

The 32-bit, 3.x version of NetWare was the first widely accepted LAN operating system. The Novell Bindery, which was the foundation for the user and directory security structure, did not integrate easily into large environments.

NetWare 4.x introduced Novell Directory Services (NDS), which was a significant change because it replaced the NetWare 3.x Bindery structure. NDS is a distributed directory services database that keeps track of all users, servers, and resources on the network regardless of the network size. The intraNetWare (NetWare 4.11) release added several Internet and TCP/IP products on top of the NDS structure.

Windows 95 can access NetWare by using one of two available clients. The two choices for clients in the Network Properties screen are the NetWare client and the Microsoft Client for NetWare Networks. The NetWare client for Windows 95 is fully integrated into NetWare. The Microsoft Client for NetWare Networks offers limited file and print sharing and can connect only by using the Bindery mode natively.

NetWare 5 provides numerous upgrades and enhancements over NetWare 4.x and contains network management features that streamline networking and consolidate resources. Some of the more significant features of NetWare 5 are the following:

➤ **Dynamic application load/unload** NetWare 5 architecture does not require the **LOAD** command to execute programs; rather, it supports dynamic load/unload of applications. It is scalable for developing and deploying kernel-level applications and network services, such as NetWare loadable modules (NLMs) and features an improved debugger and compiler.

➤ **NetWare Peripheral Architecture (NWPA)** Full NWPA support provides more reliable support for host adapters and storage devices.

➤ **Migration Gateway** The Migration Gateway provides a transparent gateway link between new NetWare 5 IP segments and existing IPX segments. During migration, you can still use IPX-based applications on the LAN and IP on your WAN segments. NetWare 5 also changes from the industry-standard IPX and implements TCP/IP as the default protocol.

➤ **Virtual memory (VM)** The VM swap file lets multiple swap files grow and shrink dynamically as memory is used. VM monitors memory usage so that only required and frequently accessed memory is available; it then swaps out other memory to the hard disk (on one or more NetWare volumes). All modules running in protected address space use virtual memory automatically. It minimizes I/O and memory fragmentation, facilitates memory resource sharing, and balances system response and utilization. Its infrastructure also supports shared memory, very large memory configurations, and expandable or compressible stacks.

➤ **Multiprocessor kernel (MPK)** MPK provides an integrated single-multiprocessor operating system to facilitate symmetric multiprocessing

(SMP)-enabled network services and applications. The scheduling algorithm lets administrators define scheduling on an application-by-application basis using either a round-robin or a priority-based scheduling algorithm.

- **PCI Hot Plug** Peripheral Component Interconnect (PCI) Hot Plug allows for dynamic modification of network PCI components, and comprises three aspects: Hot Replace, Hot Upgrade, and Hot Expansion.

  - Hot Replace permits you to replace network interface cards (NICs), LAN adapters, or host bus adapters without powering down the system.

  - Hot Upgrade allows you to replace an existing adapter with a revised card while the server is running.

  - Hot Expansion lets you add a new adapter into an open slot while the server is operating.

- **Intelligent I/O (I2O)** I2O is an open architecture for developing device drivers and runs independent of operating systems, processor platforms, or the system I/O bus.

- **ConsoleOne** This management framework has a Java-based GUI that provides a single point of administration that any Java Virtual Machine (JVM) or NetWare server can access. This lets you add network and application management utilities without developing the security and administration infrastructure. You can also browse the NDS tree; create and modify users, groups, organizations, and organizational units; and have full management rights within the directory structure.

- **Zero Effort Networks (Z.E.N.works)** Z.E.N.works is a desktop management tool suite that lets you configure, update, and maintain network workstations from a central location. It also provides directory-enabled, cross-platform networking solutions for Windows-based computers.

- **Novell Storage Services (NSS)** NSS provides backward compatibility for the NetWare File System (NWFS). It's ideal for systems with large files or large numbers of volumes, directories, and files. NSS and NWFS can run side by side, but the volume SYS must be NWFS. NSS fully utilizes hard disk space, combining any unused free space on the hard drives or in NetWare volumes (including SYS) attached to your server into a storage pool to create NSS volumes. NSS can mount any size NSS volume with as little as 4MB of memory, resulting in a smaller memory requirement on your server and more memory available for data caching. NSS can also store large objects in balanced trees (B-trees) for faster storage access.

▶ **NetWare Distributed Print Services (NDPS)** NDPS architecture supercedes queue-based print services. It centrally manages the network print environment from a single NDPS printer object and a single location. The printer setup time incorporates a configuration design that lets you resolve most network printing issues during printer installation. Because the printer drivers automatically download at setup, all you have to do to set up a printer is plug it into the network.

▶ **Compatibility mode** Through the Compatibility mode, you can run IPX applications even after you have fully migrated to NetWare 5. It has modes for both server compatibility and client compatibility for when you use an IPX application or service in an IP environment.

▶ **DNS and DHCP Services Utility** This management utility pulls network resources together into a single trusted NDS-based system. It supports Java, Java Naming and Directory Interface, CORBA/IIOP, and ActiveX. In addition, it supports IETF protocols on the front end and integrates into NDS for enterprise management on the back end. It also supports Dynamic DNS (DDNS), allowing for dynamic updates of hostnames based on changing IP addresses. NDS integrates DHCP for easy IP address management and provides NDS configuration information to clients, including initial context, NDS server name, and tree name.

▶ **Internet integration** NetWare 5 incorporates business networks and the Internet's open standards to let you run a native IP network while maintaining full support for IPX and IPX-based applications. Pure IP provides bandwidth optimization with only one protocol on the wire. It also includes Netscape FastTrack Web server and Netscape Communicator for NetWare, which support LDAP 3 and enable customers to deploy Web-publishing solutions.

▶ **Application support** The JVM provides support for Java applications and NetWare DLL support. It also provides a platform to develop and deploy new standards-based distributed Internet and intranet applications through a development environment using pure Java and Java scripting.

▶ **Security** The security services provide access to advanced security technology that supports enterprise applications on corporate networks. All the services integrate with NDS, simplify administration and access control, and integrate Internet security technology for data integrity and privacy across public networks.

▶ **Public Key Infrastructure Services (PKIS)** The PKIS allows organizations to secure their networks by verifying the identity of the server with which the user is communicating. The NDS international cryptographic infrastructure simplifies the management of applications that require encryption capabilities for multinational businesses. NDS secure authentication services (SAS) supports and integrates with additional authentication methods, such as Kerberos, SOCKS, tokens, smart cards, and biometrics.

▶ **Memory protection** In protected mode memory, NLMs can be loaded and isolated from the server code and from other NLMs. If one or more protected modules fail, a diagnostic core dump is created for the faulted address space, and only the isolated address space will fail, without bringing the server down. This lets you reload the failed address space and all its modules without affecting the network. An autostart flag is available for protected modules that allows the address space to be cleaned up and rebuilt and all modules reloaded automatically. Libraries (such as CLIB) are shared across address spaces for maximum memory efficiency. Additionally, NLMs using a CLIB interface that do not enable or disable interrupts can be loaded in a protected environment.

▶ **Configuration Manager** The Configuration Manager tracks changes to the hardware and includes PCI Hot Plug management to support EISA, MCA, and plug-and-play ISA. The Configuration Manager detects the hardware configuration on buses that support autodetection and stores the current configuration information. Each time the operating system starts up, the Configuration Manager loads and compares the currently detected hardware configuration with the saved configuration. If the hardware configuration has changed, NetWare automatically loads the appropriate installation NLM. If you make dynamic changes using Hot Plug PCI, the Configuration Manager monitors the Novell Event Bus and sends a message to the corresponding device driver to unload whenever a device is removed. When you dynamically add a device, NetWare 5 automatically loads the installation NLM to accommodate the configuration change.

NetWare Utilities

NetWare has several utilities that give you better management control over your network. A discussion of the most important utilities follows:

rconsole

rconsole takes over a NetWare server remotely from a workstation. You must set up the server to allow rconsole sessions. Any server on the network can be the controller with this utility.

Operating Systems

NetWare Administrator

NetWare Administrator (NWAdmin) runs as a service on the network to allow centralized management of network applications and Windows NT domains through one utility, ensuring data integrity and synchronization between NDS and Windows NT. With NWAdmin, you can view and manage the hierarchical directory trees in NDS to see where available network objects are located, allowing new NT objects and their attributes to be displayed and administered from within the utility.

Workstation Manager

Workstation Manager centrally manages user accounts for both Windows NT workstations and the NetWare network by storing Windows NT Workstation user and desktop configurations in NDS. It also lets you dynamically create and manage users on Windows NT workstations without Windows NT domains but still allows for central configuration of Windows NT Workstation user properties and intraNetWare client login properties.

Automatic Client Upgrade

When users log in, the Automatic Client Upgrade (ACU) automatically upgrades client software without intervention from the user or administrator. SETUPNW /ACU compares the version numbers of the currently installed client workstation software to that of the new client in the ACU installation directory to determine whether to upgrade the client. If the version number of the new client software is greater than that of the currently installed client, SETUPNW.EXE automatically installs the latest version. If the new software version number is older, SETUPNW exits without making any modifications.

IGRATE

IGRATE is an integration utility that performs the initial upload of NT users and groups to NDS, which then appear as NT user and group objects under the domain object in the NDS tree. Once you complete the initial integration, you can replicate users through NWAdmin. After the initial upload to NDS, IGRATE also integrates existing NDS users into NT and then synchronizes NT and NDS users. NDS then becomes the master repository for all user and group information. The IGRATE utility uses static NT PDC user and group information to create NDS users and groups, instead of dynamically updating the NT PDC after a change occurs in NDS.

Unix

The Unix operating system was developed at AT&T Bell Laboratories in late 1969 and early 1970 and eventually became System V Unix. The Unix operating system was written in the C programming language, which made it easy to recompile and port to other systems. In the early 1990s, Novell got into the Unix market by purchasing Unix System V, release 4 (SRV).

Unix is a multiuser operating system that runs processes, such as user applications and services. The design allows services to be added and removed easily. Unix supports distributed file systems, of which Sun Microsystems Network File System (NFS) is the most popular. Users interface with the operating system through a shell that accepts input and performs tasks. The original shells were text-based, but GUI interfaces are gradually replacing them. TCP/IP is the protocol of choice for most, if not all, current Unix operating systems. The following sections discuss the more popular Unix versions in use today.

Berkeley Software Distribution (BSD)

In the mid-1970s, AT&T released the code for Unix to the academic community. BSD is the University of California at Berkeley's edition of Unix, which adds TCP/IP networking capabilities and ports Unix to the DEC VAX.

Digital Unix

The Unix program developed and marketed by the Digital Equipment Corporation (DEC) is capable of running 64-bit applications and is scalable to every application design, from laptops to high-performance computers and networks.

HP-UX

This Hewlett-Packard answer to Unix offers a complete 64-bit operating environment for both application development and deployment of mission-critical solutions.

IBM AIX

AIX is the IBM version of the Unix operating system. It supports SMP, 64-bit systems, scalable parallel systems, and workstations. It is application-binary compatible across all AIX 4 releases and has 32- and 64-bit functionality for e-business, business intelligence, MCAD, and networking applications.

Linux

Linux is a Unix-like 32-bit operating system that is mainly user developed, and for this reason it has no standard technical support. However, Linux does have credence in that version 2 provides a 64-bit kernel that supports SMP and conforms to X/Open and POSIX standards. In addition, it also supports Java and can be used as an Internet server.

OS/2 Warp Server

OS/2 Warp Server, based on IBM's LAN Server 4, has many of the same capabilities as Microsoft Windows NT and Novell NetWare. It also uses IBM's Directory and Security Server (DSS) for distributed services. It supports SMP, can have as many as 64 processors, and can support up to 1,000 users per server. It supports a variety of clients.

SCO Unix

In the mid-1990s, Novell sold the Unix operation to the Santa Cruz Operation (SCO), which already had a successful version of Unix for the Intel-based computer market. SCO Unix is especially designed to run on Intel processor computers; SCO Unix servers can run on enterprise networks as well as on networks for small to midsize businesses.

Sun Microsystems Solaris

Solaris is essentially a BSD with many features of the industry-standard Unix SRV. It has optimizations for distributed network environments and performance enhancements for running database and Web applications. Solaris is also Java enabled and provides centralized administration for remote operating system control. In addition, Solaris uses SMP techniques and supports multithreading to allow the division of applications into segments that execute simultaneously on each processor. Solaris accommodates both intranets and enterprise networking.

Directory Services

The International Telecommunications Union (ITU) X.500 model defines the standard for the directory services industry. Most directory services vendors incorporate a subset of the ITU model and add their specific information to their directory services database. Most directory services databases are graphically represented as an upside-down tree structure, starting with the root and forming branches. At the end of each branch is a repository of information about network entities, such as users, servers, volumes, applications, files, and printers. Directory services provide a standard naming convention and description as well as location, access, management, and security information about these entities. Many NOSs implement their versions of directory services, and interoperability with one another is virtually impossible. A duplication of effort is often required to achieve interoperability in a heterogeneous NOS environment.

A directory service must meet several important requirements to be deployed in an enterprise environment:

> **Single-enterprise sign-on to the network** Single-enterprise sign-on allows end users to log on once with a single username and password to gain access to the Internet, email, and network resources, regardless of their location on the network.

> **Centralized network management** Such management provides the ability to manage all corporate resources from a central location, eliminating duplication of effort by not having to perform common management tasks (such as adding or deleting user accounts) repetitively.

> **Ability to support change easily** In the ever-changing environment of business, the directory service structure needs to be able to respond quickly to change. Competition in the marketplace demands quick response to change without a significant investment in doing so.

Several directory services vendors produce and market a directory services database. The following sections discuss the most common vendors and their products.

Novell Directory Services (NDS)

Novell deploys NDS in the NetWare 4.x and 5.x product line of operating systems. NetWare 5 has an enhanced version of NDS that offers a more flexible, secure environment for managing and administering the network resources.

Catalog services and simplified login makes it easier to create NDS-enabled applications, improves directory access performance, and allows users to sign on from any computer in any location without requiring directory knowledge. Directory information stored in catalog or index format is easily customized for searching, sorting, and reporting purposes. New *contextless login* uses the NDS catalog, allowing users to authenticate from any point on the network by entering their login name and password. This eliminates users having to know the location of their user objects in the NDS tree.

> NDS is a tree structure that contains all the objects and security for NetWare, regardless of the size of the network.

NT Directory Services

Microsoft deploys Windows NT Directory Services (NTDS) in the Windows NT 3.x and 4.x operating systems. NTDS is the directory services and security database for all Windows NT domains. It stores all the security information in a PDC and replicates the security database to BDCs within the domain.

Lightweight Directory Access Protocol

Lightweight Directory Access Protocol (LDAP) is an Internet Engineering Task Force (IETF) specification that has gained wide acceptance among the Internet community and NOS vendors who are trying to market into the TCP/IP arena. LDAP is a subset of the ITU X.500 directory service model that runs in a TCP/IP environment, and can be used as a front-end client to an X.500 directory services database. LDAP is a reduced instruction set of the Directory Access Protocol and requires less overhead. LDAP is gaining acceptance as a directory service standard because of its foundation on the TCP/IP protocol.

X.500

The ITU and ISO organizations developed the X.500 standard and it has become a foundational structure that other directory services are modeled on. X.500 is an ITU recommendation for a directory service system that is capable of providing an international global query service for people and objects. It defines how to structure usernames and objects over a national or international network; it is a hierarchical tree structure with countries forming the top level. The original intent was to set up a root X.500 server similar to the DNS root system.

The X.500 directory service is the boilerplate for several other directory services, including NDS and LDAP.

Network Clients

Windows 95 is a 32-bit multitasking desktop operating system designed to run on Intel-based computers. Windows 95 incorporates plug-and-play technology into the operating system, which also includes built-in networking, email, and a Web browser. Many applications are written for Windows 95, which has built-in support for Windows NT domain networks, Novell 3.x networks, TCP/IP networks, and third-party network support for NetWare and some Unix systems. Windows 95 is seen as a client by each of these operating systems and has no special security privileges. Windows 98, the latest version of the Windows platform, offers a new desktop that integrates with Microsoft's Internet Explorer.

Microsoft distributes TCP/IP with all Windows 9x operating systems. The TCP/IP stack offers the capability through an option tab to specify a primary and secondary WINS server within the TCP/IP protocol stack.

The WINS server setup in the TCP/IP protocol properties requires a primary and secondary WINS server to be specified.

Windows NT Workstation 4 is Microsoft's premier desktop operating system and can be fully integrated into a Windows NT domain. It was designed to work within a Windows NT domain with full domain security. When a Windows NT workstation joins a domain, the domain administrator has to authorize the transaction. The domain administrator group is added to the local administrator group of the workstation, allowing the domain administrator to control the workstation. Novell makes a NetWare client for Windows NT, and some Unix versions have clients for Windows NT.

Microsoft's Terminal Server, Sun Microsystems' Java, and Citrix Corporation's thin-client product dominate the thin-client computing arena. Thin client creates a virtual machine and provides screen, keyboard, and mouse updates to the PC or terminal.

Macintosh computers are easily integrated into Novell and Windows NT environments for file and print sharing. The Novell and Windows NT servers look like an AppleShare server to Macintosh clients.

Practice Questions

Question 1

What are the major network operating systems (NOSs) for LANs? [Choose the four best answers]

- ☐ a. Windows NT
- ☐ b. OS/2
- ☐ c. Unix
- ☐ d. DOS
- ☐ e. VMS
- ☐ f. NetWare

The correct answers are a, b, c, and f. The major network operating systems in the LAN environment are Windows NT, OS/2, Unix, and NetWare. Each one has strengths and weaknesses, and in a heterogeneous networking environment they can complement one another. DOS is an operating systems designed for the personal computer. Therefore, answer d is incorrect. VMS is a mini-computer operating system. Therefore, answer e is incorrect.

Question 2

Which clients can connect to a NetWare server under the Windows 9x configuration screen? [Choose the two best answers]

- ☐ a. Sun IPX Interchange PC-NFS client
- ☐ b. Novell NetWare Client
- ☐ c. IBM client for intraNetWare
- ☐ d. Microsoft Client for NetWare Networks
- ☐ e. Microsoft Client for Windows Networks

The correct answers are b and d. The NetWare client incorporates many advanced functions to access the full capabilities of a NetWare server. It can access the NDS tree and many NetWare utilities. The Microsoft client provides access to NetWare for basic file and print sharing in Bindery mode. The Sun IPX Interchange PC-NFS client and the IBM client for intraNetWare do not exist. Therefore, answers a and c are incorrect. The Microsoft Client for

Windows Networks does not connect to an intraNetWare server. Therefore, answer e is incorrect.

Question 3

Which International Telecommunication Union (ITU; formerly CCITT) standard is the framework for NetWare NDS?

○ a. X.319
○ b. X.400
○ c. X.25
○ d. X.500
○ e. X.1000

The correct answer is d. The X.500 electronic directory services standard is the framework for several industry directory services. NDS is the NetWare standard and LDAP is the TCP/IP standard derived from X.500. X.319 and X.1000 do not exist as an ITU standard. Therefore, answers a and e are incorrect. X.400 is a message handling standard that defines the method for exchanging electronic messages. Therefore, answer b is incorrect. X.25 is a packet switching standard, not a framework for directory services. Therefore, answer c is incorrect.

Question 4

What is the tree structure for NetWare that contains the object and security information?

○ a. NetWare Directory Services (NDS)
○ b. Bindery
○ c. NetWare Structured Directory (NSD)
○ d. Microsoft Directory Services (MDS)
○ e. Directory Services (DS)

The correct answer is a. The NDS is the electronic directory services and the security database for NetWare. The Bindery database is the user and security database used in NetWare 3.x servers and does not have a tree structure associated with it. Therefore, answer b is incorrect. The NetWare Structured Directory, Microsoft Directory Services, and the Directory Services are all fictitious answers. Therefore, answers c, d, and e are incorrect.

Question 5

What is the NT service that provides TCP/IP to NetBEUI name resolution?

○ a. DHCPNS
○ b. DNS
○ c. WINS
○ d. WINDNS
○ e. NS

The correct answer is c. The Windows Internet Name Service (WINS) is a dynamic database that associates a NetBEUI name to a TCP/IP address. The main reason to install WINS is to have one protocol installed on the network using TCP/IP. DHCPNS, WINDNS, and NS are fictitious answers. Therefore, answers a, d, and e are incorrect. DNS is a way to associate IP addresses to host names within a domain. Therefore, answer b is incorrect.

Question 6

How should you assign a WINS address in a Windows 9x workstation?

○ a. It is added as a service in the Network Properties page and requires that you specify both a primary and a secondary server.
○ b. It is added as a protocol in the Network Properties page and requires that you specify both a primary and a secondary server.
○ c. It is added as a client in the Network Properties page and requires that you specify both a primary and a secondary server.
○ d. It is an option in the TCP/IP Properties page and requires a primary and a secondary server to be specified.

The correct answer is d. The WINS server is set up on the TCP/IP Properties page under the WINS Configuration tab. The options are Disable WINS or Enable WINS. If WINS is enabled, the primary and secondary WINS servers need to be specified by IP address. WINS is not added as a service. Therefore, answer a is incorrect. WINS is not added as a protocol, it is part of the TCP/IP protocol. Therefore, answer b is incorrect. WINS is not a client in the Network Properties page. Therefore, answer c is incorrect.

Need To Know More?

 Mazda, Fraidoon, ed.: *Telecommunications Engineer's Reference Book*. Reed Educational and Professional Publishing Ltd., Woburn, MA, 1998. ISBN 0-240-51491-2. An excellent reference book explaining the intricacies of telecommunications in great detail.

 Sheldon, Tom: *Encyclopedia of Networking, Electronic Edition*. Osborne McGraw-Hill, New York, 1998. ISBN 0-07-882333-1. A good overview of general networking terms and networking characteristics. Covers everything from A to Z.

 www.microsoft.com has a detailed knowledge base on all of Microsoft's product and associated services, including Windows NT, Windows 95, Windows 98, and WINS.

 www.novell.com has a detailed knowledge base on all of Novell's product and associated services, including NetWare, NDS, and the NetWare client.

Protocols

Terms you'll need to understand:

- Internetwork Packet Exchange (IPX)
- Sequenced Packet Exchange (SPX)
- Transmission Control Protocol (TCP)/Internet Protocol (IP)
- Domain Name System (DNS)
- Windows Internet Name Service (WINS)
- Dynamic Host Configuration Protocol (DHCP)
- Address Resolution Protocol (ARP)
- Simple Mail Transfer Protocol (SMTP)
- Simple Network Management Protocol (SNMP)
- IPCONFIG/WINIPCFG
- NBTSTAT/NETSTAT
- Packet Internet Groper (Ping)
- Tracert

Techniques you'll need to master:

- Knowing how the IP, IPX, and NetBEUI protocols function
- Understanding the concept of IP default gateways
- Understanding how TCP/IP works
- Knowing the common TCP/IP, HTTP, FTP, and SMTP port numbers
- Understanding how an IP proxy server works
- Defining the TCP/IP workstation parameters
- Knowing how to use the TCP/IP utilities to test and troubleshoot IP connectivity
- Understanding DHCP, DNS, WINS, and host systems
- Identifying class A, B, and C IP addresses
- Knowing the protocols that make up the TCP/IP suite

Protocols are sets of rules and agreements that define how network components establish or end communications and exchange data. Modern networks implement the concept of layered protocols, as dictated by the Open Systems Interconnect (OSI) model. The OSI model attempted to unify network development, but because many protocols were already in use before the OSI model was developed, some (but not all) vendors redesigned their protocols to comply with the model. Although layered protocols have a significant influence on newer protocols, some protocols available today conform to the OSI, and some do not.

In this chapter we cover the three more commonly deployed protocols in local area network (LAN) and wide area network (WAN) environments. Although we do cover the main characteristics of the IPX and NetBEUI protocols, we give special emphasis to IP and TCP/IP and their associated utilities.

Internetwork Packet Exchange

Originally, Novell developed the *Internetwork Packet Exchange (IPX)* as the native protocol for the NetWare 3.x and 4.x operating systems. But in 1998, NetWare 5 changed the IPX legacy by making IP the native NetWare protocol. However, to connect a Windows NT server and a NetWare server, you can use either IPX or TCP/IP.

IPX is based on the Xerox Network System (XNS) protocol developed by Xerox in the 1970s. Several major network operating systems and most desktop operating systems support the IPX protocol. IPX is similar to IP in that it is an internetworking protocol that provides datagram services. IPX also has a Transport layer protocol, *Sequenced Packet Exchange (SPX)*, which is a connectionless-oriented datagram similar to TCP, whereas IPX and IP are connectionless datagram protocols. Table 4.1 outlines the packet structure for the IPX protocol.

An IPX protocol packet can be 30 to 65,535 bytes long. Ethernet networks have a default packet size of 1,500 bytes, and token ring networks have a default packet size of 4,202 bytes.

The IPX protocol has four Ethernet frame types and two token ring frame types. The default frame type for NetWare 4.x on an Ethernet network is IEEE_802.2, more commonly known as simply Ethernet 802.2. Table 4.2 identifies the frame types for both Ethernet and token ring networks. Figure 4.1 illustrates the Ethernet frame architectures.

The IPX datagram structure includes a network address and a node address. The network address is assigned to the network when the first NetWare server or router is installed on a segment. Each of the four frame types can be installed and bound to the same network interface card (NIC) in a server,

Protocols

Table 4.1 The IPX protocol packet structure.

Field	Size
Checksum	2 bytes
Packet length	2 bytes
Transport control	1 byte
Packet type	1 byte
Destination network	4 bytes
Destination node	6 bytes
Destination socket	2 bytes
Source network	4 bytes
Source node	6 bytes
Source socket	2 bytes
Data	Variable; determined by server or router

Table 4.2 Ethernet and token ring frame types.

Network Type	Frame Type	Description
Ethernet	Ethernet_802.2	A data-link protocol that controls the link between stations; also known as IEEE 802.2 LLC (Logical Link Control).
	Ethernet_802.3 RAW	The Novell proprietary frame type.
	Ethernet_II	Used to bind TCP/IP on a NetWare server.
	Ethernet_SNAP (Sub-Network Address Protocol)	Includes an organization code field and a type field that indicates the upper-level protocol that is using the packet. It is the frame type for AppleTalk environments.
Token ring	Token_Ring	Conforms to the IEEE 802.5 and IEEE 802.2 standards. The SAP fields indicate the protocol type and, in Novell networks, are set to 0xe0 to indicate that the upper-layer protocol is IPX.
	Token_Ring_Snap	Allows network protocol stacks to use Ethernet II frames.

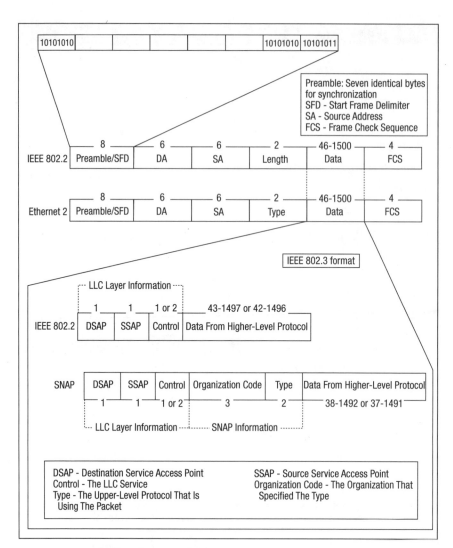

Figure 4.1 Ethernet frame architectures.

establishing a different network address for each frame type. All subsequent NetWare server installations on that network must correspond to the network address of each frame type assigned by the first server. A router that is set up to route IPX must also have a corresponding network address for each frame type it uses. The node address is the media access control (MAC) address assigned to the NIC. A socket address is included to identify a running process in a computer. An example of an IPX address is 1AB47E3F 0080D4287DE1 0121.

NetBEUI

IBM first introduced the *NetBIOS Extended User Interface (NetBEUI)* protocol in 1985. NetBEUI is an IBM proprietary specification that IBM makes available to developers. It is optimized for departmental LANs or for LAN segments of fewer than 50 people. NetBEUI has poor performance in WAN or large LAN environments but provides a fast transport protocol between clients and servers in small LAN environments. NetBEUI has relatively low memory requirements and does not need configuring. However, it is a nonroutable protocol. It uses a single-part naming scheme that cannot differentiate between multiple, interconnected networks. Each name must be unique on the network. Windows 95/98, Windows NT, and IBM LANs are the primary types of networks that deploy NetBEUI.

> Because NetBEUI is nonroutable, you should use it only for small Microsoft networks. Most large or new networks are deploying TCP/IP as the preferred protocol.

The Windows NT *NetBEUI Frame (NBF)* transport driver implements the IBM NetBEUI 3 specification. NetBEUI 3 is not a true NetBEUI because it does not extend the NetBIOS interface. However, it uses NBF to comply and interoperate with previous versions of NetBEUI. Keep in mind, though, that NetBEUI 3 exceeds the 254-session barrier of previous versions of NetBEUI. It uses a combination of two matrixes, one maintained by NBF and the other by NetBIOS, to provide a virtually limitless number of connections, memory permitting.

Network applications speaking directly to the NetBEUI 3 protocol driver must use transport driver interface (TDI) commands instead of NetBIOS commands. In Windows NT, the programming interface (NetBIOS) is separated from the protocol (NetBEUI) to increase flexibility in the layered architecture.

Internet Protocol

The *Internet Protocol (IP)* is a connectionless-oriented internetwork protocol that is the framework protocol for the Internet and other TCP/IP networks. It provides the structure that links individual networks (subnets) into a larger internetwork. Routing devices divide each subnet from the internetwork. The subnet scheme can be Ethernet, token ring, Fast Ethernet, or any of several other types of signaling architectures and need not be the same as that of the larger internetwork. IP provides a way to package information for delivery over intranets or the Internet.

The NIC driver on a subnet generates a frame when information needs to be transmitted to another device or computer on the network. The subnet signal architecture determines the frame format, and the workstation delivers the IP datagram inside the frame to the subnet node or router. Once the router receives the IP datagram, it looks at the destination IP address and determines where to send the IP datagram. The router then repackages the IP datagram into the frame format of the next subnet and sends it to either the final destination or another router in the path to the final destination.

The IP addressing scheme consists of three areas: the physical address, the IP address, and the domain name:

➤ The physical address is the hardware address, or MAC address, of the NIC connected to the LAN.

➤ A 32-bit number identifies the IP address, which identifies the host network address and the host node address on the network.

➤ The domain name is an easy way to remember a host on a network without having to remember the 32-bit IP address. The TCP/IP addressing is discussed in detail later in this chapter.

IP Default Gateway

In an IP network, the *default gateway* is the IP subnet address of the router interface connected to the same network as all the computers with that same IP subnet address. When an IP network connects to a larger internetwork, you must specify a default gateway for all devices that send and receive data beyond their subnet. In Windows 95/98, Windows NT Workstation, and Windows NT Server, the default gateway field is located in the TCP/IP settings. You can define multiple default gateways for redundancy when you need to send a packet beyond the subnet. The workstation will try sending the packet to each gateway in the order listed and will stop trying gateways when it receives the first response.

The default gateway represents a router on a subnet that all the workstations, servers, and routers point to for all traffic that is destined for a remote subnet. The default gateway must be set up for TCP/IP packets to be routed to the proper destination on a remote subnet.

IP Addressing

An IP address is a 32-bit binary number broken into four 8-bit binary numbers separated by dotted decimals. The address contains a network identifier

Protocols   **61**

(the left part of the address) and a host identifier (the right part of the address). The three classes of IP addresses are defined as follows:

➤ **Class A** If the first bit is set to 0 and it has a subnet mask of 255.0.0.0, that identifies the network as a Class A network. The remaining 7 bits identify the network address. The 7-bit network address space can accommodate 126 network addresses. The remaining 24-bit host address space can accommodate 16,777,214 hosts per network. All Class A addresses have already been assigned to organizations. The acceptable range of network addresses for a Class A network is 001.x.x.x through 126.x.x.x. The acceptable range of host addresses for a Class A network is x.0.0.1 through x.255.255.254. 127.x.x.x addresses are reserved. 127.0.0.1 is the local loopback address for the NIC that is often used to troubleshoot the TCP/IP bindings on the local NIC. If you ping 127.0.0.1 and the local bindings are working correctly, the NIC will reply to the ping request. Ping is discussed further in "TCP/IP Utilities" later in this chapter.

➤ **Class B** If the first 2 bits are set to 10 and it has a subnet mask of 255.255.0.0, that identifies the network as a Class B network. The remaining 14 bits identify the network address. The 14-bit network address space can accommodate 16,382 network addresses. The remaining 16-bit host address space can accommodate 65,534 hosts per network. The acceptable range of network addresses for a Class B network is 128.0.x.x through 191.255.x.x. The acceptable range of host addresses for a Class B network is x.x.0.1 through x.x.255.254. All Class B addresses have been assigned.

➤ **Class C** If the first 3 bits are set to 110 and it has a subnet mask of 255.255.255.0, that identifies the network as a Class C network. The remaining 21 bits define the network address. The 21-bit network address space can accommodate 2,097,150 network addresses. The remaining 8-bit host address space can accommodate 254 hosts per network. The acceptable range of network addresses for a Class C network is 192.0.0.x through 223.255.255.x. The acceptable range of host addresses for a Class C network is x.x.x.1 through x.x.x.254.

Know and be able to identify the address ranges that make up a Class A, Class B, and Class C TCP/IP address. The default subnet mask for a Class C address is 255.255.255.0, for a Class B address it's 255.255.0.0, and for a Class A address it's 255.0.0.0. You must also understand how the 127.0.0.1 TCP/IP address is used and how the NIC responds to the ping request.

Table 4.3 Class C addresses.

Subnet Mask	Binary Value Of Last Byte	Subnets Available	Hosts Per Subnet
255.255.255.254	11111111.11111110	128	0
255.255.255.252	11111111.11111100	64	2
255.255.255.248	11111111.11111000	32	6
255.255.255.240	11111111.11110000	16	14
255.255.255.224	11111111.11100000	8	30
255.255.255.192	11111111.11000000	4	62
255.255.255.128	11111111.10000000	2	126
255.255.255.0	11111111.00000000	1	254

Subnetting a network address, such as a Class C address, allows it to be broken into more subnet networks with fewer hosts per network. Table 4.3 identifies the subnet mask for Class C addresses and the subnet and hosts available per subnet mask.

IP Proxy

In a networking environment, you use IP proxy servers to protect a trusted network from untrusted networks. For example, a corporate network might represent a trusted network and the Internet an untrusted network. Because the firewall has more filtering and monitoring capabilities, it normally incorporates the proxy server functions.

Most proxy servers have two network cards installed in them. The packets are not routed between the network cards, which is an OSI layer 3 function. Instead, each packet is passed through the proxy service before determining whether it is allowed into or out of the network. The services, or ports, that are allowed to pass must be individually set up and the specific rules configured for each port. The proxy server discards all other packets. When set up properly, this method can prevent unauthorized access to your trusted network.

The proxy server sends and receives all traffic between the trusted and untrusted networks on request by a trusted computer. Here is an example of this process (the Web browser must first be configured to use a proxy server): A client on a trusted network wants to access www.coriolis.com on the Internet, and the proxy server has been set up to pass the HTTP service. The proxy server intercepts the user request to the Web server on the Internet. It reconstructs the packet, with its source address, and sends it to the Web server. The packet is returned to the proxy server, which forwards the packet to the client computer

Protocols   63

that made the original request. In this scenario, the proxy server is the only address that is broadcast to the Internet, thus protecting the trusted computer from direct attack across the Internet. It also allows the trusted network to deploy a fictitious IP address scheme because the proxy server is the only machine that needs a real IP address. Most proxy servers will cache Web sites that are frequently accessed. This keeps Internet traffic to a minimum while providing a fast response to the local user.

Use the browser to set up a workstation to point to a Web proxy server. The Web proxy server lets you gain access to the Internet and caches the most active Web pages to update changes on the locally cached Web pages.

TCP/IP

You could write an entire book on the impact that TCP/IP has had on the information technology world. However, we cover only the basic information that is included in the Network+ exam.

The *Transmission Control Protocol (TCP)* is a connection-oriented delivery service that resides at the Transport layer of the TCP/IP protocol suite. It provides reliable data delivery service by setting up end-to-end connections between two systems that need to exchange data. To do this, it establishes a virtual network between the two computers across all routers in the affected network. TCP uses the Internet Protocol (IP) as the transport to deliver information across the network.

The computer industry accepts and fully supports TCP/IP as the preferred protocol for network connectivity. Whereas Unix has always supported TCP/IP and has adopted it as its default protocol, NetWare 5 and Windows NT 5 have just begun to support it natively and now qualify it as their preferred protocol as well. The overwhelming success of the Internet has also contributed to the increasing global acceptance of TCP/IP.

You need to remember that TCP/IP is the default protocol for Unix, and the preferred protocol for the NetWare and Windows operating systems.

TCP/IP Ports

Well-known port numbers represent a common method for connecting to remote systems on IP networks. IP delivers the datagram to the appropriate computer, and the port address is used to deliver the data to the process on the host computer. When a process, such as a *Simple Mail Transfer Protocol (SMTP)* gateway, is installed on a host computer, it monitors port 25 and retrieves any data sent to that port. Each computer in a communications session creates a socket, each of which has an address (a port number). The client and server work together to set up a temporary connection using these ports to transfer data. The ports form an end-to-end connection using either TCP or the *User Datagram Protocol (UDP)*. One of the most common port addresses is port 80, which is the HTTP or Web service that allows all Internet browsers to connect to Web servers. TCP is a connection-oriented protocol that guarantees delivery of the data, whereas UDP is a connectionless-oriented protocol that does not guarantee data delivery.

To make a connection between two computers in a TCP environment, the sender makes a connection request, which the receiver grants. Because TCP is a connection-oriented protocol, it waits for authorization to send data and then checks to make sure that it was delivered in its entirety. Because the connectionless-oriented UDP does not guarantee delivery of data, if the receiving computer is busy or the data is corrupted, the receiving computer discards the packets but does not notify the sending computer of the unsuccessful delivery. Table 4.4 represents some of the more common TCP and UDP port numbers.

Table 4.4 Common TCP and UDP port numbers.

Port Number	Used By	Identifier	Description
15	UDP	NETSTAT	Network Status
21	TCP, UDP	FTP	File Transfer Protocol
23	TCP, UDP	TELNET	Telnet
25	TCP, UDP	SMTP	Simple Mail Transfer Protocol
53	UDP	DOMAIN	Domain Name System
69	UDP	TFTP	Trivial File Transfer Protocol
80	TCP, UDP	HTTP	World Wide Web HTTP
110	TCP, UDP	POP3	Post Office Protocol 3
119	TCP, UDP	NNTP	Network News Transfer Protocol
137	UDP	NetBIOS-NS	NetBIOS Name Service
220	TCP, UDP	IMAP3	Interactive Mail Access Protocol 3

Protocols 65

 Make sure that you know the port number and identifier for each protocol. In addition, be familiar with the function of each protocol and how it is used.

TCP/IP Workstation Configuration Parameters

To set up TCP/IP on a Windows 95 workstation, follow these steps:

1. From the Start menu, click on Settings|Control Panel, then double-click on the Network icon.

2. Highlight the TCP/IP protocol and go to Properties. The properties screen has seven tabs, but you'll only need to address four of them: DNS Configuration, Gateway, WINS Configuration, and IP Address.

 To set up a computer on an IP network, you need, at a minimum, a NIC, an IP address, and a subnet mask.

DNS Configuration

The *Domain Name System (DNS)* is a hierarchical routing structure that links domain names to IP addresses. You can access Web sites by either the IP address or the DNS name. However, the DNS name is usually easier to remember than an IP address, and many Web sites are recognized internationally by their DNS names.

On the Internet, DNS servers convert domain names to IP addresses. Most Internet service providers have DNS servers available for customer use. You should always specify a primary and a secondary DNS server on computers that attach to the Internet.

 You need to know that DNS is the standard protocol across all releases of TCP/IP.

When you put a URL in a Web browser, it will either query a DNS server or use a previous cache entry to acquire the host machine's IP address, and will use that information to reach the final destination and retrieve the request.

The DNS structure is hierarchical, with the root domain servers forming the top levels in the structure. Domains are then registered with the root servers and form branches from the root. For example, **coriolis.com** would be registered with the root ".com" (commercial) DNS server. The root server would then point to a branch DNS server that would register the hosts for that domain, such as **www.coriolis.com** and **ftp.coriolis.com**. The following list represents some of the more common root servers:

➤ **.net** Networks

➤ **.com** Commercial

➤ **.org** Organizational

➤ **.edu** Education

➤ **.gov** Government

➤ **.mil** U.S. military

The Internet Network Information Center (InterNIC) is the authority for assigning domain names. If your organization needs to apply for a domain name, go to the InterNIC Web site (**www.internic.net**) and follow the instructions for registering. A domain name must be unique on the root server on which it is registered, and names are registered on a first-come, first-serve basis. Remember that the InterNIC will revoke a domain name if it is in violation of a trademark.

The DNS Configuration tab offers you two options for configuring DNS:

➤ **Disable DNS** Select this option if DNS services are not required on the workstation.

➤ **Enable DNS** When you select this option, you need to fill in several fields:

  ➤ **Computer Host Name** This is the default Windows 95/98 machine name, but it can be changed if needed.

  ➤ **Domain Name** This should reflect the DNS name, not the NT domain name. The domain name is the name registered with the InterNIC.

  ➤ **DNS Server Search Order** Put the IP address or the addresses of the domain name servers in this field. The servers are queried in the order listed, and Windows 95/98 only checks the subsequent servers that are listed if no response is received from the first server. You can add three DNS servers to the list.

  ➤ **Domain Suffix Search Order** This field specifies the DNS domain suffixes that are appended to host short names during name resolution. When attempting to resolve a domain name from a short name, Windows 95/98 first appends the local domain name. If that is unsuccessful, it uses the Domain Suffix list to create additional domain names and query DNS servers in the order listed. You can add up to five domain suffixes.

Gateway

The *gateway* is the default route for all TCP/IP packets that are not destined for the local subnet. When an IP address is specified that is not part of the subnet of the workstation, the workstation must forward those packets to the default gateway or gateway router. The gateway then determines whether the IP subnet is located on any of its ports. If the packet is not destined for a local subnet connected to the gateway, it will forward the packet to its default gateway.

A Windows 95/98 machine can have a list of gateways referenced in the TCP/IP properties page, and the first gateway in the list will be the default gateway. It will send packets to the default gateway if it is functioning properly. If the default gateway does not respond, Windows 95/98 will try the next gateway in the list and will stop searching for gateways to forward packets to as soon as it finds one that responds.

WINS Configuration

Windows Internet Name Service (WINS) is a database that correlates IP addresses to NetBIOS computer names in a Windows-only networking environment. This service creates a dynamically updated database that requires very little maintenance after installation. WINS provides an avenue to deploy TCP/IP-only Windows NT networks without losing any of the functionality provided by NetBIOS names.

> The WINS address is a TCP/IP address that points to a WINS server that has the WINS database installed on it. It is a configuration tab associated with the TCP/IP protocol.

When a Windows machine makes a network device request to a NetBIOS computer name, it queries the WINS database and returns the IP address of the device that made the request.

When you are configuring WINS on a workstation, you generally have three configuration options:

➤ **Disable WINS Resolution** You should select this option if WINS resolution is not required on the network. WINS resolution is not required if the network is not using NetBIOS names.

- **Enable WINS Resolution** When you select this option, you need to specify a primary and secondary WINS server. If only one WINS server is available on the network, specify it for the primary server and leave the secondary server blank. The last field in this section is the Scope ID option, which provides a way to isolate a group of computers that are permitted to communicate only with one another. The Scope ID is a case-sensitive character string value that is appended to the NetBIOS name and is used for all NetBIOS over TCP/IP communications from that computer.

- **Use DHCP For WINS Resolution** When you select this option, the workstation will query the DHCP server for the primary and secondary WINS servers.

The minimum requirements for setting up WINS on a Windows 9x workstation are: Enable WINS resolution and then enter a primary WINS server. If you have a secondary WINS server available, enter it also.

IP Address

You can enter the IP address and subnet mask manually, or the DHCP server will supply it automatically. Whenever possible, use the DHCP server so that the TCP/IP network addresses can be maintained from a central location.

The *Dynamic Host Configuration Protocol (DHCP)* allows you to dynamically configure TCP/IP nodes and manage them from a central location. It automatically assigns IP addresses and other TCP/IP host address such as *domain name system (DNS) servers*, *Windows Internet Name Service (WINS) servers*, and *default gateways*. DHCP uses the definitions for the BOOTP protocol. Therefore, any routers that forward the BOOTP protocol can also forward DHCP, allowing a DHCP server to handle multiple subnets. Otherwise, each subnet would need a DHCP server located on it.

The DHCP server setup defines the IP address range and any other IP host services that will be automatically assigned to computers on the network. The client leases the IP address from the server and renews the lease when it reboots or when the lease is more than halfway to the expiration date. Because network nodes depend heavily on server and router IP addresses, the system engineer usually assigns server and router IP addresses statically.

The workstation can use either a static or a dynamically assigned IP address. If the workstation uses a dynamically assigned IP address from a DHCP server, the following sequence of events will take place:

1. During the workstation boot process, a broadcast message is sent out by the workstation across the network to obtain an IP address dynamically.

Protocols 69

2. One or more DHCP servers can respond to the request for an IP address. The DHCP server that assigns the address also marks the IP address as reserved in its database.

3. The client accepts the IP address and broadcasts a confirmation message.

4. The DHCP server confirms the lease with the client.

If the client changes a dynamically assigned IP address to a static IP address, when the IP address expires, the DHCP server will try to reassign it, which creates an address conflict. If, by chance, two different clients are assigned the same IP address, only the first client to access the network will receive an IP address. In addition, dynamic IP addressing requires less administrative time than static IP addressing because you do not have to resolve IP addressing conflicts, as DHCP prevents them.

You can also use a *HOSTS file* to statically assign IP addresses to domain names. Over the years, the more dynamic properties of DNS servers have replaced the static database HOSTS file. However, the HOSTS file is still in use on some older systems, especially Unix.

The HOSTS file is located in the winnt\system32\drivers\etc directory, and the addresses are assigned as follows:
192.168.10.1 coriolis_ws99 # (the pound sign # is for remarks).

TCP/IP Protocols

The following protocols provide certain services and functions to enhance communications between TCP/IP hosts. Most of them are protocols used by applications to perform communications functions between TCP/IP hosts.

Address Resolution Protocol

The *Address Resolution Protocol (ARP)* is used to correlate a MAC address with an IP address. A MAC address is a unique hardware address on the network interface card and is assigned by the NIC manufacturer.

File Transfer Protocol

The *File Transfer Protocol (FTP)* is a TCP/IP service that runs on a host computer and allows files to be uploaded and downloaded. The service monitors port 21 for incoming requests. The client software opens a TCP session on port 21 with an FTP server. Some of the more common FTP commands are GET, PUT, BINARY, and ASCII. FTP is also the protocol that Unix hosts use to transfer files.

Hypertext Transfer Protocol

The *Hypertext Transfer Protocol (HTTP)* is the Web-browser-to-server protocol for the Internet. It uses port 80 of the TCP protocol to form a connection between the workstation browser and the Web server. HTTP also has secure versions of the protocol called S-HTTP (Secure HTTP) and SSL (Secure Sockets Layer).

Post Office Protocol 3

The *Post Office Protocol 3 (POP3)* is a TCP/IP mail server protocol that delivers mail to clients on a TCP/IP network. Keep in mind that POP3 delivers mail only to a client, whereas SMTP transfers mail between mail servers on a TCP/IP network. IMAP4 is a new protocol that will replace POP3 in the future.

Simple Mail Transfer Protocol

The *Simple Mail Transfer Protocol (SMTP)* transfers mail between mail servers on a TCP/IP network. The SMTP server can be set up as a mail relay server, or it can have a post office to which it delivers mail. Mail servers that transfer mail on the Internet use the SMTP protocol.

SMTP (port 25) is used to transfer mail between Internet mail servers. POP3 (port 110) is how Internet mail clients receive mail from Internet mail servers.

Simple Network Management Protocol

The *Simple Network Management Protocol (SNMP)* is a network management protocol that collects statistics from devices on TCP/IP networks. The device loads an agent that collects information and forwards that information to a network management console. You can configure the device with specific threshold parameters. When those thresholds are exceeded, an alert message is sent to the management console, which then creates a network baseline for future reference.

Remember that SNMP is the primary protocol for managing your network.

Transmission Control Protocol

The *Transmission Control Protocol (TCP)* is a Transport layer component that provides reliable data delivery service in the TCP/IP protocol stack. It is a connection-oriented protocol that creates a tunnel for a specific port/service between two TCP/IP host computers and guarantees data delivery. TCP uses IP as the transport mechanism between the host computers.

User Datagram Protocol

The *User Datagram Protocol (UDP)* is a Transport layer component that provides unreliable data delivery service in the TCP/IP protocol stack. It is a connectionless-oriented direct interface between applications and the IP protocol in the Network layer of the OSI stack. It is used for information that is time sensitive because it does not have the overhead that TCP does and therefore can send the data much faster between two locations. It is commonly used in audio and video applications.

UDP is a connectionless protocol and does not check to see if the packet arrived at its destination. This protocol is used to transmit packets that are time sensitive, or when it's not important to know if they arrived at their destination.

TCP/IP Utilities

The following sections cover some of the more common utilities available to you for testing, validating, and troubleshooting your TCP/IP connectivity. Since most of these commands and utilities are diagnostic in nature, complete instructions for using them to troubleshoot your network are included in Chapter 14.

IPCONFIG

The IPCONFIG.EXE command displays the TCP/IP settings of a Windows NT computer. The **IPCONFIG /ALL** command displays the IP address, subnet mask, default gateway, and WINS and DNS configurations. You can also release and renew an IP address from a DHCP server using this command.

WINIPCFG

WINIPCFG is a graphical representation of all the TCP/IP configurations in a Windows 95/98 workstation. It is an effective tool for troubleshooting TCP/IP problems, to include DHCP, WINS, and DNS problems. You can execute WINIPCFG from the Run command or from the DOS prompt.

You need to know that IPCONFIG is used on Windows NT computers, whereas WINIPCFG is used on Windows 95/98 computers.

NBTSTAT

NBTSTAT is a powerful tool for troubleshooting NetBIOS name resolution problems. The NBTSTAT command removes or corrects preloaded NetBIOS entries.

NETSTAT

The NETSTAT command shows the status of all TCP and UDP port activity on a workstation or server. The best way to defend against this type of discovery is to block UDP ports 137 and 138 as well as TCP port 139 at the routers that serve your Internet connections. This way, the ports necessary for this command to work will be closed off from external traffic yet will still function inside your network.

Be familiar with the NBSTAT and NETSTAT commands and how each works in a Windows network environment.

Packet Internet Groper

The *Packet Internet Groper (Ping)* is a utility that sends an Internet Control Message Protocol (ICMP) echo request message to a host on a TCP/IP network to test network connectivity. It waits for a response from the remote host and registers the time that it takes to respond. It is a good troubleshooting tool to determine whether a route is available to a remote host. To generate a ping, go to the Windows DOS prompt and type "ping" followed by the IP address. It will look like something like this:

```
C:\WIN95>ping 220.0.0.180
```

If you specified a correct IP address, and the route to the machine is functioning, you will see a reply message. As a rule, Windows 95/98 and Windows NT machines will send the ping four times before they give up. However, on some machines, ping will continue to send packets until you stop it with a ^c or **delete** command.

Telnet

Telnet provides a terminal emulation window through which you can access remote routers and Unix systems on a TCP/IP network. It is used to modify router commands and run host applications in Unix systems. Novell and Windows NT do not support Telnet port 23 connections for terminal emulation. All TCP/IP services, such as SMTP, FTP, Telnet, or HTTP, use ports to transfer data between host computers. The TCP/IP hosts create a virtual session and these sessions use the port numbers to pass the data between them. A

Protocols

Telnet connection on port 23 is used to connect to a host machine and run an application on the connected host once the security subsystem has authenticated the user. The Telnet utility can be set up to connect to a host with a port number other than 23 to troubleshoot problems. Using the Telnet utility with port 25 instead of port 23 allow a network analyst to enter SMTP commands individually and record the results from the SMTP server and determine if there are any errors.

Telnet is one of the main utilities used to connect to ports on host computers to determine whether the port is working properly.

Tracert

This utility traces the route of a packet between two locations and displays the router hops taken to get there. It is a good tool to determine where a packet is stopping on its way to the TCP/IP destination. You can also use it to determine which route is taken on a dual port router.

Tracert is a great utility to map the route that a packet takes through an intranet or the Internet.

Practice Questions

Question 1

> Which TCP/IP service or protocol stays the same across all vendor versions?
>
> ○ a. DHCP
> ○ b. DNS
> ○ c. WINS
> ○ d. NDS

The correct answer is b. The Domain Name System (DNS) is a hierarchical tree system with the root domain server at the top of the tree. All vendor DNS systems must conform to the same standard as the root domain servers. DHCP and WINS are LAN services and can be implemented in a variety of ways. Therefore, answers a and c are incorrect. NDS is the directory services database for NetWare 4.x and above. Therefore, answer d is incorrect.

Question 2

> What is the name of the Windows NT file where IP addresses and host names are entered when static address mapping is used?
>
> ○ a. LMHOSTS
> ○ b. NTHOSTS
> ○ c. HOSTS
> ○ d. STATHOSTS
> ○ e. NBSTAT

The correct answer is c. The HOSTS file is located in the winnt\system32\drivers\etc directory, and the addresses are assigned in the following manner: 192.168.10.1coriolis_ws99 # (the pound sign is for remarks). The dynamic features of DNS are preferred over static hosts table addressing. NTHOSTS, STATHOSTS, NBSTAT are fictitious names. Therefore, answers b, d, and e are incorrect. The LMHOSTS file is a local text file that maps IP addresses to NetBIOS names of remote servers with which you want to communicate using TCP/IP. Therefore, answer a is incorrect.

Question 3

What would be the result of a user statically assigning a dynamically assigned IP address to a Windows 9x machine? [Choose the two best answers]

- a. Nothing. The DHCP server would assign that address to another user on a different subnet.
- b. The TCP/IP subnet would experience an IP bridge loop until the problem is corrected.
- c. The DHCP server would stop functioning and alert the system administrator.
- d. It could result in a duplicate IP address being assigned to another user.
- e. It could result in the address being marked duplicate in the DHCP database.

The correct answers are d and e. The statically assigned address could be assigned to another user. The DHCP server will ping an address before assigning it; if it finds that address already assigned, it will mark it as a duplicate and try assigning the next available address. Answers a and b are not within the parameters of DHCP; therefore they are incorrect. The DHCP server has code to anticipate this type of problem. Therefore, answer c is incorrect.

Question 4

What would be the result of two workstations being assigned the same IP address?

- a. The default gateway would identify the conflict and reassign one of the workstations a different IP address.
- b. Neither of the workstations would be able to connect to the IP network.
- c. The first workstation on the network would be allowed to use the address, and the second workstation would not be allowed to connect to the IP network.
- d. The second workstation would connect to the network, and the first workstation's IP would be disabled as a result.

The correct answer is c. The TCP/IP stack on a client workstation looks for another machine on the network with a duplicate address; if it is found, it will shut down TCP/IP on the second machine connecting to the network. The default gateway routes packets and is not responsible for IP conflict resolution. Therefore, answer a is incorrect. The first workstation to connect to the network would get the IP address. Therefore, answers b and d are incorrect.

Question 5

Which TCP port does the Network News Transport Protocol (NNTP) use?

○ a. 25

○ b. 119

○ c. 110

○ d. 23

○ e. 80

The correct answer is b. The TCP port used by NNTP is 119. Port 25 is SMTP; therefore answer a is incorrect. Port 110 is POP3; therefore answer c is incorrect. Port 23 is Telnet; therefore answer d is incorrect. Port 80 is HTTP; therefore answer e is incorrect.

Question 6

Which TCP port does the File Transfer Protocol (FTP) use?

○ a. 21

○ b. 23

○ c. 25

○ d. 15

○ e. 53

The correct answer is a. The TCP port used by FTP is 21. Port 23 is Telnet; therefore answer b is incorrect. Port 25 is SMTP; therefore answer c is incorrect. Port 15 is a UDP, NETSTAT port; therefore answer d is incorrect. Port 53 is a UDP, Domain Name System port; therefore answer e is incorrect.

Question 7

Which TCP port does the Hypertext Transfer Protocol (HTTP) use?
- a. 21
- b. 23
- c. 80
- d. 110
- e. 119

The correct answer is c. The TCP port used by HTTP is 80. Port 21 is FTP; therefore answer a is incorrect. Port 23 is Telnet; therefore answer b is incorrect. Port 110 is POP3; therefore answer d is incorrect. Port 119 is NNTP; therefore answer e is incorrect.

Question 8

Which TCP port does Telnet use?
- a. 21
- b. 23
- c. 80
- d. 110
- e. 220

The correct answer is b. Telnet uses port 23. Port 21 is FTP; therefore answer a is incorrect. Port 80 is HTTP; therefore answer c is incorrect. Port 110 is POP3; therefore answer d is incorrect. Port 220 is IMAP3; therefore answer e is incorrect.

Question 9

Which TCP/IP application would you use to connect to a host and see whether the SMTP portion of a mail server is working correctly?

○ a. SNMP

○ b. TFTP

○ c. FTP

○ d. Telnet

○ e. None of the above

The correct answer is d. The Telnet utility uses port 23 by default to connect to TCP/IP hosts. If you change the Telnet port number to 25, connect to a mail host, and issue some SMTP commands, you will be able to determine if the mail host is operating correctly. SNMP is a network management protocol. Therefore, answer a is incorrect. TFTP and FTP are used to transfer files. Therefore, answers b and c are incorrect.

Question 10

What tool would you use to set up a Windows 95/98/NT workstation to use a proxy server?

○ a. Telnet utility

○ b. FTP utility

○ c. Web browser

○ d. Network Neighborhood

The correct answer is c. The Web browser has an option to use a proxy server. The Telnet utility connects to a host to run an application on the host. Therefore, answer a is incorrect. The FTP utility transfers files between hosts. Therefore, answer b is incorrect. The Network Neighborhood lists other computers on the LAN. Therefore, answer d is incorrect.

Question 11

> Which shared network product caches the most often accessed Web pages on a local area network?
> ○ a. Microsoft Internet Information Server
> ○ b. Netscape FocalPoint Web Server
> ○ c. Stateful inspection firewalls
> ○ d. HTTP proxy server
> ○ e. IP proxy server

The correct answer is d. A proxy server will identify and precache updates of the most active Web sites during low network traffic. Microsoft Internet Information Server and Netscape FocalPoint Web Server both publish Web sites. Therefore, answers a and b are incorrect. A stateful inspection firewall looks at the patterns of the data that is being transferred and does not cache it. Therefore, answer c is incorrect. An IP proxy server does network address translation. Therefore, answer e is incorrect.

Question 12

> Which utility traces the route of a TCP/IP packet and identifies delays or bottlenecks?
> ○ a. TRACEIT
> ○ b. TRACERT
> ○ c. NBTSTAT
> ○ d. NETSTAT
> ○ e. TRACEIP

The correct answer is b. The TRACERT utility identifies the route a packet takes through a TCP/IP network. It identifies the routers and any delays that the packet experiences in getting from one router to another. TRACEIT and TRACEIP are not utilities. Therefore, answers a and e are incorrect. NBTSTAT is used to troubleshoot NetBIOS name resolution problems. Therefore, answer c is incorrect. NETSTAT is used to show all TCP and UDP port activity on a server. Therefore, answer d is incorrect.

Question 13

What is the best TCP/IP protocol to use when transferring files between two Unix hosts?

○ a. TFTP

○ b. Telnet

○ c. FTP

○ d. COPY

○ e. XCOPY

○ f. ARP

The correct answer is c. File Transfer Protocol (FTP) is the standard for file transfer between systems on the Internet and between Unix systems. Many network operating systems, such as Windows NT and NetWare, are implementing TCP/IP as their default protocols, and their respective file copying utilities use TCP/IP as the transport. Unix has always used FTP and will continue to do so. TFTP is used to transfer the configuration from a router or switch to a TFTP server. Therefore, answer a is incorrect. The Telnet utility connects to a host to run an application on the host. Therefore, answer b is incorrect. The **COPY** and **XCOPY** commands are DOS/Windows commands. Therefore, answers d and e are incorrect. The **ARP** command is used to correlate an IP address to a MAC address. Therefore, answer f is incorrect.

Question 14

Which utility is used to view the TCP/IP configuration on a Windows 95/98 machine?

○ a. WINIPCFG

○ b. WINIPCONFIG

○ c. WIPCFG

○ d. IPCONFIG

The correct answer is a. The WINIPCFG utility is used to display the IP address, MAC address, subnet mask, default gateway, DNS information, DHCP information, and WINS information. This utility is also used to release and renew a lease from a DHCP server. WINIPCONFIG and WIPCFG are not utilities. Therefore, answers b and c are incorrect. IPCONFIG is used to view the TCP/IP configuration of a Windows NT machine. Therefore, answer d is incorrect.

Question 15

Which utility is used to view the TCP/IP configuration information on a Windows NT machine?

○ a. WINIPCFG
○ b. WINIPCONFIG
○ c. WIPCFG
○ d. IPCONFIG

The correct answer is d. The IPCONFIG utility is used to display the IP address, MAC address, subnet mask, default gateway, DNS information, DHCP information, and WINS information. This utility is also used to release and renew a lease from a DHCP server. WINIPCFG is used to view the TCP/IP configuration of a Windows 95/98 machine. Therefore, answer a is incorrect. WINIPCONFIG and WIPCFG are not utilities. Therefore, answers b and c are incorrect.

Question 16

Which utility would you use to determine whether another IP host is reachable?

○ a. SAP
○ b. PING
○ c. OSPF
○ d. RIP
○ e. NLSP

The correct answer is b. The PING command is used to determine whether a TCP/IP host is accessible and whether a host on one network can see a host on the same or a different network. SAP is used to update NetWare server routing tables. Therefore, answer a is incorrect. OSPF, RIP, and NLSP are all routing protocols used by routers. Therefore, answers c, d, and e are incorrect.

Question 17

What are the minimum requirements necessary to attach a node to a TCP/IP network?

- ○ a. NIC and IP address
- ○ b. NIC, IP address, and subnet mask
- ○ c. NIC, IP address, subnet mask, and DNS address
- ○ d. NIC, IP address, subnet mask, DNS address, and gateway address

The correct answer is b. A NIC, IP address, and subnet mask are the minimum requirements to communicate on a TCP/IP network. Therefore, answer a is incorrect. The DNS address is necessary to associate a TCP/IP address to a fully qualified domain name (FQDN). Therefore, answer c is incorrect. A gateway address is only necessary to communicate beyond the local subnet. Therefore, answer d is incorrect.

Question 18

What is the minimum information necessary to manually set up WINS on a Windows 95/98 machine?

- ○ a. Select the Enable WINS Resolution option and specify a primary WINS server address.
- ○ b. Select the Enable WINS Resolution option and specify a primary and secondary WINS server address.
- ○ c. Scope ID.
- ○ d. Using DHCP for WINS resolution.

The correct answer is a. At a minimum, you must select the Enable WINS Resolution option and specify a primary WINS server address. A secondary WINS address is recommended, but isn't mandatory. Therefore, answer b is incorrect. The Scope ID is used to group workstations together and is also not mandatory. Therefore, answer c is incorrect. Using DHCP for WINS resolution is a good idea but it is not mandatory. Therefore, answer d is incorrect.

Question 19

Which TCP/IP field is required before a packet can be transmitted to another subnet?

- ○ a. WINS
- ○ b. DHCP
- ○ c. FTP
- ○ d. Default gateway
- ○ e. NNTP

The correct answer is d. The default gateway address is needed before a packet can be transmitted beyond the local subnet. The default gateway is usually a router that is connected to the Internet or another router that would be the default path for the packets. The workstations at a remote office would point to the router connected to the corporate office as the default gateway address.

WINS is used to correlate NetBIOS names to IP addresses. Therefore, answer a is incorrect. DHCP is used to automatically assign TCP/IP parameters to a host computer. Therefore, answer b is incorrect. FTP is used to transfer files between TCP/IP hosts. Therefore, answer c is incorrect. NNTP is used for Network News Transfer Protocol. Therefore, answer e is incorrect.

Question 20

Which TCP port does the Trivial File Transfer Protocol (TFTP) use?

- ○ a. 21
- ○ b. 23
- ○ c. 25
- ○ d. 110
- ○ e. 69
- ○ f. None of the above

The correct answer is f. TFTF uses a UDP port not a TCP port. Therefore, none of the answers are correct. The correct answer is UDP port 69.

Need To Know More?

 Mazda, Fraidoon, ed.: *Telecommunications Engineer's Reference Book*. Reed Educational and Professional Publishing Ltd., Woburn, MA, 1998. ISBN 0-240-51491-2. An excellent reference book explaining the intricacies of telecommunications in great detail.

 Sheldon, Tom: *Encyclopedia of Networking, Electronic Edition*. Osborne McGraw-Hill, New York, 1997. ISBN 0-07-882333-1. A good overview of general networking terms and networking characteristics. Covers everything from A to Z.

 Microsoft has a CD subscription service called TechNet that covers the procedures necessary to set up TCP/IP in a Microsoft environment. Search the TechNet CD for "TCP/IP", "WINS", "DHCP", and "DNS".

 Novell has a CD subscription service called Novell Support Connect that covers the procedures to set up TCP/IP on a network containing NetWare. Search the Novell Support Connect CD for "TCP/IP", "WINS", "DNS", and "DHCP" to find the latest articles on configuring NetWare in a TCP/IP environment.

 Visit **www.microsoft.com**, which has a detailed knowledge base that explains the specifics of setting up TCP/IP in a Microsoft networking environment.

 Visit **www.novell.com**, which has a knowledge base that explains how to set up TCP/IP on a NetWare network.

Fault Tolerance

Terms you'll need to understand:

- Redundant Array of Inexpensive Disks (RAID)
- Mirroring
- Disk duplexing
- Striping
- Volumes
- Server fault tolerance (SFT)
- Digital audio tape (DAT)
- Digital linear tape (DLT)
- Normal backup
- Copy backup
- Incremental backup
- Differential backup
- Daily backup
- Removable media

Techniques you'll need to master:

- Understanding the concept of data redundancy
- Explaining the different types of hard drive redundancy
- Understanding the function and applications of fault tolerance
- Explaining the concept of clustering
- Knowing the appropriate uses for normal (full), copy, incremental, differential, and daily tape backups
- Knowing the different tape rotation types

Network fault tolerance is essential to providing your network with database redundancy to safeguard against losing valuable information stored on the network. Establishing system-level fault tolerance allows seamless failover by the redundant disk during a disk failure or by the redundant server during a server failure. This gives the network the ability to continue operations, despite the failure of significant network subsystems, and to prevent costly system downtime.

In addition to *clustering*, in which two or more servers share the same hard disk array that looks like one physical drive, fault tolerance schemes include methods such as disk mirroring, disk duplexing, and disk striping to provide recovery from system failures. Almost every network operating system (NOS) includes software components that help you establish network fault tolerance. This chapter helps you understand the different levels of fault tolerance and explains how they work.

Disk-Level Fault Tolerance

The importance of the data on your network is directly related to how much fault tolerance you need to implement. In areas of critical operations (such as production or accounting servers), you will need the maximum amount of fault tolerance. However, in areas of lesser importance (such as a low-use remote access server), you will not need to implement as much fault tolerance.

RAID Level 0: Stripe Sets Without Parity

Stripe sets without parity combine areas of unformatted free space on two or more hard drives into one logical volume (or logical drive if you are using Windows NT). Stripe sets can combine areas on different types of drives, such as small computer system interface (SCSI), enhanced small device interface (ESDI), and integrated drive electronics (IDE) drives. However, system and boot partitions cannot be part of a stripe set. In a stripe set, the system writes data to identically sized strips of disk space across each disk in the volume in logical order, one row at a time, and at the same rate.

Because the system evenly distributes the data over the stripe sets, all the drives collectively perform the same function done by a single drive in a normal configuration. For this reason, stripe sets without parity provide the best performance and data access of any of the RAID (redundant arrays of inexpensive disks) levels. However, stripe sets without parity are RAID level 0 and do not provide any redundancy. If a drive in the stripe set fails, you must replace the drive and restore the data from backup.

RAID Level 1: Disk Mirroring And Duplexing

When you initially implement *disk mirroring*, the system makes an exact copy of all the data on the first drive and writes it to a second, mirror drive. Both drives use the same controller, and the secondary drive must be of equal or greater size than the primary. Any remaining space on the secondary drive becomes free space. After initial implementation, the system exactly duplicates data simultaneously to both the primary and secondary hard drives to provide data redundancy. You can mirror any existing partition, including system and boot partitions, using the same controller. RAID hard drive controllers can perform hardware mirroring, but the SCSI and IDE controllers shipped with computers do not have that capability. Microsoft Windows NT and Novell NetWare have hard drive mirroring capability through the operating system.

If the primary drive fails, the system uses the mirrored hard drive to recover and allow the systems to continue operations in a nonmirrored state until you replace the failed hard drive. The redundant data on the mirror drive protects data from media and controller failure.

Mirror sets are more expensive than stripe sets with parity in terms of dollars per megabyte because they use one hard drive of equal or greater size to mirror the data. However, the initial cost is lower because they require only two disks, whereas stripe sets with parity require three or more disks and might also require a RAID controller.

Most SCSI disk drives can load-balance read operations across the mirrored drives to increase read performance over that of a single-drive installation. However, disk-write operations are less efficient because the system must individually write the data to both disks, causing a slight performance penalty.

In addition to no loss in performance when a member of a mirror set fails, mirror sets have better overall read and write performance than stripe sets with parity because of I/O load balancing between the two drives.

Disk duplexing is similar to disk mirroring in that it implements hard drive mirroring, but duplexing incorporates two controllers instead of one to reduce the chance of a bad controller causing a system failure. Disk duplexing allows the system to write the same data to all disks simultaneously. Because the disks are on different controllers, data transfer is faster than with disk mirroring, in which data is written to the disks sequentially over the same controller. Disk duplexing also allows *split seeks*, which allow the system to send read requests to whichever disk can respond first. Multiple read requests are also split between the duplexed disks for simultaneous processing.

You should know the difference between mirroring and duplexing hard drives. Mirroring uses the same hard disk controller, whereas duplexing uses two separate hard disk controllers. Both mirroring and duplexing are considered RAID level 1.

RAID Level 4: Independent Data Disks With Shared Parity

In RAID 4, which is seldom implemented, each entire block of data is written on a data disk. The parity for same-rank blocks is generated on writes, recorded on the parity disk, and checked on reads. RAID 4 uses one disk as the parity disk, unlike RAID 5, which stripes parity data across all the disks in the array. RAID 4 has a very high read data transaction rate and a low ratio of ECC (parity) disks to data disks, which means high efficiency.

However, because of its complex controller design, it has a terrible write transaction rate and aggregate transfer rate. It also has an inefficient data rebuild in the event of disk failure, and the block read transfer rate equals that of a single disk.

RAID Level 5: Stripe Sets With Parity

RAID level 5, also known as *disk striping with parity*, stripes the data and parity in large blocks across all the disks in the array and requires a minimum of three drives of equal size. Level 5 differs from level 4 in that it writes the parity data across all the disks, whereas level 4 writes the parity data to only one disk. RAID level 4 is seldom implemented because RAID level 5 offers greater speed and data redundancy. The parity information provides data redundancy because the system arranges the data and parity information on the disk array so that the two are always on different disks.

Stripe sets with parity have better read performance than mirror sets, except when a drive fails or is missing from the array. When a drive is missing, the read performance is degraded because it has to recover the data that was on the missing drive with the parity information. A RAID 5 configuration is more efficient when you have applications that are primarily read-only oriented.

Even though RAID 5 uses less disk space to implement redundancy than does mirroring, write operations are slower than mirroring because the system must write the parity information and then write the data. The parity calculations reduce the efficiency of write operations and require more memory to perform than read operations.

Remember that after a disk failure, no fault tolerance occurs until you repair the fault, and currently RAID 1, 4, or 5 implementations cannot withstand two simultaneous failures. However, once you replace the failed disk, the system can regenerate the data using the redundant information. Data regeneration occurs without bringing in backup tapes or performing manual update operations to cover transactions that took place since the last backup. When data regeneration is complete, all data is current and again protected against disk failure. Providing cost-effective, high data availability is the most important advantage of disk arrays.

> You need at least three hard drives to perform RAID level 5. The parity information uses the space that totals the size of one hard drive and is not counted in the total available user space.

Server Fault Tolerance

Both NetWare and Windows NT support a server fault model. The systems differ in the way they are set up, but the result is the same. If one server fails because of a hardware problem, the other server seamlessly continues network operations.

Server Fault Tolerance III

The Novell model is *Server Fault Tolerance (SFT) III*, which is composed of two identical servers with the same hardware configuration. The servers are connected with a mirrored server link. In the event that one server fails, the other server provides a seamless takeover.

Clustering

The Windows NT answer to SFT III is the cluster server. The cluster server requires two servers with similar hardware that are connected to a shared external hard drive cabinet. As with SFT III, if one of the servers fails, the other one takes over without a glitch.

Tape Backup

The most widely used method for offline storage is the tape backup method using digital audio tape (DAT) or digital linear tape (DLT). If you establish a regular schedule to back up data on hard drives, you will minimize data loss or damage caused by disk failures, user error, power outages, virus infection, theft, fire, and many other problems. If you check your backup operation regularly for data consistency and successful backups, restoring a file or even an entire system should be successful.

You should clean the tape drive regularly by using a cleaning tape according to the manufacturer's recommended schedule. Some organizations fail to emphasize this practice and neglect regular cleaning of the tape drives. Dirty tape drives result in data loss because the write heads on the drive cannot write the data properly to the tape.

 If you experience an error during a backup session, you should first clean the tape drive, then try the backup session again.

It is important that you install all backup software modules on a server to guarantee the quality of backed-up data. You will commonly need additional modules when you back up a database server or mail server. The modules shut down certain portions or, in some cases, the entire database and then perform a backup of the data. After the data backup is complete, the backup software will restart the database automatically. Before you begin your database backup, there are a few things that you should know and do, such as:

➤ Know what data you will be backing up.

➤ Be familiar with the size of the tape backup hardware you are using.

➤ Establish the type of backup procedure or tape rotation you will use.

➤ Define a specific time that the backup is scheduled to start.

➤ Set aside a tape storage area for both short- and long-term access.

➤ Perform system backups when the fewest people are on the network. If many files are in use, the backup might not correctly reflect the data.

You can perform five types of tape backup: normal (full), copy, incremental, differential, and daily. You will use the normal, incremental, and differential backups most often.

Normal (Full) Backup

The *normal backup* copies all the selected files and marks each one as backed up. Normal backups allow you to restore files quickly and with minimal data loss because the most current files are on the last system tape or tape set. However, restoring from a normal backup tape is the most time consuming, and if the files do not change, the backups are redundant.

Copy Backup

The *copy backup* copies all the selected files but does not mark each file as backed up. You will normally use the copy backup if you want to back up files between normal and incremental backups. In this case, the copy backup is preferred because it does not invalidate other full or incremental backup operations.

Incremental Backup

The *incremental backup* copies only those files that have been created or changed since the last normal or incremental backup and will be marked as backed up. If you use a combination of normal and incremental backups, restoring the files requires that you start with your last normal backup and then work through all the incremental backup tapes. This can pose a problem, as files can be difficult to find because they can be on several tapes. The advantages of this type of backup are that it is the least time consuming and requires the least amount of data storage space.

Differential Backup

The *differential backup* copies those files that have been created or changed since the last normal or incremental backup. However, it does not mark files as backed up. If you perform normal and differential backups, restoring the system requires only the last normal and last differential backup tapes. Although the differential backup is less time-consuming than normal backups, file recovery takes longer than if the files were on a single, normal backup tape. However, if large amounts of data change daily, differential backups can be more time consuming than incremental ones.

Daily Backup

The *daily backup* copies only the selected files that have been modified on the day that you perform the daily backup. The backed-up files are not marked as backed up. The daily backup does not reset the archive bit; therefore, the files can be backed up during a full or incremental backup. The daily backup is a fast way to back up files that have changed during the current day.

 The system changes the file archive bits to indicate that a file has been backed up on a normal (full) or incremental backup. In copy, differential, and daily backups, the archive bit is not changed.

Tape Rotation

Once you have implemented a backup operation, you should document your backup and restore procedures. After your backup system is in place, it is a good idea to periodically practice restoring both files and entire servers. In addition, you should run periodic tests to validate the established restore procedure and to verify that the backup data is actually on the tape. You can choose from two types of backup rotation: the grandfather rotation method and the 10-tape rotation method.

Grandfather Rotation

To use the grandfather rotation method, you need 21 storage media tapes. Label four tapes as daily sets—Monday, Tuesday, Wednesday, and Thursday—and use these tapes to perform incremental or full backups as desired. Label five tapes as weekly sets—Friday1, Friday2, Friday3, Friday4, and Friday5—and use these tapes to perform full backups. Label the other tapes as monthly sets—January, February, March, April, May, June, July, August, September, October, November, and December—and use these tapes to perform full backups as well. Substitute the tape for the last Friday of the month with the monthly tape.

10-Tape Rotation

To use the 10-tape rotation method, you will need 10 tapes, each one labeled with a number from 1 through 10. Doing this divides the backup into a 40-week period with 10 4-week cycles. This method uses each tape an equal number of times during the 40 weeks. A 12-week-old copy of your data is on at least one tape. Use the same tapes for the Monday (tape 1), Tuesday (tape 2), Wednesday (tape 3), and Thursday (tape 4) backups during the first 4 weeks. Use the next sequence of four tapes (tapes 5 through 8) for the first four Fridays. After the 4 weeks, increment the daily tape set numbers by one. For example, Monday will be tape 2, Tuesday will be tape 3, and so on. Use this numbering scheme during the second 4-week cycle. You should also increment the Friday tape numbers by one during the second 4 weeks so that they become tapes 6 through 9. Continue this method through the tape rotation, and at the end of 40 weeks you will be back at tape 1.

Tape Archiving And Storage

No matter which backup or rotation method you use, keep a written log of all backups that you perform in case the electronic log and error files are destroyed. Record the date, backup type, what data you backed up, the media set identification name or number, session log path, and the initials of the person performing the backup. The tapes should be stored offsite in a secure and environmentally controlled area. Do not leave the tapes in your car or in any other environmentally unstable area, because extreme heat and cold can affect the integrity of the data stored on the tape. You should also avoid storing tapes in close proximity to magnetic fields, such as computer monitors, televisions, and microwave ovens, because they can cause data corruption or deletion.

Backup tapes should be stored in a secure location offsite as a precaution against theft, fire, and other disasters. You should also institute, as part of the standard operating procedures, a contingency plan to get a server back in operation in case of theft or disaster.

Removable Media

Removable media provide a means of data redundancy besides that provided by tape backup (*offline storage*) or redundant internal disks (*online storage*). Removable media ensures that you still have your network data intact should the network completely fail. In addition to tape backup, which provides the slowest recovery, removable media include optical storage disks and removable hard drives.

Optical Storage Disks

Optical disks provide *near-line storage*, meaning that although the data is not instantaneously available, it is available in one to two minutes. The optical disk carousels can store hundreds of gigabytes of information, which is available upon user request, and can support document imaging systems. Optical drives use two types of CD-ROMs: rewritable, to which you can store, erase, and overwrite data; and write once, read many (WORM) disks, to which you can only write data once.

Removable Hard Drives

Removable hard drives are just that: hard drives that you can pull out of your computer for remote storage. They can also store gigabytes of data and have a fast backup speed. Removable hard drives provide a higher level of security for your data, not only against tampering, but against natural catastrophes as well. The biggest downfall of removable hard drives is that data recovery is considerably slower as compared to optical or online data storage.

Chapter 5

Practice Questions

Question 1

> Which RAID level makes an exact copy of the data on the first hard drive and writes it to the second hard drive?
>
> ○ a. RAID 0
> ○ b. RAID 1
> ○ c. RAID 3
> ○ d. RAID 4
> ○ e. RAID 5

The correct answer is b. RAID 1 uses hard disk mirroring and hard disk duplexing. An exact image of the first hard drive is copied to the second drive. If a hard disk fails, the system continues to operate in a broken mirrored state until the failed hard disk is replaced and the mirror is reestablished. RAID 0 is disk striping without parity. Therefore, answer a is incorrect. RAID 3 and RAID 4 write the parity data to one disk in the array. Therefore, answers c and d are incorrect. RAID 5 is disk striping with parity. Therefore, answer e is incorrect.

Question 2

> Which two types of tape backup reset the archive bit after backing up a file? [Choose the two best answers]
>
> ❑ a. Normal
> ❑ b. Copy
> ❑ c. Incremental
> ❑ d. Differential
> ❑ e. Daily

The correct answers are a and c. The archive bit is reset after a normal or full backup and after an incremental backup. The copy, differential, and daily backups do not reset the archive bit. Therefore, answers b, d, and e are incorrect.

Question 3

What is the first thing you should do when the tape backup log shows verification errors or any type of errors indicating that it had trouble writing data to the tape?

- ○ a. Clean the tape drive
- ○ b. Reformat the tape and try it again
- ○ c. Call technical support
- ○ d. Discard old tapes and use new tapes

The correct answer is a. Cleaning the tape drive should be the first thing that you try. If the tape drive is dirty, the other options will not work. Reformatting the tape, calling technical support, and replacing the tapes are viable options but should not be the first choice. Therefore, answers b, c, and d are incorrect.

Question 4

Which method of offline storage is the most widely used for network operating systems?

- ○ a. Server mirroring
- ○ b. Hard drive mirroring
- ○ c. Tape backup
- ○ d. Internet site mirroring
- ○ e. Rewritable optical drives

The correct answer is c. Tape backup is the most widely used offline storage method. The most popular tape drives are the 4mm DAT drives and the DLT drives. Server mirroring, hard drive mirroring, and Internet site mirroring are online storage options. Therefore, answers a, b, and d are incorrect. Rewritable optical drives are considered near-line storage. Therefore, answer e is incorrect.

Question 5

> Why should backup tapes be stored in an offsite location? [Choose the three best answers]
>
> ❏ a. In case of fire
> ❏ b. In case of theft
> ❏ c. For security
> ❏ d. For safety

The correct answers are a, b, and c. The primary reason for taking tapes offsite is to protect business data in the unlikely event of fire or theft. If the business data is safely stored on a backup tape, a replacement server can be installed and business transactions can resume with the least possible impact. Safety is not an issue, therefore answer d is incorrect.

Question 6

> RAID Level 0 can combine areas of what types of drives? [Choose the three best answers]
>
> ❏ a. SCSI
> ❏ b. 3.5" floppy
> ❏ c. ESDI
> ❏ d. IDE
> ❏ e. CD-ROM

Answers a, c, and d are correct. Stripe sets without parity (RAID level 0) can combine areas of unformatted free space on different types of drives, such as small computer system interface (SCSI), enhanced small device interface (ESDI), and integrated drive electronics (IDE) drives. However, it cannot do so for 3.5" floppies or CD-ROMs. Therefore, answers b and e are incorrect.

Question 7

Disk duplexing is different from mirroring in what ways? [Choose the two best answers]

- ❏ a. It is more expensive than mirroring.
- ❏ b. It uses two controllers instead of one.
- ❏ c. Data transfer is faster.
- ❏ d. There is no loss in performance when a member fails.

Answers b and c are correct. Disk duplexing uses two disk controllers, unlike mirroring, which uses one. In addition, disk duplexing has a faster data transfer rate than mirroring. Answer a is incorrect because the cost between the two is negligible. Answer d is also incorrect, because this attribute is the same for both duplexing and mirroring.

Question 8

Which RAID level can perform stripe sets with parity, to include the system and boot partitions?

- ○ a. Software RAID 0
- ○ b. Software RAID 1
- ○ c. Software RAID 5
- ○ d. Hardware RAID 1
- ○ e. Hardware RAID 5

Answer e is correct. The hardware controller makes the three drives required for RAID 5 look like one drive to the NOS. Answers a and c are incorrect because although they are a type of software stripe set, the boot partition cannot be a part of a stripe set. Answers b and d are incorrect because they are for mirroring and duplexing.

Need To Know More?

 Sheldon, Tom: *Encyclopedia of Networking, Electronic Edition*. Osborne McGraw-Hill, New York. ISBN 0-07-882333-1. A good overview of general networking terms and networking characteristics; covers everything from A to Z.

 Microsoft has a CD subscription called TechNet that is an invaluable reference when setting up redundancy using Microsoft products. Search for "cluster", "RAID", and "backup" on the Microsoft TechNet CD to learn more about fault tolerance.

 Novell also has a CD subscription service, called Support Connection, which is an invaluable reference when setting up redundancy using NetWare products. Search for "SFT 3", "RAID", and "backup" on the Novell Support Connection disk to learn more about fault tolerance.

 Visit **www.cai.com**, the home of Cheyenne ARCserve backup software. ARCserve can back up NetWare servers, Windows NT servers, and many network clients and hosts.

 Visit **www.microsoft.com**, which has a knowledge base that explains in detail the specifics of hard disk redundancy and tape backup methods.

 Visit **www.novell.com**, which has a knowledge base that explains how to set up hard disk redundancy and tape backup methods.

 Visit **www.seagatesoftware.com**, which offers BackupExec software. Seagate BackupExec can back up NetWare servers, Windows NT servers, and many network clients and hosts.

Remote Connectivity

Terms you'll need to understand:

- Serial Line Internet Protocol (SLIP)
- Point-to-Point Tunneling Protocol (PPTP)
- Link Control Protocol (LCP)
- Network Control Protocol (NCP)
- Integrated Services Digital Network (ISDN)
- Point-to-Point Protocol (PPP)
- Virtual Private Network (VPN)
- Basic Rate ISDN (BRI)
- Primary Rate ISDN (PRI)
- Broadband ISDN (B-ISDN)
- Plain Old Telephone Service (POTS)
- Public Switched Telephone Network (PSTN)

Techniques you'll need to master:

- Knowing the different modem configurations
- Understanding the concept of remote connectivity
- Explaining the differences between PPP and SLIP
- Understanding the function of PPTP
- Explaining the attributes of, and differences between, ISDN and PSTN

The area of remote connectivity has grown tremendously over the past several years. The largest dial-in network in the world is the Internet, the global reach of which is growing every day. Telephone companies are starting to offer a wider selection of services to meet the diverse needs of their clients. In addition, most cable companies offer Internet access. The Web browser is rapidly becoming the default user interface to access all types of data. With the Internet driving the standards for remote connectivity, corporate clients are requiring the same type of access to corporate data that they get from the Internet. The requirement to connect remote clients to corporate local area networks (LANs) across the Internet has led to the development of a whole new breed of protocols that create secure tunnels through the Internet.

Encapsulation Protocols

The two most prevalent encapsulation methods for remote connectivity are the *Serial Line Internet Protocol (SLIP)* and the *Point-To-Point Protocol (PPP)*. However, PPP has become the standard encapsulation protocol because it supports encapsulation of many different types of protocols and incorporates extensive error checking and correction. The following sections discuss the attributes of the encapsulation protocols and the environments in which they are deployed.

Serial Line Internet Protocol

SLIP was the popular, although unofficial, encapsulation protocol before PPP became the adopted standard. SLIP connects one TCP/IP system with another TCP/IP system over a modem link. It then encapsulates the IP packets into the Data Link layer and transmits them between the modems. Compared to PPP, which can transport many different protocols, SLIP can transport only IP packets. SLIP supports V.90 asynchronous communication, but only up to speeds of 56Kbps. In addition, it cannot use synchronous links at all, and it does not support compression. For more information on the Data Link layer, see Chapter 8.

> *Note: Although PPP is the emerging standard, some exceptions exist. For example, some Unix systems still use SLIP for asynchronous modem connections, and some cellular telephone companies use it to connect workstations to their Cellular Digital Packet Data (CDPD) network. SLIP only supports IP encapsulation and it does not support compression.*

Point-To-Point Protocol

PPP was originally developed to overcome the lack of an official, standard Internet encapsulation protocol. PPP addresses issues such as asynchronous (start/stop) and bit-oriented synchronous encapsulation, network protocol multiplexing, link configuration, link quality testing, error detection, Network layer address negotiation, and data compression negotiation. PPP can operate across any DTE/DCE interface, provided that the circuit is duplex (either dedicated or switched), and can operate in either an asynchronous or synchronous bit-serial mode. PPP frame construction is shown in Table 6.1.

PPP is a Data Link layer protocol that encapsulates other Network layer protocols, such as TCP/IP and IPX, for transmission on synchronous and asynchronous communication lines. It establishes connections across many different

Table 6.1   The PPP frame structure.

Field	Description
Flag	A single byte containing the binary sequence 01111110, indicating the start or end of a frame.
Address	A single byte containing the binary sequence 11111111, the standard broadcast address. PPP does not assign individual station addresses.
Control	A single byte containing the binary sequence 00000011, calling for transmission of user data in an unsequenced frame. It provides a connectionless link service similar to the Logical Link Control (LLC).
Protocol	2 bytes identifying the protocol encapsulated in the information field of the frame. It specifies the protocol field values in the most recent Assigned Numbers Request For Comments (RFC).
Data	Zero or more bytes containing the datagram for the specified protocol. The end of the information field is found by locating the closing flag sequence and allowing 2 bytes for the frame check sequence (FCS) field. The default maximum length of the information field is 1,500 bytes. Consenting PPP implementations can use other values for the maximum information field length.
Frame check sequence (FCS)	Normally 16 bits (2 bytes). Consenting PPP implementations can use a 32-bit (4-byte) FCS for improved error detection.

communications links and in environments that use varied vendors and devices. PPP connects computers with asynchronous modems, bridges, routers, ISDN devices, and X.25 devices and assigns and manages IP addresses. In addition, PPP can encapsulate multiple protocols in a given session and can keep links active over each of the individual protocols. PPP has three components that allow it to transmit datagrams over serial point-to-point links:

➤ The Data Link layer is based on the High-Level Data Link Control (HDLC) frame structure, which acts as a basis for encapsulating datagrams over point-to-point links.

➤ An extensible Link Control Protocol (LCP) establishes, configures, maintains, and terminates the data-link connection.

➤ A Network Control Protocol (NCP) establishes and configures different Network layer protocols.

Link Control Protocol

To establish point-to-point communications, the originating PPP first sends *Link Control Protocol (LCP)* frames to configure and test the data link. The LCP also negotiates the highest reliable speed that can support the connection. The LCP can negotiate modifications to the standard PPP frame structure but can discern modified frames from standard frames. LCP goes through four discrete stages:

1. **Link establishment and configuration negotiation** Before the PPP can exchange Network layer datagrams, the LCP must open the connection and negotiate configuration parameters. When a configuration acknowledgment frame is both sent and received, the LCP goes to the next phase: link quality determination.

2. **Link quality determination** This is an optional stage in which the LCP tests the link quality to see whether it is sufficient to bring up Network layer protocols. LCP can delay transmission of Network layer protocol information until this is complete.

3. **Network layer protocol configuration negotiation** Next, the originating PPP sends *Network Control Protocol (NCP)* frames to establish a connection with and configure one or more Network layer protocols. The Internet Protocol Control Protocol (IPCP) then negotiates and configures the link to carry TCP/IP packets. After each Network layer protocol is configured, packets from each protocol can be sent over the link.

Remote Connectivity

4. **Link termination** The link remains configured until an LCP or NCP frame closes the link. The NCP can close Network layer sessions, but the LCP closes the entire link. If the LCP closes the link, it informs the Network layer protocols so that they can close out their sessions. The LCP can terminate the link at any time. Usually, a user will request the termination, but it can also terminate because of a physical event, such as the loss of carrier or the expiration of an idle-period timer.

Make sure that you select PPP when you are connecting to remote locations over an asynchronous connection. Communications errors commonly occur because one side of the communications link is set for PPP and the other side is set for SLIP.

PPP is a fast and reliable Data Link layer protocol that is the emerging standard encapsulation protocol for asynchronous and synchronous communications. Table 6.2 compares SLIP and PPP performance.

Point-To-Point Tunneling Protocol

The *Point-To-Point Tunneling Protocol* (PPTP) is a networking protocol that supports multiprotocol, virtual private networks (VPNs). The VPN enables remote users to access corporate networks through a secure connection across the Internet. This access is available by dialing into an Internet Service Provider (ISP) or by connecting directly to the Internet. PPTP also enables secure

Table 6.2 A comparison of PPP versus SLIP.	
PPP	**SLIP**
Dynamically negotiates IP addresses.	Requires user intervention to mediate IP addresses.
Transports multiple protocols on a single serial connection.	Transports only IP data.
Uses the LCP to negotiate reliable connections at the highest possible speed.	Lacks error correction capabilities.
The NCP negotiates the Network layer protocols that it will pass.	Supports only TCP/IP.
Supports bandwidth-on-demand using the PPP Multilink Protocol or the Bandwidth Allocation Control Protocol.	Cannot strap two channels together to increase the bandwidth beyond 56Kbps.

data transfer of PPP packets from a remote client to a private corporate server by creating a VPN across TCP/IP-based data networks.

Because PPTP allows multiprotocol encapsulation, you can send any type of packet, such as Internetwork Packet Exchange (IPX) or NetBIOS Extended User Interface (NetBEUI), over the network. PPTP uses the Password Authentication Protocol (PAP) and the Challenge Handshake Authentication Protocol (CHAP) encryption algorithms to provide secure, password-protected access to data over the tunnel.

PAP sends the user's name and password over the wire to a secure server for comparison with a database of user account names and passwords. PAP is not secure because the password is sent over the wire.

CHAP is a secure authentication protocol that does not send passwords over the wire because it uses a challenge/response technique. Once the server authenticates the user by their username and gives them access to the server, it uses the user's password as the encryption key but still does not send the password across the wire.

In addition to supporting encrypted PPP links across the Internet, PPTP also allows the Internet to become a backbone for carrying TCP/IP, IPX, and NetBEUI traffic. PPTP can create an IPX tunnel because it encapsulates and encrypts PPP packets that ride TCP/IP to the destination.

Both Windows NT Server 4 and Windows NT Workstation 4 include PPTP, and Windows 95/98 have provisions to add PPTP. With PPTP, computers running these operating systems can securely connect to a private network using a public data network such as the Internet. You do not need an ISP or a modem pool to create a PPTP tunnel as long as the PPTP client connects to a LAN.

PPTP secure communication consists of three processes: the PPP connection, the PPTP connection, and PPTP packet tunneling.

The PPP Connection

A PPTP client uses PPP to establish a connection over the Internet to an ISP using a regular telephone line or an ISDN line, and then serves to encrypt the data packets.

The PPTP Connection

After the client makes the initial PPP connection to the ISP or modem pool, it makes a second connection, called a *control connection*, from the PPTP client to the PPTP server over the existing PPP connection. The control connection

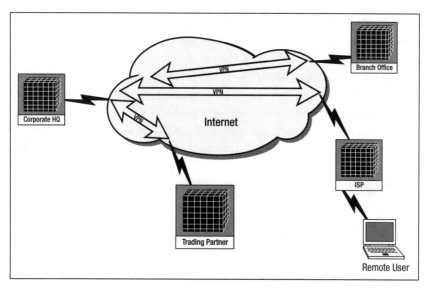

Figure 6.1 Virtual private network.

uses TCP to create the VPN connection, called a tunnel, to a PPTP server on the LAN, as shown in Figure 6.1. The tunnel is a "secret passageway" that carries communications over a secure channel using the original PPP connection.

PPTP Packet Tunneling

Tunneling is the process of sending encapsulated packets to a computer on a private LAN by routing them over some other network, such as the Internet, by using a VPN. The PPTP client and server use tunneling to securely route packets to a computer on a private, corporate LAN by using routers that know the address of only the private LAN server.

After the client establishes the PPTP connection, the PPTP encapsulates and compresses the PPP packets into IP datagrams. These datagrams are transmitted over the Internet through the PPTP tunnel (VPN) to the PPTP server that connects the Internet to the private LAN.

The PPTP server disassembles the IP datagram into a PPP packet, decrypts the PPP packet using the network protocol of the private LAN, and routes the decrypted packets to the private LAN.

 The PPTP uses TCP/IP as the transport to establish the VPN across a TCP/IP network and encrypts the packets between the two locations.

Integrated Services Digital Network

The Integrated Services Digital Network (ISDN) is a digital, circuit-switched telephone network that was designed to replace the analog telephone system. A digital telephone network provides more reliable data transmissions, faster transmission, and increased scalability than an analog system. Currently, modems translate digital signals from a computer into analog signals and transmit them across the analog telephone network. The modem at the other end translates the analog signal back into a digital signal and forwards the packet to the computer or the Internet. ISDN circumvents the translation steps and allows the computer, which transmits data digitally, to connect to the Internet or another computer directly. ISDN comes in three implementations: Basic Rate ISDN, Primary Rate ISDN, and Broadband ISDN.

Basic Rate ISDN

The *basic rate ISDN (BRI)* signal has three channels: two 64Kbps data transmission channels, called B channels, and one 16Kbps network signaling channel, called the D channel. Figure 6.2 shows the BRI channel circuits.

> When using a BRI connection for voice and data, the data will use both B channels until a voice connection is requested. When the ISDN circuit detects an incoming or outgoing telephone call during a data transmission, the BRI will automatically scale back to use only one channel of the ISDN circuit.

BRI is a circuit-switched network that uses the existing copper wire installed by the telephone company and is the most commonly installed ISDN line for home consumers. The ISDN line can be set up to use one of the data channels for voice and the other for data. This permits the data channel to dynamically use the voice channel when no voice traffic is transmitting. When the ISDN circuit detects an incoming or an outgoing call, the data signal automatically releases the voice channel to complete the voice call.

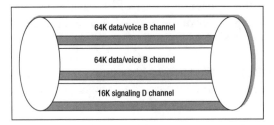

Figure 6.2 BRI channel circuits.

The telephone company installs a network termination device (NT1) for the ISDN line at the customer site. The NT device has a terminal equipment (TE) port and a terminal adapter (TA) port. The TE port supports ISDN-compatible devices, and the TA port supports non-ISDN devices, such as analog telephones and computers.

> BRI is deployed to achieve data speeds of 128Kbps. The V.90 asynchronous modem standard is most commonly deployed at 56Kbps. However, the V.90 asynchronous modem standard can strap two modems together to achieve 128Kbps, but it is seldom deployed. A BRI data connection is faster than an analog V.90 asynchronous data connection.

Primary Rate ISDN

The *primary rate ISDN (PRI)* signal consists of 23 64Kbps ISDN B channels and one 64Kbps D channel for a total bandwidth of 1.544Mbps. The 64Kbps channels can be dynamically strapped together to provide the maximum bandwidth of 1.544Mbps within the PRI circuit. It is a circuit-switched network that creates a dedicated circuit between two points like the existing analog telephone network, but is equivalent in bandwidth to a T1 leased line. You will find the PRI signal deployed most commonly in organizations that need large bandwidth to remote locations. In that case, the telephone company will install a network termination device (NT2) that supports multiplexing and switching systems at the customer site.

Broadband ISDN

The *broadband ISDN (B-ISDN)* service was developed for rates above 155Mbps. The Physical layer uses the Synchronous Optical Network (SONET) standard, and the Data Link layer uses an asynchronous transfer mode (ATM)-based cell-switching service that gives network providers flexibility in allocating transmission capacity among diverse user needs. B-ISDN provides high-capacity, high-performance voice, video, data, and integrated multimedia services to users on a worldwide basis. B-ISDN information transport is through the ATM. B-ISDN signaling is accomplished using switchable B-ISDN channels and provides users with call management.

B-ISDN uses a three-plane approach: the user plane, the control plane, and the management plane. The user plane is responsible for user information transfer, including flow control and error control; the control plane manages the call-control and connection-control functions; and the management plane includes plane and layer management.

B-ISDN also adopts a layered approach consisting of the Physical layer, the ATM layer, the ATM adaptation layer (AAL), and higher layers. The Physical layer provides the base network functions. Because B-ISDN handles both packet and circuit-mode applications, it uses ATM, also called fast packet switching. The AAL handles non-ATM protocols, such as Link Access Protocol-D. Higher layers consist of services layers for video, SMDS, frame relay, access, and network signaling.

Plain Old Telephone Service

Whereas ISDN is a digital system, the *plain old telephone service (POTS)* is the circuit-switched, analog telephone system that has been around since the original Bell telephone system. POTS is a more casual name for the *public switched telephone network (PSTN)*, but the two are the same. It uses twisted-pair wire to connect homes and businesses to a central office (CO). The CO is connected to other COs and long-distance carriers to form the largest network in the world. The maximum distance from the CO to the home or office without installing a repeater is between 7 and 10 kilometers.

Circuit switching sets up a dedicated communications channel between two end systems. In a company, the local, private branch exchange (PBX) will set up a local switched circuit to accommodate internal calls. The next level out would be connecting to the local exchange and making a call within the local exchange. The next level would be making a long-distance call and creating a switched circuit from the local PBX to the branch exchange, and then to the long-distance carrier.

Modem Configuration

Whether you are accessing the Internet or remotely connecting to your corporate office, you must have your modem connected properly if you want to successfully connect to the network. In the following discussion, we address the steps of setting up an internal modem in a computer running Windows 95.

Configure the modem to use an available serial port, interrupt, and I/O address range. The interrupt and I/O address should match the default values for the COM port that the modem is using. However, some plug-and-play modems do not need manual configuration because the computer will automatically find and configure them on bootup. If you install plug-and-play devices along with non-plug-and-play devices, you can cause resource conflicts that you will have to resolve later.

If the modem is configured to use an existing serial port, go into the computer's CMOS and disable that serial port to release the resource for modem use. In a plug-and-play BIOS, this might not release the resource for modem use, and you might have to reinstall Windows 95 using the **setup /p i** command. The **setup /p i** switch does not report the existence of a plug-and-play BIOS. Then, when you disable the serial port in your computer's CMOS settings, the resources that the serial port was configured to use are freed.

If Windows 95 does not detect the modem automatically on startup, you should run the Install New Modem Wizard. The wizard will automatically try to detect the serial port and type of modem and install all the drivers for it. If the wizard cannot determine the type of modem installed, you might need to supply the manufacturer's driver disk to finish the installation.

The process of adding a modem to a computer system is relatively easy if the modem is an external modem. An internal modem can cause conflict with existing devices and serial ports. It can be a greater challenge to install an internal modem because of the troubleshooting methods necessary to make it work.

Maximum Port Speed

The serial ports on all new computers use the 16550 UART chip, which can reach speeds of 256Kbps. The predecessor to the 16550 chip was the 16450 UART chip, which could achieve a maximum speed of only 115.2Kbps. The original UART chip was an 8-bit 8250 chip. When connecting a modem to a serial port, make sure that the UART chip is a 16550 chip.

You should know the speeds of the 16550 UART chip (256Kbps) and the 16450 UART chip (115.2Kbps).

Serial Port IRQ And I/O Address

Most computers come with two serial interfaces built into the motherboard, which by default assigns each serial interface two communication ports. It assigns serial interface 1 to COM1 and COM3 and assigns serial interface 2 to COM2 and COM4. The default interrupt for serial interface 1 is IRQ 4, and the default interrupt for serial interface 2 is IRQ 3. The COM ports assigned to each serial interface share the same interrupt but have separate memory I/O addresses. Table 6.3 shows the relationship among the serial interfaces, COM ports, I/O addresses, and interrupts.

Some manufacturers produce multiport communications boards that use minimal system resources yet still make the COM ports available for system use. If you install more than two serial interface boards into a computer, you can cause resource conflicts that result in unstable communications.

Table 6.3 Serial port IRQ and I/O addresses.

Serial Interface	Port	I/O Address	Interrupt (IRQ)
1	COM1	03F8	4
1	COM3	03E8	4
2	COM2	02F8	3
2	COM4	02E8	3

Requirements For Remote Connectivity

To establish a remote connection, you must meet a few absolute requirements, the most basic of which are the following:

➤ Both the remote client and the dial-in host must be using the same asynchronous protocol, such as PPP, SLIP, or PPTP.

➤ Make sure that the dial-in host is set up for security.

➤ Set up the dial-in host for DHCP or static IP address mapping (for more detail on DHCP, see Chapter 3).

➤ Select autonegotiation if you are using the PPP so that it can attain the fastest possible speed. Remember that the SLIP does not perform autonegotiation and that you must set the modem speed manually.

Practice Questions

Question 1

> Which asynchronous communications protocol is the most commonly used protocol today?
>
> ○ a. SLIP
> ○ b. PPP
> ○ c. POTS
> ○ d. PSTN
> ○ e. PPTP

The correct answer is b. PPP is used to connect to most ISPs. It is also very popular when connecting remote sites using a point-to-point connection. SLIP can encapsulate only TCP/IP and lacks error correction capabilities. Therefore, answer a is incorrect. POTS and PSTN are not protocols. Therefore, answers c and d are incorrect. PPTP is a secure communications protocol that creates a VPN through a TCP/IP network. Therefore, answer e is incorrect.

Question 2

> Which protocol creates a VPN across a TCP/IP-based network?
>
> ○ a. ISDN
> ○ b. PPP
> ○ c. POTS
> ○ d. PSTN
> ○ e. PPTP

The correct answer is e. PPTP creates a secure tunnel through a TCP/IP-based network (a VPN). Answer b is incorrect because PPP is the protocol that establishes the connection to the ISP, and PPTP creates a VPN using the PPP connection to a TCP/IP-based network. ISDN, POTS, and PSTN are switched networks that provide the physical connections. Therefore, answers a, c, and d are incorrect.

Question 3

> What is the maximum speed of a basic rate ISDN (BRI) with two B channels?
>
> ○ a. 33Kbps
>
> ○ b. 56Kbps
>
> ○ c. 128Kbps
>
> ○ d. 256Kbps
>
> ○ e. 1.544Mbps

The correct answer is c. The ISDN BRI channel is composed of two 64Kbps channels with an aggregate bandwidth of 128Kbps for data traffic and a 16Kbps channel (called a D channel) for network signaling. The benefit of ISDN over analog modems is the speed. The maximum speed of an analog modem is 56Kbps, whereas an ISDN modem can attain speeds of 128Kbps. Therefore, answers a and b are incorrect. Answers d and e are incorrect because 1.544Mbps and 256Kbps are the speeds of a T1/FT1 circuit.

Question 4

> Which UART chip works at speeds greater than 115.2Kbps?
>
> ○ a. 8250
>
> ○ c. 16450
>
> ○ c. 16550
>
> ○ d. 16650
>
> ○ e. 16750

The correct answer is c. The 16550 UART chip can attain speeds of 256Kbps. Answer a is incorrect because the 8250 UART chip is an 8-bit chip and was installed in old PC XT and AT computers. The 16450 UART chip, which is capable of a maximum speed of 115.2Kbps, replaced the 8250 UART chip. Therefore, answer b is incorrect. Answers d and e are incorrect because 16650 and 16750 are not UART chips.

Question 5

> Which asynchronous protocol can encapsulate TCP/IP, IPX, and several other protocols?
>
> ○ a. SLIP
> ○ b. PPP
> ○ c. POTS
> ○ d. ISDN
> ○ e. PSTN

The correct answer is b. PPP is capable of encapsulating more than one LAN protocol for transmission between two sites using asynchronous modem connections. SLIP can encapsulate TCP/IP only for transmission between two sites using modems. Therefore, answer a is incorrect. Answers c, d, and e are incorrect because ISDN, POTS, and PSTN are switched networks that provide the physical connections.

Question 6

> What type of circuit can a PPP connection use? [Choose the two best answers]
>
> ❏ a. ISDN
> ❏ b. Ethernet
> ❏ c. PSTN
> ❏ d. Token ring

The correct answers are a and c. PPP can be used on an analog (PSTN) or a digital (ISDN) network. Ethernet and token ring are not circuits; they are LAN topologies and they do not support PPP. Therefore, answers b and d are incorrect.

Question 7

What COM port(s) use IRQ 4? [Choose the two best answers]

- ❑ a. COM1
- ❑ b. COM2
- ❑ c. COM3
- ❑ d. COM4

The correct answers are a and b. COM2 and COM4 use interrupt 3. Therefore, answers b and d are incorrect.

Question 8

A BRI circuit has three channels, what are they?

- ❑ a. A channel(s)
- ❑ b. B channel(s)
- ❑ c. C channel(s)
- ❑ d. D channel(s)
- ❑ e. X channel(s)

Trick! question

The correct answers are b and d. Although the question asks for three channels, there are two B channels and one D channel. Answers a, c, and e are incorrect because those channels do not exist in a BRI circuit.

Need To Know More?

 Jones, James G. and Craig Landes: *A+ Exam Cram*. The Coriolis Group, Scottsdale, AZ, 1998. ISBN 1-57610-251-3. A great reference book covering PC hardware, peripherals, 16-bit Windows, Windows 95, and basic troubleshooting.

 Mazda, Fraidoon, ed.: *Telecommunications Engineer's Reference Book*. Reed Educational and Professional Publishing Ltd., Woburn, MA, 1998. ISBN 0-240-51491-2. An excellent reference book explaining the intricacies of telecommunications in great detail.

 Sheldon, Tom: *Encyclopedia of Networking, Electronic Edition*. Osborne McGraw-Hill, New York, 1998. ISBN 0-07-882333-1. A good overview of general networking terms and networking characteristics. Covers everything from A to Z.

 Microsoft's TechNet CD is invaluable when setting up a network that has Microsoft products. Search for "PPP" and "PPTP" to learn more about them.

 www.microsoft.com has a knowledge base that explains the specifics of setting up PPTP and PPP in a Microsoft networking environment.

Security

Terms you'll need to understand:

- √ Security model
- √ Dial-in security
- √ Password policies
- √ Security equivalences
- √ Data encryption
- √ Data encryption standard (DES)
- √ Public key encryption
- √ Virus protection
- √ Firewalls

Techniques you'll need to master:

- √ Defining and implementing a security model that suits your network
- √ Selecting a user- and share-level security model
- √ Establishing standard password practices and procedures
- √ Understanding the need for and different methods of employing data encryption
- √ Being familiar with the different types of computer viruses
- √ Knowing the different firewall types

Security is a major concern of many corporations and government agencies, and security breaches can come in several guises. Often, an organization's security is relatively lax until someone outside the organization compromises the network. Most organizations will openly discuss virus problems within their organization but seldom openly discuss network security breaches. However, it is comforting to know that you, as the network professional, can do something to prevent network compromises. In this chapter, we touch on the high points of information security as it relates to local area networks (LANs), wide area networks (WANs), dial-in, and the Internet.

Security Model

Every organization sets its own level of access that individuals, both inside and outside the organization, have to information that is stored on the network. These access levels comprise the security model for that network.

Security is implemented at both the server and the desktop within some constraints: Your security procedures should not be so difficult for users that it hampers their work, but it must still effectively protect corporate information. We discuss these implementations further in this section.

Setting up your security model entails two steps. First, you need to determine the levels of both physical security and data security that you need to implement on your network. Then, you present your implementation plan to management, who must agree to provide the resources necessary to implement your proposed security model.

The Desktop

Many software vendors have built extensive security measures into their network operating systems (NOSs) but have overlooked desktop operating system security. Someone who wants to penetrate a network will most likely focus on a desktop system that has no logging, very little security, and the password written on a piece of paper under the keyboard. Because the desktop is often neglected in the overall security model, receiving little more than cursory mention, the following are some procedures that you can implement at the desktop to secure both it and the LAN:

➤ Implement power-on passwords to protect data on the local machine.

➤ If data security is a major concern, install Windows NT Workstation and set up the NTFS partition on the hard drive. The NTFS file system—the same file system used on Windows NT Server—allows you to implement extensive file security.

► Store sensitive information on an NOS, such as Microsoft Windows NT Server or Novell NetWare Server. This is an important precaution because Windows 95 is based on the FAT file system and has very little file security built into it. Someone can boot a desktop machine by using Safe mode or a DOS boot floppy to gain access to the hard drive.

► Institute mandatory screensavers with passwords on all workstations.

► Turn local password caching off. Password caching leaves the door open for someone to try to gain unauthorized access to a protected resource. If the password is in a cache, that person can access the desktop without ever entering a password. In addition, several utilities can read local passwords and gain access to password-protected systems, such as the NOS. Often, the local password is the same as the NOS password; make sure that you assign the NOS and the local machine different passwords.

► Institute system policies that require Windows NT or NetWare server validation before allowing a user to access a Windows 95 workstation. If you allow users to enable peer resource sharing, you can implement either of two different security levels: user-level security or share-level security. *User-level security* provides greater security because the NOS must authenticate the username and password before the system grants access to the resource. *Share-level security* protects shared network resources on a Windows 95 computer with individually assigned passwords or no password at all. If you do not assign a password to a shared resource, it is open to every user on the network. File and printer sharing for NetWare Networks does not support this option, so you need to define system policies and profiles that restrict users from configuring system components, applications, desktop settings, and network connections.

You should know the difference between user-level and share-level security as defined in the previous paragraphs.

Network Operating System

NetWare and Windows NT have many of the same security attributes but implement them in different ways. A basic implementation of either NOS provides file and print sharing with a security database that protects access to resources. However, both NetWare and Windows NT have gone far beyond the basic NOS security.

Dial-In Security

You should assign the network access device or modem pool its own username and password list or have it use the NOS user and password list to authenticate users before allowing access to the network. For added security protection, you should blind the username and password on the screen and set the system so that it locks out the port if a preset number of login attempts have failed. In addition, the system should have caller ID (a log that records the telephone number that calls each port) and call-back capability. You should set up the system so that once the network access device authenticates a user, the user must enter a username and password so that the NOS can authenticate them.

Windows NT Security Model

Windows NT security consists of several components that work together to control users' access rights. Figure 7.1 illustrates how these components interact with one another to ensure optimum network security. These components are the following:

▶ **Logon processes** The mandatory logon process handles user logon requests. This process includes the local workstation logon and the remote logon, the latter of which allows users to remotely access a Windows NT domain. The user logon initiates two authentication processes: Netlogon and WinLogon. The Netlogon service is the transparent part of the process that the user does not see, whereas WinLogon provides the user interface.

▶ **Local Security Authority (LSA)** The LSA ensures that the user has permission to access the system. It creates access tokens, controls the local security policy, and provides interactive user authentication services. The LSA also manages the audit policy and logs the audit messages. This is the most important component of the Windows NT security subsystem.

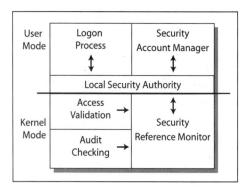

Figure 7.1 The Windows NT security procedure.

Security   121

- **Security Account Manager (SAM)** The SAM, also known as the NTDS database, maintains the user accounts database, which contains information for all user and group accounts and the access level they have in the NOS. The LSA uses the user validation service that the SAM database provides.

- **Security reference monitor** The security reference monitor checks to see whether the user has permission to access an object; if the user does have permission, the monitor performs the requested user action. It enforces the access validation and audit generation policy defined by the LSA and generates audit messages when appropriate.

The NetWare Security Model

The heart of the NetWare security model is NetWare Directory Services (NDS), which allows the user to log in to the tree from any place on the network. The security model, illustrated in Figure 7.2, is a hierarchical tree structure starting with the root of the tree. The components of the model are the following:

- **Access control list (ACL)** The ACL uses authentication information to determine the functions that users can perform. Administrators can protect all the objects at the server level from unauthorized access. Trustee rights can be assigned at the directory and file levels for users and groups, to restrict a user's access to specific directories, files, and print and job queues.

- **NetWare Directory Services (NDS)** NDS is a global, object-oriented, hierarchical database for naming and referencing entities on the network. The security functionality for NDS objects and attributes are implemented using the ACL, inheritance, and security equivalences. The ACL attribute specifies which objects have rights to access and modify an object

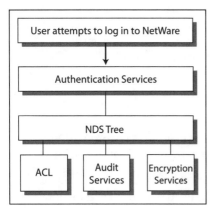

Figure 7.2   NetWare security model.

and its associated attributes. *Security equivalences* allow one object to receive the same rights that are assigned to another object. The NDS administrative tools manage enterprise-wide security in NetWare.

➤ **Authentication services** Authentication services verify the authenticity of a user for each login and for each access to other network resources. NetWare 4.x NDS authentication services use the RSA public key encryption technology. The authentication process uses the private key attribute to verify a user's identity. The combination of NDS and authentication services provides the mechanism for a single-login process.

➤ **Audit services** The NetWare 4.x audit services maintain transaction logs on the network independently of administrators and users. An independent auditor can monitor security-related NDS transactions, such as logins, logouts, object creation, attribute changes, trustee modifications, and equivalence changes. The audit service can also audit file system transactions, such as reads, writes, creations, deletions, and modifications.

➤ **Encryption services** The NetWare Core Protocol (NCP) packet signature is a security feature that protects communication between servers and clients. It deters forged packets between a server and a workstation by requiring the server and the client to "sign" each NCP packet. The packet signature changes with each packet.

Password Policy

You might be wondering whether you should enforce maximum password security at all times. Rigid password policies can occasionally restrict users from working efficiently, thus bringing complaints to the IS department. In addition, if a password is difficult to remember, some users will write it down instead of calling the IS department. Still other users will share protected resources if the security is so tight that they cannot get their work done as easily as they want. On top of that, some users will circumvent security whenever possible to get their jobs done more efficiently. However, it is your job to ensure that password policies keep your network secure. Several password-cracking programs are available on the Internet, and this can be a major security hole if you have not implemented password security properly. The following are some ideas for optimum password security:

➤ Set a minimum length of seven characters for user passwords and require passwords to have letters, numbers, and special characters.

➤ Do not allow users to create a password that can be found in any language (i.e., that is composed of just words), to prevent a dictionary attack against the password.

- Do not allow usernames and passwords to be the same.
- Set the password expiration so that users must choose a different password on a regular basis. The ideal expiration date is monthly.
- Create different passwords for Windows 95/98 desktops and the Windows NT or NetWare network.
- Require users to receive validation from the NOS before they can log on to a Windows 95/98 workstation.

 Know the password security tips in the preceding list. Remember that networks connected to the Internet are vulnerable if poor password security is in place.

Your first priority is to make an accurate assessment of which files or applications need to have password security, then determine the level of security that you will implement. Ensure that your users know why security is important and what their role is in effective network security. No security program is valid unless you can monitor it and make adjustments accordingly.

Data Encryption

Data encryption uses an algorithm key that takes plain text and produces cipher text from it. The algorithm is usually well known, and the strength of the cipher relies on the key and the length of the key.

Data Encryption Standard

A very common encryption algorithm is the *Data Encryption Standard (DES)*, which is a private-key 56-bit block cipher that divides the message into blocks and processes the blocks in multiple iterations. Both parties have to know the key that encrypted the message. DES has been compromised on the Internet and thus is not a good choice.

Public-Key Encryption

In contrast to DES, *public-key encryption* uses two keys. All users get a copy of the public key, and the private key is kept secret. To send a message to someone, you get the public key of the person to whom you want to send a document and use it to encrypt the message. The message can be decrypted only by using the recipient's private key. Public-key servers that house and retrieve keys are available on the Internet. Public-key encryption is currently playing a major role in verifying electronic message origination. An encrypted message will contain a date and time stamp, and because the sender's public key is the only way to open the document, you can guarantee that it was not tampered with during transmission.

Viruses

A virus is a computer program that infects other programs with copies of itself, much like a biological virus does. It reproduces and hides in other computer code. When the infected program executes, the virus executes. Viruses can infect only executable code. Previously, only executable files were at risk, but some current viruses can infect macro executables.

> Viruses work only if you execute them, either by running the program to which they have attached or by booting your system from an infected disk.

A virus is a software program that has been deliberately created by a source other than a software manufacturer. To classify a program as a virus, it must meet these requirements:

➤ It must replicate itself to carry out a mission (generally data destruction).

➤ It depends on a host to carry out that mission.

➤ It damages the infected computer system.

The virus attaches to the software and infects any computer on which the software is installed. Viruses are not always visible from the moment that your computer is infected. Some are keyed to activate on a specific date or time in the system clock or after a set of keystrokes. Each virus has a unique program code, called a *signature*. Virus infections can manifest themselves in a variety of ways, but only three types of software viruses exist:

➤ **Destructive** These are the most devastating viruses. They affect the hard drive and data so that it cannot be recovered, and they can cause total hard drive erasures.

➤ **Nuisance** These viruses are more annoying than destructive. They commonly cause intermittent problems that might go away when you reboot but then reappear later. A virus might be revealing itself if your software cannot print or if your software locks up but then works fine when you back out of the application and restart it.

➤ **Nondestructive** These viruses are simply the result of someone's bad sense of humor and have no adverse effect on your data or computer. The only evidence of such a virus might be an occasional message on your computer screen to apprise you of its presence.

Viruses can have a variety of effects on your hard drive, in varying degrees of severity. For example, a virus with a trivial effect simply reproduces or displays messages and is nondestructive. A virus with an unlimited effect will discover the system administrator's password and mail it to other users so that they can use it for illegal purposes. Although the severity of an unlimited-effect virus can have catastrophic, secondary repercussions, the virus itself is only a nuisance. A virus with a minor effect will alter or delete infected files. A moderate infection will wipe out your entire disk drive. A major infection will slowly corrupt data with a pattern, making restoration difficult, and a severe infection will slowly corrupt data without a pattern, making restoration impossible. Minor, moderate, major, and severe infections are all destructive.

Virus Classifications

Viruses are classified by the part of the system that they affect. The following sections discuss the main types of virus classifications as outlined by the National Computer Security Association (NCSA).

Boot Sector Virus

A boot sector virus attaches itself to the boot block of a floppy disk or an executable file. It then copies all or part of itself onto the boot sector of your hard drive when you turn on your system or launch an executable file. You can get a boot sector virus from an infected disk or from the Internet.

| If you have recently installed a program onto your computer that you downloaded from the Internet and the computer subsequently exhibits hard disk problems, you will want to check for a boot sector virus.

File-Infecting Virus

These viruses attach themselves to executable files associated with other programs, usually appending the virus code to the file where new versions can hide the virus. Most of them attach to EXE or COM files, but they can infect any file that launches a program, such as SYS, DLL, and BIN files. When you launch a program that contains a virus, the virus loads into your computer's memory and then infects any other executed program.

Macro Virus

Macro viruses are a variation of program viruses. These viruses affect the Microsoft Word and Excel templates (in PCs, usually the normal.dot file), which is used to create documents and spreadsheets. Once a template is infected, every document or spreadsheet opened with the program becomes corrupted. Because macro viruses infect common office applications and can spread between platforms, they have recently become widespread.

Polymorphic Virus
Polymorphic viruses can infect boot sectors, files, or both. They modify their appearance and change their signature periodically, which allows them to escape signature-scanning detection methods. Because virus scanners detect viruses by their characteristic code, polymorphic viruses use code alteration and encryption so that search strings cannot recognize them. Polymorphic viruses encrypt the main part of their code with a variable key and leave only the decryption executor unencrypted. The decryption code uses an algorithm that alters the decryption code at each incidence of infection, thus preventing detection with a search string.

Stealth Virus
All viruses try to hide their presence in some way, but stealth viruses make a greater effort to do so. This type of virus infects a program by adding bytes to an infected file and then subtracting the same number of bytes from the directory entry of the infected file. This makes it appear as if no change has taken place. Stealth viruses stay in memory to intercept attempts to use the operating system and hide changes made to file sizes. Thus, you must detect these viruses while they are in memory.

Multipartite Virus
Multipartite viruses combine the characteristics of memory-resident, nonresident file, and boot sector viruses and incorporate stealth and polymorphic characteristics to prevent detection. Multipartite viruses infect both boot sectors and executable files.

Meta Virus
Meta viruses are the first viruses that were known to infect data files and work on multiple platforms. The data files for Microsoft Word and AmiPro documents normally carry them. An example of a meta virus is "Concept," which infects the global template and all files loaded thereafter.

Virus Protection Software
Before you use any antivirus software package, make a boot disk from a clean, uninfected, write-protected floppy with your antivirus software loaded on it. If your antivirus software is loaded on the same hard drive where the virus exists, the software might not be able to see the virus. Furthermore, the virus can infect the antivirus software to render it useless.

Several antivirus software packages on the market assess the hard drive to detect viruses and eliminate them. The software's documentation tells you everything you need to know to run the software. The following sections give you an overview of the most popular antivirus software packages.

McAfee VirusScan

VirusScan is fast, easy to install and use, and effective at saving infected files. It provides choices for typical, custom, or compact installation. In addition to having it check the default file, you can select program files, all files, compressed files, or all of these. It also includes diskettes for installation on DOS, Windows 3.x, Windows 95, Windows NT, and OS/2 machines.

You can set VShield, a component of VirusScan, to scan your system at startup, shutdown, and screensaver activation. When VirusScan detects a virus, it identifies the virus and explains what kind of damage that virus can cause. It then gives you the option of cleaning the file or deleting it and generating a report. It can also scan zipped files and has a routine for creating an emergency disk.

VirusScan contains SecureCast, which allows the program to regularly self-update. It checks your Internet connection for inactivity and then downloads information on virus signatures, virus alerts, and product announcements. When you reactivate your connection, SecureCast will stop.

Dr. Solomon's Anti-Virus

This software includes a boot disk that clears viruses from your PC's memory and hard drive even before you install the antivirus program. WinGuard, a component of Anti-Virus, can detect a wide range of viruses, including rogue programs that are embedded in email and compressed files. However, WinGuard does not alert you to infection on downloaded and zipped files until you try to access them.

You can launch a scan by right-clicking on a file or folder in Explorer. You can make default settings for scanning target drives, directories, and files. When you scan an infected drive manually, you receive a warning message to let you know that a virus exists on that drive. To clean an infected file, you open the main utility and launch the separate Clean tool. If a file cannot be cleaned, you can delete or rename it, an option that must be preset in the configuration menu before you start the scan.

By using the Update button, you can connect to the Dr. Solomon's Web site or BBS and automatically download virus signature files and program upgrades. In addition, when the company discovers a new strain, it notifies you by pager or email.

Norton AntiVirus

Norton AntiVirus has joined forces with IBM AntiVirus to provide a comprehensive antivirus package. The IBM features include disks that run on DOS, Windows 3.x, Windows 95/98, Windows NT, and OS/2, as well as a boot disk for deleting viruses before you install the software onto your hard drive. IBM's antivirus technology provides the Norton AntiVirus program with a neural network that detects new viruses automatically, and can detect previously unknown viruses, analyze them, and distribute a cure worldwide, all automatically and within minutes of discovering a new virus.

Norton AntiVirus provides protection for the desktop, groupware, server, Internet, and gateway levels. It recognizes most viruses, even in zipped files and email. However, it gives no alarm until you try to open the file, rather than when you receive the virus in your inbox. Although Norton AntiVirus does not always repair the infected files, you can remove macro viruses without being forced to delete the whole file.

You can customize the scans to limit them to only programs or data files or limit them to a list of 18 different file extensions. When the program detects a virus, the Repair Wizard pops up with a list of the invaders. You can select automatic repair or manual repair, the latter of which allows you to fix or delete viruses one by one.

LiveUpdate automatically connects you to Symantec's FTP site or its BBS and downloads updated virus signatures and programs.

PC-cillin

PC-cillin can catch infected email files, including zipped files, as you receive them in your inbox and before you open them. The program's Clean Wizard purges viruses on disks while the infected floppy is still spinning. PC-cillin can identify both the virus and the source. In addition to recognizing the signatures of more than 10,000 known viruses, PC-cillin uses code analysis and rule-based searching to identify unknown viruses. You can manually update the program through the company's BBS.

Nonviral Destructive Programs

Destructive programs other than viruses—including worms, Trojan horses, and logic bombs—can infect your system.

Worms

A worm, often mistaken for a virus, is a single, destructive program on a single system that is often planted by someone with direct access to the system. Worms have the same characteristics as viruses, but do not replicate themselves or spread in the same manner as viruses.

Trojan Horses

A Trojan horse is a program that appears to be simply another program, and waits for an unsuspecting user to execute it. A Trojan horse can infect other files on the system or on other network computers. In some cases, a Trojan horse is not destructive. Instead, it collects information such as logon passwords or copies sensitive files to another computer on a network without the host user knowing what is happening.

Logic Bombs

A logic bomb is essentially a Trojan horse with a timing device that is keyed to go off on a certain day or time. The damage that it inflicts can range from destroying data on a local hard drive to releasing a virus.

Preventing Virus Infections

Common sources of virus infection are diskettes that have been on other computers, freeware, and software downloaded from online sources. Software that comes directly from the manufacturer is generally (but not always) virus free. Here are some rules of thumb for virus awareness:

➤ Keep virus protection software active at all times and scan your hard disk periodically as an added precaution. No computer in a networking, disk-sharing environment should be without antivirus software. Make sure that you update the virus signature file frequently because new viruses appear all the time.

➤ Be wary about inserting floppy disks from unknown sources into your disk drive, especially if several other people have shared the disks. If you have to use a suspect disk, you should scan the disk with antivirus software before installing it onto your computer. Make sure that you scan every file on the disk, not just the program files.

➤ You should also run virus software on shrink-wrapped software, including CD-ROMs, because some manufacturers have released viruses on their vendor software in the past.

➤ When you give a floppy to someone else, always write-protect it. That way, a virus on someone else's machine will not be passed to your disk.

➤ Be careful when you download files. Most viruses travel through shared disks or files on a network. For maximum safety, download all files into a special folder, whether they are from disk, from the Internet, or over the network. Then be sure to scan those files before you open them.

➤ Scan attachments before reading them. Although you cannot get a virus by reading an email message, you can get one through an executable email attachment. Some email programs will automatically open attachments. This makes reading your email easier, but it is a potential virus nightmare. Disable this function in your email program and then scan any attachments that you receive before you open them.

➤ If you want to share data on a network server while keeping your computer virus-free, save all files in RTF or ASCII format. This makes your document presentation a little ragged because neither file format saves macros or formatting information. However, it will help prevent macro viruses.

➤ Back up all your work files and system configuration files regularly and then store these backups in a safe place, separate from your hard drive. This way, you will not lose everything if a virus irreparably infects your system.

If information is shared among your network users by means of a floppy disk, a LAN, a WAN, or the Internet, you need to implement total virus defense throughout your organization. Total defense protects your workstations, servers, and email and checks packets as they enter the network.

Firewalls

A firewall is a device that controls data traffic between networks by providing a barrier between them. Most commonly, organizations deploy firewalls between themselves and the Internet. However, they can be deployed internally as well between the corporate financial information and the rest of the company. A firewall is usually a standalone device that provides only firewall protection.

A firewall provides protection from untrusted networks, such as the Internet.

Most firewalls have a minimum of two network cards—one connected to the trusted network and the other to the untrusted network. Firewalls are available in three types:

➤ **Packet-filtering firewall** Many routers employ packet-filtering capabilities and are classified as screening routers. Packets can be filtered on the basis of a media access control (MAC) address; an IP address; a specific service, such as HTTP or Simple Mail Transfer Protocol (SMTP); or a combination of the three. A packet-filtering firewall can be set up to reject all packets destined for the trusted network except for specific IP addresses and ports associated with those IP addresses.

➤ **Proxy service firewall** This firewall hides the internal network by taking the request from the trusted network and applying it against a rule set. If the packet passes the rule set and then manages to exit the network, the proxy service firewall will reconstruct the packet and send it out on the untrusted network using its IP address. When it receives the packet back from the untrusted network, it will reconstruct the packet with the trusted network IP address of the workstation that originally sent the request.

➤ **Stateful inspection firewall** The bit patterns of the packet coming from the untrusted network are compared to the bit patterns of the packets that are known to be trusted. When a user on the trusted network accesses an outside service, the firewall remembers the port numbers of the source and destination addresses. This is known as "saving the state."

Practice Questions

Question 1

> How can you protect your private network from a public network, such as the Internet? [Choose the two best answers]
>
> ❑ a. Firewall
> ❑ b. Password security
> ❑ c. Bridge
> ❑ d. Nonfiltering router

The correct answers are a and b. A firewall in conjunction with password security makes a good defense when connected to a public network. A bridge does not provide any protection. Therefore, answer c is incorrect. A nonfiltering router cannot provide any protection from a public network. Therefore, answer d is incorrect.

Question 2

> What is the best password security model?
>
> ○ a. Expires once a year; is a minimum of 7 characters; contains alpha and numeric characters
> ○ b. Expires once a month; is a minimum of 4 characters; contains alpha, numeric, and special characters
> ○ c. Expires once a month; is a minimum of 7 characters; contains alpha, numeric, and special characters
> ○ d. Expires once a month; is a minimum of 17 characters; contains alpha, numeric, and special characters

The correct answer is c. Password security must maintain a balance between functionality and data protection. If a security system is too difficult to use, trusted users will find a way to circumvent it. If security is too lax, a trusted system can be penetrated and vital data lost. Answers a and b are incorrect because both represent password security that is too lax. Answer d is incorrect because such security is too stringent in password length.

Question 3

How would you centrally control access to shared resources on a Windows 9x workstation?

○ a. NTFS-level access control

○ b. User-level access control

○ c. Group-level access control

○ d. Share-level access control

○ e. Windows NT SAM security database

The correct answer is b. User-level access control uses the NOS to authenticate the username and password before access to the resource is granted. NTFS access control is available only on Windows NT computers. Therefore, answer a is incorrect. Group-level access control and the Windows NT SAM security database do not exist in Windows 9x computers. Therefore, answers c and e are incorrect. Share-level access control individually assigns a password or no password to allow access to local resources on a Windows 9x workstation, and you must manage the access on each Windows 9x workstation. Therefore, answer d is incorrect.

Question 4

If you download a significant amount of information from the Internet, which type of protection should you have in place?

○ a. Antivirus software on the workstations, servers, and proxy servers/firewalls with the capability to check inbound email. Total antivirus defense

○ b. A central FTP server as the only location to store all the downloaded files

○ c. A central Web server as the only location to store all the downloaded files

○ d. Encrypted passwords on the internal network

The correct answer is a. Total antivirus defense is a mandatory investment if you download a significant amount of information from the Internet. Central FTP and Web servers would not provide any protection against information downloaded from the Internet. Therefore, answers b and c are incorrect. Encrypted passwords are always a good security measure but will not provide any protection from information downloaded from the Internet. Therefore, answer d is incorrect.

Question 5

> If your system experiences a hard drive error and cannot boot the day after a user downloads and installs a program from the Internet, what should you check first?
>
> ○ a. Hard drive failure
>
> ○ b. System board failure
>
> ○ c. Boot sector virus
>
> ○ d. Microsoft Word macro virus
>
> ○ e. Trojan horse

The correct answer is c. A boot sector virus can stop a computer from loading the operating system on a bootable hard drive or bootable floppy drive. A hard drive failure and a system board failure are possible causes of a computer not booting but should not be the first thing to check in this case. Therefore, answers a and b are incorrect. The Microsoft Word macro virus and a Trojan horse will not corrupt the system boot partition. Therefore, answers d and e are incorrect.

Question 6

> With total antivirus defense installed on a corporate LAN, what should be your first response when you receive an email that states that you have just been infected by opening this email?
>
> ○ a. Assume that it is just another hoax and conclude that you should follow only serious leads
>
> ○ b. Find out who sent it and report the incident to the proper authorities
>
> ○ c. Treat it as a threat to your system and work with your antivirus vendor to determine the level of the threat, if any even exists
>
> ○ d. Send a virus back to the originator to teach them a lesson

The correct answer is c. When you suspect that your computer has been infected and your antivirus software does not detect it, you should contact your antivirus vendor. All viruses or suspected viruses should be researched. Therefore, answer a is incorrect. If a virus exists, you should notify the proper authorities. However, that should not be your first response. Therefore, answer b is incorrect. It is not your place to execute judgment in this case. Therefore, answer d is incorrect.

Need To Know More?

 Feibel, Werner: *Encyclopedia of Networking*. Sybex Network Press, San Francisco, CA. 1996. ISBN 0-7821-1829-1. A reference book explaining general hardware and networking terms.

 Sheldon, Tom: *Encyclopedia of Networking, Electronic Edition*. Osborne McGraw-Hill, New York, 1998. ISBN 0-07-882333-1. A good overview of general networking terms and networking characteristics. Covers everything from A to Z.

 Microsoft has a CD subscription called TechNet that is invaluable when setting up shared resources in a Microsoft Windows 9x environment. Search on firewalls, virus protection, security model, and NTFS security.

 www.checkpoint.com is a good resource for installation and integration information and white papers discussing setting up firewalls.

 www.cnet.com also has a lot of good information on the latest viruses and appropriate counteractions.

 www.datafellows.fi has some of the latest virus information and tactical solutions.

 www.mcafee.com has the latest information on virus alerts and its products that provide total antivirus defense.

 www.microsoft.com has a knowledge base that explains in detail the specifics of setting up shared resources in a Microsoft Windows 9x environment.

 www.norton.com has the latest information on virus alerts, antivirus products, and its strategy for total antivirus defense.

 www.raptor.com has installation, integration, and reference papers containing information on deploying a firewall.

ISO Open Systems Interconnect (OSI) Model

Terms you'll need to understand:

- Open Systems Interconnect (OSI) model
- Physical layer (OSI layer 1)
- Ethernet/Fast Ethernet hubs
- Repeaters
- Multistation access unit (MAU)
- Transceiver
- Media filter
- Data Link layer (OSI layer 2)
- Bridge
- Switch
- Brouter
- Network layer (OSI layer 3)
- Routers
- Connectionless-oriented service
- User Datagram Protocol (UDP)
- Connection-oriented service
- Transport layer (OSI layer 4)
- Session layer (OSI layer 5)
- Presentation layer (OSI layer 6)
- Application layer (OSI layer 7)
- Department of Defense (DoD) model

Techniques you'll need to master:

- Knowing the difference between a repeater, a hub, and an MAU
- Understanding how a bridge works
- Defining a MAC address
- Being familiar with the IEEE 802 specifications
- Understanding how a router functions
- Distinguishing between routable and nonroutable protocols
- Knowing the difference between connection-oriented and connectionless-oriented protocols

The *International Organization for Standardization (ISO)* develops standards for international and intranational data communications. In the 1980s, the ISO developed the *Open Systems Interconnect (OSI)* reference model, which provides a complete framework for multivendor computer systems to communicate with one another (see Figure 8.1). The OSI model is also known as CCITT X.200. The ISO also developed the OSI protocol, which followed this framework but never became popular as the standardized protocol for the OSI model.

The OSI network architecture determines which components may exist on the network, how they must operate, and what form they may take. This includes the hardware, software, data link controls, standards, topologies, and protocols within the network. The OSI architecture is composed of seven layers, according to their design and function within the telecommunications process. Each layer builds on the last, so that each layer adds a different dimension of functionality to the services provided by the previous layers. This chapter discusses each of these layers in detail.

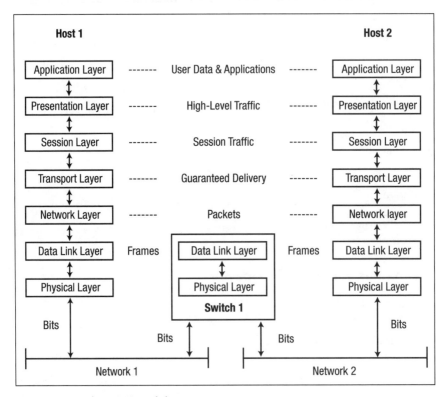

Figure 8.1 The OSI model.

ISO Open Systems Interconnect (OSI) Model   139

Make sure that you thoroughly know the layers of the OSI model, understand how they interconnect, and can explain the functionality of each layer.

Layer 1: Physical Layer

The *Physical layer* delivers data from one computer to another, translating bits of data into a format suitable for transmission, or receives a transmission and translates it back into bits. It also determines the following attributes:

➤ The physical interconnection attributes to the physical media and electronic components

➤ The signal's electrical specifications (for example, which voltages and currents are used) and transmission schemes

➤ The mechanical specifications, including the shape and size of the connectors

➤ The functional aspects of the network, such as the pin-outs

Layer 1 hardware and software specifications dictate the types of connectors, signaling, and media-sharing schemes that a network uses.

Note: Be aware that the Physical layer (OSI layer 1) is not the same as the physical media (cabling plant) that is detailed in Chapter 2.

In concept, the Physical layer deals only with the electrical and mechanical level of data communication, which builds the foundation to allow higher OSI layers to talk through it. The most common Physical layer devices are discussed in the following sections.

Know the Physical layer devices and the fact that they are responsible for transmitting packets on the network.

Network Interface Cards

A basic network interface card (NIC) consists of a network connector, a setup disk, a diagnostic disk, and a set of operating system driver disks. To fully test a NIC, you need a loop-back connector, which Chapter 13 explains in detail. This cable crosses the transmit and receive pins in the same connector so that the diagnostic utility can test the transmit and receive functions without using the entire network to do so.

Before you install a NIC that is not plug-and-play (PnP), you need to know an open IRQ, memory address, and I/O address for all non-PnP cards. PnP cards automatically look for an available IRQ, memory address, and unregistered I/O address on the computer. If you install a non-PnP card in the computer and then install a PnP card later, the PnP card might use some of the resources assigned to the non-PnP card and cause a resource conflict.

Ethernet/Fast Ethernet Hubs

This device is an Ethernet/Fast Ethernet repeater with multiple RJ-45 connection ports (see Figure 8.2). When a signal arrives on one of the ports, the hub repeats the signal on all the active ports. You can stack hubs to provide a larger port density, and many hub manufacturers provide a cascade port to allow you to stack hubs in one closet. In this case, when signals pass between the hubs, it counts as only one repeater hop.

In an Ethernet/Fast Ethernet network that has only hubs, the entire network is one collision domain. Intelligent hubs have the capability to perform remote administration, which allows them to disable ports, monitor traffic, send Simple Network Management Protocol (SNMP) traps to a management station, and remotely troubleshoot the network equipment.

A hub is a multiport repeater that, when it receives a signal, retransmits that signal on all ports. A hub does not segment the network like a switch does.

Repeaters

A repeater is a device that you add to a network to extend the signal on the cable. As a signal travels the length of a network cable, it tends to lose strength, or attenuate. A repeater compensates for this attenuation, reconstructs the signal,

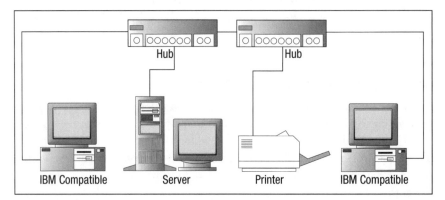

Figure 8.2 An Ethernet hub configuration.

and retransmits it on the network. You can install a hub to function as a multiport repeater, which it does by repeating the signal on all ports within the collision domain. However, repeaters are not commonly installed on individual unshielded twisted pair (UTP) cable runs but are used to extend backbone segments. More often, the main distribution facility (MDF) connects to the intermediate distribution facilities (IDFs) by means of fiber-optic cable, although the connection can be of UTP.

Multistation Access Units

A *multistation access unit (MAU)* is a device in a token ring network that is similar to a hub in an Ethernet network. It contains an internal ring and acts as a central point to which token ring workstations can connect (see Figure 8.3). If the MAU detects an error on a port, it automatically bypasses that port, thus maintaining the ring integrity. You can also stack MAUs by connecting the ring-in port to the ring-out port between the two devices.

You need to connect the ring-in port of one MAU to the ring-out port of another MAU and vice versa to maintain the ring integrity.

Transceivers

A transceiver converts one type of media topology to another type while maintaining the integrity of the network signal. Unlike other network devices (such as hubs, switches, and routers), which have several types of connectors for the

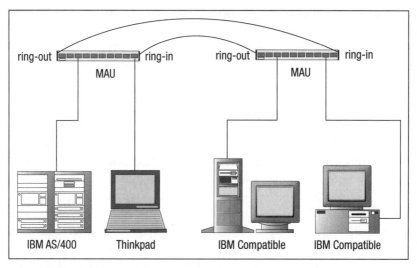

Figure 8.3 MAU configuration.

same type of network—such as RJ-45, AUI, and fiber optics—a transceiver only has two types of connectors. Transceivers are most commonly used to extend a backbone segment as a standalone device or as an expansion module in a hub.

A transceiver converts a network segment from one media type to another. Some of the more common transceivers convert AUI to UTP. Some hubs, switches, and routers have expansion ports that support fiber-optic modules, AUI modules, and other network topology modules.

Media Filters

A media filter balances token ring signals that are expecting to connect to shielded twisted pair (STP) cable but that really connect to a UTP cable. The media filter removes the high-frequency signal and adjusts the signal parameters to work with the media.

In a token ring network, a media filter adjusts the signal parameters from those that are compatible with an STP cable to those compatible with a UTP cable.

Layer 2: Data Link Layer

The *Data Link layer* provides flow and error control and synchronization for the Physical layer. It is a point-to-point link between devices on the same network and is responsible for taking information from the Network layer, generating packets, and sending them by means of the Physical layer across the network to the address of the destination device (as shown previously in Figure 8.1). The Data Link layer uses the *media access control (MAC)* address, often referred to as the *physical address*, to send packets to the devices. The Logical Link Control (LLC) and MAC sublayers of the 802.2 standard define the Data Link layer. Layer 2 supports the connectionless-mode and connection-mode transmissions of the LLC.

In a nonbridged Ethernet environment, the sending device broadcasts the signal on the network, and the receiving device processes the data packet. In a bridged/switched network, the bridge/switch, which stores a list of MAC addresses and the corresponding port on which the device is located, reads the packet and retransmits it only on the port where the device resides. If a packet has a MAC address that the bridge/switch has not seen before, it retransmits it on all ports and waits for a device to respond. MAC addresses direct data within the same network but cannot send data across routers. Bridges and switches are examples of layer 2 devices, and are discussed in the following sections.

Bridge

A bridge is a layer 2 local area network (LAN) device that connects two or more LAN segments to effectively make those segments one logical network. Previously, a bridge was commonly used to segment two or more coaxial networks. Currently, a bridge can connect two different types of topologies and forward network traffic between the two segments. It can also have an analog or digital port to connect remote locations, and it provides network segmentation by filtering traffic between the segments.

A bridge stores the MAC address of the device located on each port in a process known as *transparent bridging*. Token ring networks use mainly *source route bridging*, in which the packet contains the routing information. A bridge generally operates in promiscuous mode, meaning that it listens to all traffic on the network. When it receives a packet, it determines whether the destination device is located on the segment the packet came from or whether it is located on a different segment. If it is on the same segment, the bridge discards the packet; if it is on a different segment, the bridge forwards the packet to the proper segment. If the bridge does not know the port on which the device is located, it will retransmit the packet on all ports except the port of origin.

Switch

Switch-based networks are rapidly replacing hub-based and bridge-based networks, as the price of workgroup switches competes more evenly with the price of hubs. In a switched network, each device connects to a workgroup switch over a point-to-point UTP cable and shares the media with any other device (see Figure 8.4). This allows for a full-duplex connection between the switch and the device, provided that both support full-duplex operation. The backplane speed of a switch is at least the aggregate of all the inbound and outbound ports.

Workgroup switches are hierarchical in design and can connect to individual workstations as well as large enterprise switches, making it possible to have an entirely switched network. A switch is similar to a bridge in the way in which it forwards packets through a network, and some enterprise switches incorporate layer 3 routing functions and VLAN functions. A switch is similar to a brouter in that it has some built-in Data Link layer and Network layer functions.

A switch can segment a network into as many ports as the switch has and can forward packets between those ports simultaneously at the maximum speed of each port.

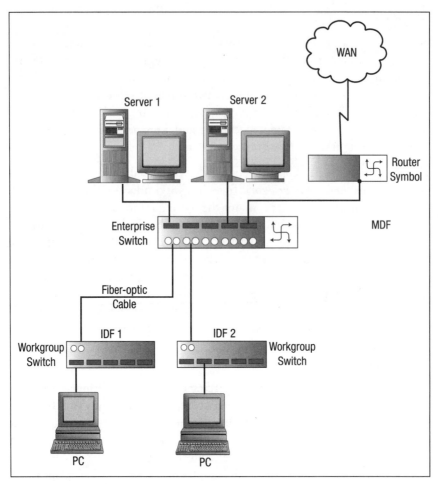

Figure 8.4 A switched network.

Protocols

The LAN protocols are shared media protocols, whereas the Point-to-Point Protocol (PPP) is a point-to-point connection over a nonshared link. The Data Link layer protocols define the access to the physical media and enforce the rules for communication. The most common layer 2 protocols are the following:

➤ Point-to-Point Protocol (PPP)

➤ Serial Line Internet Protocol (SLIP)

➤ High-Level Data Link Control (HDLC)

➤ Logical Link Control (LLC)

➤ Link Access Protocol (or Procedure) (LAP)

Because Ethernet is a carrier sense multiple access/collision detection (CSMA/CD) protocol, it listens to the Physical layer before transmitting; if it does not hear a signal on the wire, it transmits its packet. The receiving device then performs a cyclic redundancy checksum (CRC) on the packet. If the packet passes the checksum, the packet has arrived without colliding with another packet (shared media). If the packet collided with another packet, the CRC will fail, and both the sending and receiving stations will request a retransmission. The stations will generate a random number and retransmit according to that random number to avoid another collision.

IEEE 802

For communications standardization, the OSI model adheres to the IEEE 802 specifications. The Institute for Electrical and Electronics Engineers (IEEE) is a professional organization that develops computing and electrical engineering standards. The IEEE 802 committee focuses on physical network devices, such as cables, connectors, NICs, bridges, and switches, as well as the electrical signaling and access methods used to make physical network connections.

The ISO has adopted the IEEE 802.1 through IEEE 802.11 committees and has given them new designations, namely, ISO/IEC 8802-1 through ISO/IEC 8802-11. The International Electrotechnical Commission (IEC) is responsible for setting electrical standards and contains members from more than 30 countries.

IEEE 802 consists of several subgroups that define specific mediums of communication (see Figure 8.5). The duties of these groups are as follows:

> **IEEE 802.1 Internetwork Definition (ISO/IEC 8802-1)** This working group is responsible for LAN optimization, bridging, and switching in the internetwork. It brought the spanning tree algorithm forward as a standard. It is in the process of establishing VLAN standards and works closely with the Internet Engineering Task Force (IETF) and the Asynchronous Transfer Mode (ATM) forum.

> **IEEE 802.2 Logical Link Control (ISO/IEC 8802-2)** This working group defines the LLC sublayer of the OSI Data Link layer. The LLC defines an interlink between the media access methods and the Network layer of the OSI model. It also provides framing, addressing, and error control. Ethernet II does not use this sublayer, but 802.3 Ethernet does.

 IEEE 802.2 provides logical link control for IEEE 802.3, 802.4, 802.5, 802.6, 802.12, and 802.14.

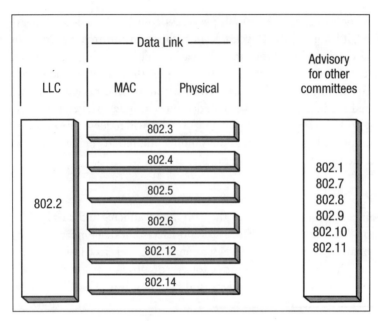

Figure 8.5 IEEE 802 subgroups.

▶ **IEEE 802.3 Ethernet (CSMA/CD) Networks (ISO/IEC 8802-3)** This working group defines the manner in which twisted-pair cable, fiber-optic cable, and coaxial cable work with CSMA/CD networks, such as Ethernet, Fast Ethernet, and Gigabit Ethernet. IEEE 802.3u adopted the 100BaseT standard on the same day that the IEEE 802.12 100BaseVG standard was adopted.

IEEE 802.3 is the standard for CSMA/CD networks, such as Ethernet, Fast Ethernet, and Gigabit Ethernet.

▶ **IEEE 802.4 Token Bus Networks (ISO/IEC 8802-4)** This working group defines a broadband networking standard that is mainly implemented by the manufacturing industry. This is because it has roots in the manufacturing automation protocol. It uses a token passing scheme on a broadcast network and is not widely implemented in LANs.

▶ **IEEE 802.5 Token Ring Networks (ISO/IEC 8802-5)** This working group defines the cabling, interfaces, and access methods for token ring networks. It uses a token passing ring network that is in a star configuration and connects to an MAU. The speeds are 4Mbps and 16Mbps.

IEEE 802.5 is the standard for 4Mbps and 16Mbps token ring networks.

- **IEEE 802.6 Metropolitan Area Networks (MANs) (ISO/IEC 8802-6)** This working group defines a high-speed protocol by which stations share a dual fiber-optic bus using an access method called *distributed queue dual bus (DQDB)*, which is the access method for switched multimegabit data service (SMDS).

- **IEEE 802.7 Broadband Technical Advisory Group (ISO/IEC 8802-7)** This working group provides technical direction to other working groups for broadband networking (cable television). It specifies the minimum physical, electrical, and mechanical features of the broadband cable.

- **IEEE 802.8 Fiber-Optic Technical Advisory Group (ISO/IEC 8802-8)** This working group provides technical direction to other working groups for fiber-optic networks. It specifically supports the IEEE 802.3 through 802.6 committees.

- **IEEE 802.9 Integrated Data and Voice Networks (ISO/IEC 8802-9)** This working group is responsible for the integration of voice, data, and video on IEEE 802 LANs. The Integrated Services Digital Network (ISDN) is transmitted on Ethernet networks and is sometimes referred to as *ISO-Ethernet*.

- **IEEE 802.10 Network Security Technical Advisory Group (ISO/IEC 8802-10)** This working group is developing a security model that will incorporate authentication and encryption for transmission over diverse networks.

- **IEEE 802.11 Wireless Networking (ISO/IEC 8802-11)** This working group is responsible for defining standards for wireless networks that transmit narrow-band radio frequency (RF), spread-spectrum RF, and infrared.

- **IEEE 802.12 Demand Priority (100VGAnyLan) (ISO/IEC 8802-12)** This working group is responsible for defining the demand priority access method for 100VGAnyLan. The hub determines the priority of each station connected to it and controls the signal flow accordingly.

- **IEEE 802.14 Cable Modems** This working group is responsible for creating standards for the transmission of data over cable television networks. The focus is on Ethernet and ATM traffic.

CSMA/CD

Because many of the Ethernet standards employ carrier sense multiple access/collision detection (CSMA/CD), we will briefly discuss it. CSMA/CD allows a client to sense the transmission channel and transmit data when the line is clear. The client can monitor the line during the transmission and detect any collisions that occur on the line. After that, the client waits before sensing the line again. This allows the client to know whether a packet got to its destination intact, and will resend it if it did not. CSMA/CD also serves to minimize bandwidth during packet transmissions.

Brouter

A brouter (bridging router) is a device that effectively sits between layers 2 and 3 of the OSI model. As a bridge, it is protocol independent and can filter LAN traffic; as a router, it can forward network packets between layers 2 and 3. Brouters can bridge multiple protocols and provide routing for those protocols, provided that they are routable. Brouters are being replaced by switches and are quickly becoming obsolete.

Layer 3: Network Layer

The Network layer manages communications routing for packets that are destined for addresses that are not on the LAN. Whereas the Data Link layer uses MAC addresses to communicate with devices on the same LAN, the Network layer uses routable protocols to deliver packets across interconnected networks joined by routers. Although enterprise switches or brouters have some layer 3 routing capabilities, they still rely on layer 2 addresses to achieve the speed necessary to forward packets in a LAN environment. The two most prevalent routable protocols are TCP/IP and IPX/SPX, in that order. NetBIOS Extended User Interface (NetBEUI) is not included because it is not a routable protocol. A routable protocol must have a source and a destination network address located in the packet; otherwise, it assumes that all the packets are destined for the LAN. NetBEUI does not have a source and destination network address in the packet.

 Remember that NetBEUI is not a routable protocol because it does not have a source and destination address in the packet.

Routers

In an IP-based network, each device must have a place to send packets that are not destined for the local subnetwork. This is called a *default gateway*, and it

ISO Open Systems Interconnect (OSI) Model   **149**

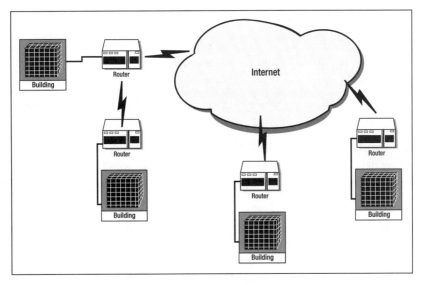

Figure 8.6 A routed network.

must be set up on a workstation that is going to communicate beyond its local subnetwork (see Figure 8.6). The gateway is commonly a router that is connected to another router or several routers to allow a packet to travel beyond its own subnetwork.

Let's use the Packet Internet Groper (PING) utility as an example of how a rooted network operates. When a user tries to ping a device that is not located on the local subnetwork, the packet is forwarded to the default gateway. The default gateway then determines whether the destination address is physically connected to any of its ports. If it is, then the packet is directly routed to the appropriate port. If it is not, the router sends the packet to the other routers to which it is connected.

Routers use routing protocols such as Open Shortest Path First (OSPF) and Routing Information Protocol (RIP) to determine the best method to forward a packet destined for a remote network. Both OSPF and RIP provide routers with a dynamic routing table without which an administrator would need to statically assign each route.

Connectionless-Oriented Service

A *connectionless-oriented service* does not require the sender and receiver to establish a session before sending packets to the destination. This service can be implemented in the Network layer or the Transport layer of the OSI model. The following are characteristics of connectionless service:

- Packets can arrive at the destination out of sequence, but must be reassembled in sequence.
- No time is required to establish a session, and data can be sent immediately.
- Connectionless-oriented service does not use acknowledgments to check for packet delivery.
- Connectionless-oriented service is analogous to a radio broadcast or letter delivery. The sender receives no acknowledgment for receipt of the letter delivery or radio broadcast.

The Internet is the largest connectionless-oriented network in the world, and it uses IP to deliver the packets to their destination. IPX is the connectionless-oriented protocol used by Novell NetWare systems, and it is used to deliver packets to their destination. The *User Datagram Protocol (UDP)* is a connectionless-oriented protocol that works at the OSI Transport layer. We will discuss UDP in the next section. The Trivial File Transfer Protocol (TFTP) is another connectionless-oriented protocol.

Layer 4: Transport Layer

The Transport layer manages the end-to-end control and error checking by providing an end-to-end connection between the source and the destination node to ensure reliable data delivery. In addition, it is responsible for providing end-to-end recovery and flow control and for releasing the connection.

The Transport layer is essentially a virtual circuit that uses connection-oriented protocols and gives each packet a sequential number. The receiving station then sends an acknowledgment to the transmitting station stating that the packet was received. You might compare the concept of a connection-oriented protocol to that of a certified letter, whereas a postcard might represent a connectionless-oriented protocol.

Connectionless-Oriented Protocols

UDP provides a connectionless-oriented protocol at the Transport layer. This protocol is used for information that is time sensitive and does not need to be retransmitted, such as realtime video and audio. If a packet is not received, it would be pointless to retransmit the packet once the remaining packets in that sequence have been sent to the video/audio processing software. Connectionless-oriented protocols are needed at the Transport layer of the OSI protocol to take advantage of the port structure already in place.

For example, say that we have two hosts, one transmitting realtime audio and the other connecting to the first host to receive the transmission. The second host would receive the transmission on a UDP port identified by the software that is receiving the realtime audio transmission. No error correction or packet acknowledgment would be coordinated between the two hosts, but both would use the same port for the transmission and receipt of the data.

Connection-Oriented Service

Connection-oriented service provides reliable data delivery by establishing a virtual circuit between the sending host and the receiving host. Some characteristics of connection-oriented service are the following:

➤ The initial request for a session involves some setup time between the hosts.

➤ The connection is considered a virtual circuit.

➤ Acknowledgments of data receipt are used to guarantee data delivery.

➤ Long transmissions are common.

Connection-Oriented Protocols

Both Transmission Control Protocol (TCP) and Sequenced Packet Exchange (SPX) are connection-oriented protocols. SPX is the NetWare protocol for providing connection-oriented service. TCP uses ports between hosts to create a virtual circuit between two host computers on an IP network. It is not concerned with the process of routing through the network but is concerned with the data delivery in the datagram.

For example, if two host computers want to transfer Simple Mail Transfer Protocol (SMTP) traffic between each other, the sending host requests a session with the receiving host on TCP port 25. Once the initial protocol negotiation is complete, the virtual circuit is established, and the two hosts can guarantee data delivery. File Transfer Protocol (FTP), SNMP, SMTP, and Post Office Protocol 3 (POP3) are all TCP connection-oriented protocols.

Remember that IP, IPX, and UDP are connectionless-oriented protocols, which are similar to sending a letter or a radio broadcast because the sender is not concerned with whether the recipient actually received the packet. TCP and SPX are connection-oriented protocols, which is similar to sending a certified letter because the sender ensures that the recipient received the packet.

Layer 5: Session Layer

The Session layer manages the establishment of a continuing series of requests and responses between the applications at each end. In the past, mainframe and terminal communications used the Session layer, but modern networking does not.

Layer 6: Presentation Layer

The Presentation layer is usually part of the operating system. It prepares incoming data for the Application layer and formats outgoing data that the Application layer sends and receives. It also offers applications a set of data transformation services, such as graphics, binary, or ASCII data. Data compression and data encryption also occur at this level.

Layer 7: Application Layer

The Application layer is the top layer of the OSI model. It provides distributed information services and is the layer at which users can access the OSI environment. In TCP/IP, the applications at this layer communicate directly with the Transport layer. Some of the most common TCP/IP applications are FTP, Telnet, and SMTP.

> You should know that FTP and Telnet access the OSI model at the Application layer.

How The OSI Layers Work

Now that we understand what each independent layer does, let's put the layers into an interactive, functional perspective. The applications use OSI layers 5 through 7 to define how to communicate with an application running on another computer using the same protocol. OSI layers 3 and 4 define how to set up and ensure reliable data delivery between computers that use the same protocol. OSI layers 1 and 2 define the physical characteristics and electrical signal characteristics. Each OSI layer knows how to communicate with the layer above it and below it, excluding layers 7 and 1. Layer 7 applications pass information to layer 6 and then to layer 5 and so on, all the way down to layer 1, which then transmits the packet to the remote computer. As the information is processed using the OSI model, each layer performs its function; when the information arrives at the Physical layer, it has all the information it needs to perform the required task.

DoD Network Model

Initially, the Department of Defense (DoD) four-layer model was developed as part of the DARPA Internetwork Project, which produced what we know as the Internet. This model uses the core Internet protocols, although the OSI seven-layer model is preferred for new designs. Figure 8.7 illustrates the four DoD model layers and shows how they correspond to the OSI model layers.

Network Access Layer

The Network Access layer corresponds to the both the Physical layer and the Data Link layer of the OSI model. It is responsible for delivering data over the particular hardware media and selecting different protocols, depending on the type of physical network.

Internet Layer

The Internet layer corresponds to the Network layer of the OSI model and delivers data across a series of different physical networks that interconnect a

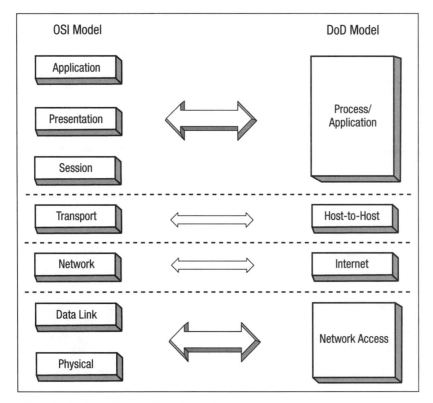

Figure 8.7 The DoD network model.

source and a destination machine. Routing protocols, to include IP, are most closely associated with this layer.

Host-To-Host Layer

The Host-to-Host layer corresponds to the Transport layer of the OSI model and handles connection rendezvous, flow control, retransmission of lost data, and other generic data flow management commands. TCP and UDP are important members of this layer.

Process Layer

Also called the Process/Application layer, the Process Layer accomplishes the duties performed by the Application, Presentation, and Session layers of the OSI model. It contains protocols that implement user-level functions, such as mail delivery, file transfer, and remote login.

Practice Questions

Question 1

> Where does the MAC address on an Ethernet card originate?
>
> ○ a. The InterNIC
>
> ○ b. The root DNS server
>
> ○ c. A DHCP server
>
> ○ d. The NIC manufacturer

The correct answer is d. The Ethernet NIC manufacturers are assigned a range of unique MAC addresses, and all Ethernet NICs should have a unique MAC address regardless of the manufacturer. The InterNIC is responsible for domain name assignment and the root DNS servers. Therefore, answers a and b are incorrect. A DHCP server assigns IP addresses to a network host. Therefore, answer c is incorrect.

Question 2

> What is the first thing you should do when your NIC is not functioning properly?
>
> ○ a. Replace it with a working NIC.
>
> ○ b. Use the manufacturer's diagnostics to test the NIC.
>
> ○ c. Replace the transceiver.
>
> ○ d. Uninstall and reinstall the NIC driver with the latest driver.

The correct answer is b. The manufacturer's diagnostics will test all the hardware components of the NIC. Replacing the NIC may become necessary, but not until it is diagnosed as defective. Therefore, answer a is incorrect. You cannot identify defective components until you test the NIC. Therefore, answer c is incorrect. Reloading the NIC driver might become necessary, but not until a diagnostic test has ruled out hardware failure. Therefore, answer d is incorrect.

Question 3

> Why would a loop-back connector be used on a NIC?
> - a. To test the physical connector pin integrity during diagnostic testing.
> - b. To test the transmit and receive capability of the NIC during diagnostic testing.
> - c. A loop-back connector and a crossover cable are the same thing. Just plug in the crossover cable during diagnostic testing, and it will test the physical connector pin integrity.
> - d. NICs do not use loop-back connectors.

The correct answer is b. A loop-back connector uses one piece of cable and crosses the transmit and receive wire pairs to the same connector. The physical connector pin integrity is accomplished by visual inspection. Therefore, answer a is incorrect. A crossover cable has two connectors on it, whereas a loop-back connector has one connector on it. Therefore, answer c is incorrect. NICs require loop-back connectors during diagnostics. Therefore, answer d is incorrect.

Question 4

> Which OSI layer is responsible for transmitting the packets on the network?
> - a. Data Link layer
> - b. Transport layer
> - c. Physical layer
> - d. Network layer

The correct answer is c. The Physical layer defines the characteristics of the connection to the physical media and the electrical aspects of the signal. The Data Link layer is responsible for generating frames and sending the data across the network to the destination device. Therefore, answer a is incorrect. The Transport layer provides an end-to-end connection between the source and the destination node to ensure reliable data delivery. Therefore, answer b is incorrect. The Network layer manages communications that are destined for a location that is not on the LAN. Therefore, answer d is incorrect.

Question 5

Which of the following network devices do not segment a network? [Choose the two best answers]

- ❏ a. Switch
- ❏ b. Bridge
- ❏ c. Hub
- ❏ d. Router
- ❏ e. Repeater

The correct answers are c and e. A hub and a repeater will retransmit the signal on all available ports. A switch and a bridge will use the destination MAC address to determine which port to forward the packet to. Therefore, answers a and b are incorrect. A router forwards packets based on the network destination address. Therefore, answer d is incorrect.

Question 6

Which LAN device has a primary function of segmenting a network into multiple segments that are capable of forwarding packets to all ports simultaneously at the maximum rated speed for each port?

- ○ a. Switch
- ○ b. Hub
- ○ c. Router
- ○ d. Gateway

The correct answer is a. A switch is designed to segment a large network into smaller networks. The backplanes of most switches are rated in the gigabits-per-second range and are designed to forward all ports at the maximum rated speed. A hub does not segment a network. Therefore, answer b is incorrect. The primary function of a router is to connect a LAN to a WAN. Therefore, answer c is incorrect. The primary function of a gateway is to translate from one protocol to another. Therefore, answer d is incorrect.

Question 7

> Which network device operates in both the Data Link layer and the Network layer?
> - a. Hub
> - b. Router
> - c. Brouter
> - d. Gateway

The correct answer is c. A brouter is a device that performs bridge/router functions. A hub works at the Physical layer. Therefore, answer a is incorrect. A router works at the Network layer only. Therefore, answer b is incorrect. A gateway translates from one protocol to another. Therefore, answer d is incorrect.

Question 8

> What are the three types of ports on the front of a token ring MAU? [Choose the three best answers]
> - a. Ring-left
> - b. Ring-right
> - c. Ring-in
> - d. Ring-out
> - e. Token ring port

The correct answers are c, d, and e. A token ring MAU has a ring-in port that connects to a ring-out port on another MAU. The ring-out port connects to a ring-in port on another MAU. The token ring port is where the NIC connects to the MAU. The MAU creates an internal ring as long as it is the only MAU in the network. The ring-left and ring-right are not ports. Therefore, answers a and b are incorrect.

Question 9

Which network topology uses an MAU?

- a. FDDI
- b. Token ring
- c. Ethernet
- d. ATM

The correct answer is b. An MAU is used in a token ring network. FDDI uses a concentrator. Therefore, answer a is incorrect. Ethernet uses a hub. Therefore, answer c is incorrect. ATM uses a switch. Therefore, answer d is incorrect.

Question 10

Which device works at the Data Link layer of the OSI model?

- a. NIC
- b. Hub
- c. Router
- d. Gateway
- e. Switch

The correct answer is e. A switch is a Data Link layer device. A NIC and a hub are Physical layer devices. Therefore, answers a and b are incorrect. A router is a Network layer device. Therefore, answer c is incorrect. A gateway can work at layers 5 through 7 of the OSI model. Therefore, answer d is incorrect.

Question 11

Which OSI layer uses the MAC address to forward packets to their destination?

- a. Physical layer
- b. Network layer
- c. Transport layer
- d. Data Link layer
- e. Application layer

The correct answer is d. The Data Link layer uses the MAC address to forward packets to their destination. The Physical layer defines the characteristics of the connection to the physical media and the electrical aspects of the signal. Therefore, answer a is incorrect. The Network layer manages communications that are destined for a location that is not on the LAN. Therefore, answer b is incorrect. The Transport layer provides an end-to-end connection between the source and the destination node to ensure reliable data delivery. Therefore, answer c is incorrect. The Application layer has the network programs, such as FTP and Telnet. Therefore, answer e is incorrect.

Question 12

Which network device works mainly at the Network layer of the OSI model?

- a. Hub
- b. Router
- c. Switch
- d. Repeater
- e. Gateway

The correct answer is b. The Network layer manages communications that are destined for a location that is not on the LAN or that need to be routed using network destination addresses. A hub and a repeater work at the Physical layer of the OSI model that defines the characteristics of the connection to the physical media and the electrical aspects of the signal. Therefore, answers a and d are incorrect. A switch works at the Data Link layer and uses the MAC address to forward packets to their destination. Therefore, answer c is incorrect. A gateway works at the Application layer of the OSI model and translates from one protocol to another. Therefore, answer e is incorrect.

Question 13

Which of the following protocols are connection-oriented? [Choose the two best answers]

- a. IPX
- b. SPX
- c. IP
- d. TCP
- e. UDP

The correct answers are b and d. SPX and TCP provide guaranteed data delivery by receiving a confirmation that the data was delivered. IPX, IP, and UDP are connectionless-oriented protocols that do not check to see if the packet has arrived at its destination. Therefore, answers a, c, and e are incorrect.

Question 14

Which of the following protocols provide unreliable data delivery? [Choose the two best answers]

- a. SPX
- b. IPX
- c. TCP
- d. UDP

The correct answers are b and d. IPX and UDP are connectionless-oriented protocols that do not check to see whether packets have arrived at their destination. SPX and TCP are both connection-oriented protocols that guarantee data delivery. Therefore, answers a and c are incorrect.

Question 15

Which layer of the OSI model does TCP, UDP, and SPX use?

- a. Application layer
- b. Session layer
- c. Transport layer
- d. Network layer

The correct answer is c. TCP and SPX are connection-oriented protocols that work at the Transport layer, and UDP is a connectionless-oriented protocol that works at the Transport layer. The Application layer is where programs such as FTP and Telnet are used. Therefore, answer a is incorrect. The Session layer is rarely used in modern networking. Therefore, answer b is incorrect. IP and IPX use the Network layer. Therefore, answer d is incorrect.

Question 16

Which protocols are similar to a certified letter or a telephone call in their delivery method? [Choose the two best answers]

- ❏ a. IP
- ❏ b. IPX
- ❏ c. TCP
- ❏ d. UDP
- ❏ e. SPX

The correct answers are c and e. TCP and SPX are connection-oriented protocols that require proof of delivery. A certified letter requires a receipt of delivery and a telephone call is a virtual circuit through the public-switched telephone network. IP, IPX, and UDP are connectionless-oriented protocols and rely on TCP or SPX to determine proof of delivery. IP, in combination with UDP, does not require proof of data delivery and is commonly used in time-sensitive realtime video in which retransmission of data would be too late to matter. Therefore, answers a, b, and d are incorrect.

Question 17

Which protocols are similar to a radio broadcast in their delivery method? [Choose the three best answers]

- ❏ a. SPX
- ❏ b. IP
- ❏ c. IPX
- ❏ d. TCP
- ❏ e. UDP

The correct answers are b, c, and e. IP, IPX, and UDP do not require a receipt of delivery. They broadcast the data and rely on higher-layer protocols to guarantee receipt of delivery. SPX and TCP guarantee data delivery. Therefore, answers a and d are incorrect.

Question 18

> FTP and Telnet operate at which layer of the OSI model?
>
> ○ a. Presentation
>
> ○ b. Application
>
> ○ c. Session
>
> ○ d. Transport
>
> ○ e. Network

The correct answer is b. FTP and Telnet operate in the Application layer of the OSI model. The Presentation and Session layers are seldom used with network operating systems. Therefore, answers a and c are incorrect. The Transport layer provides reliable data delivery. Therefore, answer d is incorrect. The Network layer uses routable protocols to deliver packets across interconnected networks joined by routers. Therefore, answer e is incorrect.

Question 19

> Which of the following protocols is connectionless-oriented?
>
> ○ a. FTP
>
> ○ b. TFTP
>
> ○ c. POP3
>
> ○ d. SNMP
>
> ○ e. SMTP

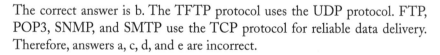

The correct answer is b. The TFTP protocol uses the UDP protocol. FTP, POP3, SNMP, and SMTP use the TCP protocol for reliable data delivery. Therefore, answers a, c, d, and e are incorrect.

Need To Know More?

 Fraidoon, Mazda, ed.: *Telecommunications Engineer's Reference Book*. Reed Educational and Professional Publishing Ltd., Woburn, MA, 1998. ISBN 0-240-51491-2. An excellent reference book explaining the intricacies of telecommunications in great detail.

 Sheldon, Tom: *Encyclopedia of Networking, Electronic Edition*. Osborne McGraw-Hill, New York, 1998. ISBN 0-07-882333-1. A good overview of general networking terms and networking characteristics. Covers everything from A to Z.

 www.3com.com publishes information on NICs, switches, routers, and the OSI model.

 www.baynetworks.com publishes information on switches, routers, and the OSI model.

 www.cisco.com publishes information on switches, routers, and the SI model.

 www.iso.ch is the official Web site for the International Standards Organization.

Designing The Network

Terms you'll need to understand:

✓ Total cost of ownership (TCO)
✓ Direct costs
✓ Indirect costs
✓ Migration
✓ Implementation

Techniques you'll need to master:

✓ Translating business needs into equipment
✓ Determining the most effective equipment for the job
✓ Understanding equipment compatibility
✓ Costing out the new system/upgrade
✓ Developing an installation plan
✓ Developing and executing a migration and implementation plan
✓ Securing vendor support

In an ideal networking scenario, all the hardware features work exactly as the vendor said they would, money is unlimited, and you do not have to worry about integrating the new hardware with older equipment. In addition, you have the resources to implement the new system without affecting the IS staff or users, and equipment vendors are as helpful after the sale as they were before the sale. However, the networking world is far from perfect, and you must consider all these issues before you undertake the design of a new network or upgrade.

In this chapter, we cover all the steps necessary to help you design a network and then effectively implement it. Our focus starts with hardware compatibility and integrating equipment with existing systems and then moves to migrating and implementing the system.

Evaluating Business Requirements

One of your most difficult tasks as an IS professional is that of translating a business' needs and goals into the appropriate hardware and software. When you are designing a new network or upgrading an existing one, you should have the right people involved in the process from the very beginning.

You need to involve senior management, so that they can provide a vision of the company's direction in terms of information technology. You should also involve the department managers and workers in the design process, so they can supply you with their needs. Then, the IS department must translate the combined needs and goals of senior management, department managers, and workers into suitable hardware and software.

If you determine that you need best-in-the-class equipment to do the job, you will need to provide justification for this to management that is based on a sound business decision. Your selection of equipment should reflect the needs and goals that you identified during the design process.

Determining Equipment Compatibility

When you begin designing a network, it is imperative that you have an inventory of all existing network devices that you can reference to determine compatibility with new equipment. Before you define an equipment list for the new network or upgrade, you need to do the following to ensure that the equipment is compatible with current technology:

➤ Check the operating system version of the existing equipment. Then, check the technical bulletins and reports to ensure that the old network operating system (NOS) will integrate with the new one. Discovering any known bugs will help you minimize integration problems. Generally, the newer operating systems are backward compatible, but in some cases older operating systems cannot integrate with the newer ones.

➤ Determine the network topology of existing equipment to ensure that the topology is compatible with the new one. For example, if you are upgrading from Ethernet to Fast Ethernet, you need to ensure that all the network interface cards (NICs), print servers, and all other devices (such as hubs, switches, and routers) can communicate at the new speeds. If they do not, you will need to install a dual speed hub.

➤ Make sure that your equipment has the latest firmware versions because manufacturers use firmware upgrades to fix known bugs in systems.

➤ Make sure that all intelligent switches and hubs are installed with the latest operating systems and service packs.

Sometimes an IS department will install or upgrade a network system without upgrading the routers, switches, bridges, servers, and NOS with the latest patches. In such a case, the department's job becomes one of fixing problems that should not have occurred in the first place, and you will be spending most of your time focusing on corrective maintenance instead of preventive maintenance.

If a business neglects its system, it will soon become outdated. In such a case, adding new equipment to legacy equipment becomes an integration nightmare. To lessen the impact of integrating new equipment with legacy equipment, you can contact the legacy equipment vendors and bring the old equipment up to the most current revision. If you let a system get too far out of date, upgrading might require hardware upgrades in flash and RAM memory. Often, you will have to decide whether you will design a system to integrate into the existing network or redesign the existing network to integrate into the new system.

Costing Out The System

When you are costing out a system, you must consider several financial factors beyond the general outlay for the physical pieces of the system. These factors include the following:

➤ The cost of bringing existing equipment into compliance with the new system

➤ Installation costs for the new system

➤ Maintenance costs of the new system

➤ The total cost of ownership

Total Cost Of Ownership (TCO)

You can define total cost of ownership as the cumulative financial requirements of owning and operating the network. This includes everything from having a vendor provide networking recommendations to the purchase price of continuing software upgrades. You can generally divide these expenses into two categories: direct costs and indirect costs. The total expense of these factors will determine the overall cost of your network or upgrade.

Direct Costs

Direct costs are those that you will see almost immediately once you begin installing a new network or upgrade. Such costs include the following:

➤ **Hardware and software** This entails the outright price for all the devices, cabling, cards, and software that you will purchase to upgrade or assemble the network. Your selection of hardware and software should not be limited to your immediate needs but should encompass your projected needs for the next three to five years.

➤ **Support and network management** This is the cost of the personnel who will support the network. Several options are available for network support, including contracting an outside vendor or hiring a full- or part-time employee. If the company decides to hire someone to support the network, you will need to calculate the cost of training in addition to the salary of that individual. This includes both immediate training and training that will be necessary in the future to keep that person up to date with late-breaking networking technology.

➤ **Data communications fees** These include both internal and external connections. The connectivity options that you will likely need to consider include connecting business units to other business units, connecting to the Internet, and providing for remote dial-in connectivity. Telecommunications between business units and business partners is rapidly becoming a major business focus, the scope of which promises only to grow in the future. Given these considerations, you should allow generous room for expansion in that area.

Indirect Costs

Indirect costs are those that are not accurately quantifiable. End-user support entails user training and the amount of time that network support personnel must spend remedying user errors. Another ambiguous figure is that of calculating the company cost of network downtime or the cost of providing electricity and other environmental considerations. Although you need to consider indirect costs, you usually do not calculate these directly into the total cost of purchasing the network.

Identifying Equipment Availability

In the fast-paced environment of computers and networking, you need to make sure the equipment that you specify is available and compatible.

Leading-Edge Technology

Although the latest-and-greatest equipment might seem to be the best choice, you do need to be careful when using such equipment. Marketing is always ahead of production, and sometimes it is even ahead of engineering. The best source through which to determine new equipment availability is the vendor or a local reseller. You can either call the vendor or visit its Web site. Most companies will tell you about the availability of new equipment on their Web sites.

In addition, be wary of extremely new technology that incorporates new interface concepts or that claims to do things that no other equipment has done before. If this technology has not been on the market for at least a short time, it might not integrate well with your existing network. Unforeseen integration glitches might arise that cause conflict in your system or that render the old (or new) equipment less than efficient or even useless. New equipment needs to be in use for a time so that the manufacturer can work out any bugs.

Older Equipment

Although old equipment might not be as expensive as newer equipment, designing a network with equipment that is at the end of its life cycle is not a good idea. Software requirements continue to place increasing demand on machines for more memory, faster speed, or more communications diversity. Equipment that was leading-edge technology just four years ago now lags behind considerably and is unable to handle the latest software or modem speeds. Although you might save money up front, ultimately you will spend more maintaining old equipment.

> *Note: When purchasing a dual-processor-capable machine, you should populate the second processor in anticipation of future need. Most processor chip manufacturers have a life cycle for each processor chip, and when they stop producing that chip, obtaining another one becomes very difficult.*

Developing An Installation Plan

After you have determined your equipment needs for the new network or upgrade, you must evaluate the floor plan to determine exactly where you will put the new equipment. You can use old floor plans or cable plant diagrams as a basis for determining where existing equipment and cabling are located, but you should not rely exclusively on these. In some cases, small changes to the footprint are not documented, so the floor plans might give you a false idea of where equipment and cabling is located. After you look at the floor plan, you should perform a walk-through of the installation area and note any discrepancies between the floor plan and the actual equipment layout. The server room and the main distribution facility (MDF) for the network are usually, but not always, located in the same place. If your installation is large, an intermediate distribution facility (IDF) will house the network hubs and switches that connect to the MDF.

The environment in which you will install the network components will determine the life of the components. When you lay out the equipment footprint, you will need to consider several environmental and physical factors. The following sections outline these considerations.

Humidity And Temperature

To assess the humidity and temperature tolerances of the equipment, refer to the vendor manuals. The ambient temperature and humidity should be well inside the parameters for the least-tolerant piece of equipment. Placing equipment in an environment in which tolerances are borderlined or exceeded regularly will decrease the life expectancy of the electronic components. The MDF especially should be located in a well-ventilated room that has a good air conditioning system and some form of humidity control.

Remember that excessive heat can cause servers and network equipment to fail or have intermittent problems.

Airborne Debris

You should place the IDF and any other network equipment so that they are not exposed to airborne debris, such as occurs in manufacturing areas. Electronic equipment that is subjected to excessive levels of dust, dirt, and manufacturing byproducts have shorter life spans.

Interference

The location of computers and network equipment with respect to other electrical devices is an important consideration. Many electrical devices can interfere with network signals if they are close enough to communications cables. Because the MDF is usually in a controlled environment, devices that cause communication interference are normally not located near the MDF. However, interfering devices can be located throughout the workplace near communications components, such as workstations and cable runs. Some common scenarios are the following:

➤ UTP (unshielded twisted pair) runs are installed near fluorescent lights.

➤ Space heaters are located adjacent to network outlets or devices.

➤ Microwave ovens are in operation near network outlets or devices.

Any equipment that generates an electrical field, especially heavy industrial equipment, and that is close enough to an unshielded network cable can cause interference.

Space heaters or microwave ovens that operate too closely to a cable run or network equipment can overload a circuit or cause network interference.

However, you can take steps to compensate for unavoidable interference. An uninterruptible power source (UPS) or a line conditioner installed between the power source and the equipment will condition the power supply and protect the main components from interference. They can also detect line anomalies, such as a missing ground or an overloaded neutral wire. In addition, they give you short-term protection against unexpected power outages and power sags.

Note: Keep in mind that although a UPS has surge protection capability built into it, it is not the same as a surge protector. A surge protector levels out variances in the electrical stream, such as voltage spikes, whereas the UPS protects against power outages, provides interference protection, and corrects line anomolies.

In addition, consider installing fiber-optic cable instead of UTP for transmission in high-interference areas. Fiber-optic cable is commonly installed to compensate for areas in which industrial equipment is generating massive electrical fields.

Connectivity

Although this might sound obvious, you need to make sure that you can plug in your equipment. You need to consider two types of connectivity: electrical lines and data lines.

Electrical Lines

Make sure that all your equipment has a sufficient, accessible power source. Survey the power drain on the existing service to see whether it will be enough for the new equipment. You will also want to check the power usage on the individual circuit onto which you plan to install the equipment to make sure that you do not overload the circuit. It is a good idea to have the MDF and the servers on their own circuits.

Data Lines

Once you determine that you can plug your equipment into the electrical system, you need to determine whether you can run communications cables to your equipment. This will include the modem lines and the cabling from the backbone or server. You will need to survey the floor and the ceiling to assess how you are going to run the cables. If you are installing equipment in a room with a raised floor, you should have no problems. However, in a room without a raised floor, you will need to run the communications lines through the ceiling. Most businesses have dropped ceilings to compensate for ventilation ducting. Your task is to determine where to place the equipment and to arrange to have poles installed to house the cabling from the ceiling to the equipment.

Traffic Flow And Accessibility

Once you determine where the network equipment will go, you will need to consider how much passerby traffic it will receive. Equipment that is out in the open will often be a temptation for any novice who feels that he or she can fix the equipment or network.

Although you need to minimize casual traffic, you do not want to make access to the network equipment difficult for the people who need to operate or maintain it. Your IDF will contain most of your remote network equipment, and you should place it in a locked cabinet in a low-traffic area.

Physical Security

Make sure that the network equipment is in a locked facility. This might entail locating the MDF or server equipment in a cipher-locked room or the IDF in a locked cabinet. A secure facility will safeguard against preventable catastrophes, such as tampering, theft, and other malicious activities. However, it provides no protection from natural catastrophes, such as flood or fire.

Developing A Migration Plan

Although migration from one system to another can be accomplished in several ways, one thing remains constant: Minimal user and system downtime is mandatory. You can accomplish system migration either by replacing everything in one weekend or by gradually introducing new components. Keep in mind that you must document the plan and get management's approval before you can effect implementation.

Phased Implementation

Although phased implementation will take longer to complete than one-time implementation, you can control the cause-and-effect of phased implementations better than you can that of total integration. Phased implementation allows you to integrate one or two pieces of equipment or software at a time. Then, when network problems arise, you can quickly narrow the field of suspects and take prompt action.

One-Time Implementation

Implementing all the new network equipment at one time over a weekend or holiday gives you the advantage of controlling network demand and minimizes the amount of downtime. However, you cannot control the cause-and-effect of one-time, total migrations, and you might be setting yourself up for many nasty, unforeseen surprises. You might bring the network up again only to find that entire sections of the network do not operate or that a specific function or utility did not integrate as it was supposed to. Because you integrated everything at one time, you might not be able to easily identify the culprit, and you might spend most of your time in the following days and weeks solving nuisance problems.

Coordinating With Vendors

Once management approves the network design, you should contact several vendors or resellers to take the network design and provide a quote for all the equipment and labor to do the job. You should also encourage the vendors to make any recommendations for changing or improving the network design. It is of the utmost importance that the vendors provide maintenance and technical support and that this is included in the quotes. In addition, be sure that the resources of a local vendor or vendor representative are available throughout the implementation process.

If your company has the internal resources to complete the task of implementation, it is still a good idea to have a close relationship with the equipment manufacturer, which can provide experienced guidance during the integration and is also the best resource for troubleshooting. A vendor often has manufacturers' representatives working throughout the country.

Practice Questions

Question 1

> What device conditions the power to network equipment?
> - a. A media filter
> - b. A UPS
> - c. A transceiver
> - d. A cheap power strip

The correct answer is b. A UPS conditions the power input from the power source before it gets to the equipment, leveling any results of interference. In addition, it provides protection against power outages and power surges. Answer a is incorrect because a media filter is used in token ring networks. Answer c is incorrect because a transceiver connects network media from one type to another. Answer d is incorrect because a cheap power strip provides no power conditioning benefits.

Question 2

> With whom should you confer when you are specifying a business' networking needs? [Choose the four best answers]
> - a. Senior management
> - b. The IS department
> - c. The workers
> - d. Department managers
> - e. Vendors

The correct answers are a, b, c, and d. You need to include the vision and requirements of the company and then provide the vendors with a set of goals and work with them to provide a solution. The vendor does not specify a business need but, rather, provides a solution to a business need. Therefore, answer e is incorrect.

Question 3

What is the greatest advantage of integrating leading-edge equipment into a network or upgrade?

- ○ a. It is brand new, and few people have equipment like it.
- ○ b. It comes with new cables and software.
- ○ c. It has a greater life expectancy than older equipment.
- ○ d. You can redesign your whole network around it.

The correct answer is c. Leading-edge equipment has the potential to extend the life expectancy of existing networks or new networks. For example, say you have an existing network with five 24-port Ethernet hubs. If the network is experiencing slowdowns, a switch placed at the MDF with the servers and hubs connecting to the switch will decrease the traffic in one collision domain. Answers a and b are incorrect because such considerations are irrelevant when choosing new equipment. Answer d is incorrect because the last thing that you want to do is completely redesign your existing network.

Question 4

Which of these factors are direct costs? [Choose the three best answers]

- ❑ a. The cost of the servers
- ❑ b. The cost of the software
- ❑ c. The cost for training
- ❑ d. Money lost during network outages

The correct answers are a, b, and c. Servers, software, and training are considered direct costs. Network outages are considered an indirect cost. Therefore, answer d is incorrect.

Question 5

What do data communications fees encompass? [Choose the four best answers]

- ❑ a. Connecting business units together
- ❑ b. Long-distance telephone calls
- ❑ c. Connecting to the Internet
- ❑ d. Conference calls
- ❑ e. Remote dial-in connectivity

The correct answers are a, b, c, and e. Connecting to business units, long-distance calls (which can be for data communications), the Internet, and remote dial-in are data communications costs. Answer d is incorrect because conference calls are not considered data communications costs.

Question 6

How do you determine network equipment availability? [Choose the two best answers]

- ❑ a. Go to your local computer store and see what they have
- ❑ b. Confer with a local reseller of networking equipment
- ❑ c. Read magazine advertisements
- ❑ d. Search the Internet

The correct answers are b and d. A local network reseller will assist in determining network equipment availability along with network design, and the Internet is available for determining network equipment availability. A local computer store would not likely be able to provide a total network solution. Therefore, answer a is incorrect. Magazine advertisements would not provide availability data. Therefore, answer c is incorrect.

Question 7

What is the best medium to install in a high-interference area caused by electromagnetic interference?

- ○ a. UTP
- ○ b. STP
- ○ c. Fiber-optic cable
- ○ d. Coaxial cable

The correct answer is c. Fiber-optic cable is immune to electromagnetic interference. Answer a is incorrect because UTP is a poor choice in a high-interference area. Answers b and d are incorrect because STP and coaxial cable are more shielded than UTP but not as shielded as fiber-optic cable.

Question 8

Why is physical security for the main network components important? [Choose the three best answers]

- ❑ a. For protection against fire
- ❑ b. For protection against theft and vandalism
- ❑ c. For protection against industrial espionage
- ❑ d. For protection against floods
- ❑ e. For protection against malicious tampering

The correct answers are b, c, and e. Physical security protects against theft, vandalism, industrial espionage, and malicious tampering. Physical security does not protect against fire or floods. Therefore, answers a and d are incorrect.

Question 9

What can happen if an MDF or server room is constantly above 95 degrees Fahrenheit?

- ○ a. Nothing. All network equipment and servers are engineered to withstand sustained room heat of 100 degrees Fahrenheit, which conforms to ISO 9002 electronic heat standards.
- ○ b. The life of the equipment could be decreased, and the equipment could experience intermittent problems.
- ○ c. You would not get people to work in such an environment.
- ○ d. All network equipment and server rooms have a temperature-controlled environment that does not exceed 72 degrees Fahrenheit.

The correct answer is b. The equipment could start to fail because of the excessive heat. Answer a is incorrect because no electronic heat standard for network and server equipment is specified in ISO 9002. Answer c is incorrect because that issue is irrelevant in this case. Answer d is incorrect because not all network and server equipment is in a temperature-controlled environment.

Question 10

On very cold days, the accounting department experiences excessive problems with computers shutting down and intermittent network problems. What could be the problem?

- ○ a. The UTP cables in exterior walls are too cold to work within specifications and are causing ground loops between the network device and the computer.
- ○ b. The space heaters distributed throughout the accounting office are causing network interference and an excessive power drain on the circuit.
- ○ c. The equipment is experiencing random thermal shutdown.
- ○ d. The electrical phase in the accounting department is faulty and becomes apparent during cold weather.

The correct answer is b. Space heaters can easily overload a circuit, and if placed in close proximity to network devices they can cause network interference. Answer a is a fictitious answer and is, therefore, incorrect. Thermal shutdown is not usually a problem during cold snaps. Therefore, answer c is incorrect. Faulty electrical problems will not become apparent just because it is cold. Therefore, answer d is incorrect.

Need To Know More?

 Jones, James G. and Craig Landes: *A+ Exam Cram*. The Coriolis Group, Scottsdale, AZ, 1998. ISBN 1-57610-251-3. A great reference book covering PC hardware, peripherals, 16-bit Windows, Windows 95, and basic troubleshooting.

 Mazda, Fraidoon, ed.: *Telecommunications Engineer's Reference Book*. Reed Educational and Professional Publishing Ltd., Woburn, MA, 1998. ISBN 0-240-51491-2. An excellent reference book explaining the intricacies of telecommunications in great detail.

 Sheldon, Tom: *Encyclopedia of Networking, Electronic Edition*. Osborne McGraw-Hill, New York, 1998. ISBN 0-07-882333-1. A good overview of general networking terms and networking characteristics. Covers everything from A to Z.

Installing The Network

Terms you'll need to understand:

√ Bayonet nut connector (BNC)

√ Attachment unit interface (AUI) connector

√ DB-9 serial connector

√ DB-25 serial connector

√ Small computer systems interface (SCSI) connectors

√ Single connector attachment (SCA) connector

√ Fiber channel connector

√ Universal serial bus (USB) connector

√ RJ-45 connector

√ Type 1 connector

√ Network operating system (NOS) server

√ Print server

Techniques you'll need to master:

√ Preparing to install the network

√ Deciding on an implementation strategy

√ Identifying hardware interfaces and devices by description

√ Identifying cabling characteristics

√ Staging the system

√ Installing the system

After you have nailed down a feasible design for the network, you face the task of staging and testing the network equipment and installing it at the site. Ideally, you will purchase, test, and institute a comprehensive implementation plan before you install or upgrade the network. This chapter discusses the benefits of these steps and provides a functional and physical description of the most common network components. At the end of this chapter, we also provide an implementation checklist that will help ensure that you have properly laid the groundwork for all aspects of your network.

Getting Prepared

You have developed a plan, had it approved, and ordered the equipment. Now comes the next stage: receiving, testing, and installing the equipment. Although this task might seem overwhelming at first, the implementation will go much smoother and will not seem so daunting if you have prepared yourself well.

Getting Your Equipment Together

You have placed your equipment orders, and now all the equipment seems to be arriving at the same time. To ease the task of accounting for everything, you should have made a list of every piece of hardware and software that you will need for the network installation. You should also have a designated area to put the boxes of equipment after they arrive. Make sure that this is an out-of-the-way place and that it is well marked so that everyone knows what the equipment is for and are not tempted to borrow any of it.

Scheduling System Downtime

You will also need to schedule time to take the network down. Preferably, this will be a time when network usage is minimal, such as over a weekend, during a holiday, or in the evening. The length of time that you have the network down depends on the kind of implementation you plan to do. You have two choices: phased or total.

Phased (Partial) Implementation

A phased implementation will take longer than a total integration to implement, but you can control the cause-and-effect of a phased implementation better than you can that of a total integration. A phased implementation allows you to integrate one or two pieces of equipment or software at a time. Then, when network problems arise, you can quickly narrow the field of suspects and take prompt action. A phased implementation should be planned with time allotted to address the network problems as they arise. Once the implementation starts, it should progress at a steady pace to minimize transition time.

Total (One-Time) Implementation

Implementing the new network equipment all at one time over a weekend or during a holiday gives you the advantage of controlling network demand and minimizes the amount of time that you have the network down. However, you cannot control the cause-and-effect of total, one-time migrations, and you might be setting yourself up for many unwanted surprises. You might bring the network up again, only to find that entire sections of your network do not operate or that a specific function or utility did not integrate like it was supposed to. Because you integrated everything at one time, identifying the problem might be difficult, and you might spend most of your time in the following days and weeks solving nuisance problems. Total implementation leaves no room for error. The implementation must be planned and time allotted to perform the implementation.

If you have any equipment that will not affect the existing users when you install it, then you should install it first. This will allow you to work out as many problems as possible during this time. Then set up the phased or total implementation schedule and proceed with the plan.

Preparing The Installation Site

To prepare the installation site, you might need to move some existing equipment or even reconfigure the whole footprint. Your main objective in site preparation is to ensure that once you have staged the network, you can seamlessly integrate the new network equipment or upgrade. You should be able to do this in a way that minimizes both traffic flow in the work area and the time required to install the equipment.

Identifying And Configuring Network Components

To effectively install and maintain a network, you need to be familiar with all the devices, cabling, and connections that are associated with network equipment. The following sections discuss the more common components associated with computers and network devices and explain how to identify them. The vendor manual for each piece of equipment discusses in detail how to install and configure the equipment.

Serial Connectors

The world of connectors can be a confusing one because many connectors are associated with specific types of equipment, others are associated with specific communications media, and still others have a wide range of applications. Whether you are installing an all-new network with the most recent equipment or you are integrating upgrades to legacy equipment, you will run across a myriad of connectors, some of which you might have never seen before. The following sections discuss the most common serial connectors.

Bayonet Nut Connector

A *bayonet nut connector (BNC)* on a network card is a round, protruding connector with a female center pin. The BNC connects the computer to a Thinnet (10Base2) network. The network is an RG-58 coaxial cable network with devices connected using BNCs. Refer to the discussion on network interface cards (NICs) and Figure 10.3 later in this chapter for an illustration of a BNC connector.

Attachment Unit Interface Connector

An *attachment unit interface (AUI)* connector is a 15-pin connector with pins 1 through 8 on the top row and pins 9 through 15 on the bottom row. The AUI connector connects network devices to a Thicknet (10Base5) network. The popular RJ-45 connector has replaced most AUI connectors for local area network (LAN) connectivity. Refer to the discussion on NICs and Figure 10.3 later in the chapter for an illustration of an AUI connector.

DB-9 Serial Connector

This 9-pin male connector is used for serial communications. The typical speed ranges from 110 bps to 115,200 bps, but sometimes can run higher. A DB-9 connector on a computer is a data terminal equipment (DTE) device, whereas a DB-9 connector on a modem is a data communication equipment (DCE) device. Many network components use a DB-9 serial port for out-of-band management, both during initial equipment setup and for subsequent equipment management. Any time you make a DTE-to-DTE connection, including when you are connecting a computer to a network device using the serial port, you will need a null modem cable. The signaling standard for this application is Electronic Industries Association/Telecommunication Industry Association standard 574 (EIA/TIA-574). Figure 10.1 illustrates a DB-9 serial connector.

DB-25 Serial Connector

This 25-pin male connector is used for serial communications and has the same signal characteristics as the DB-9 serial connector. The DB-9 connector

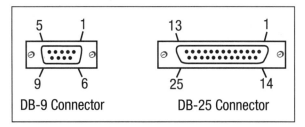

Figure 10.1 DB-9 and DB-25 serial connectors.

is generally preferred over the DB-25 connector because it takes up less physical space on the back of the computer without losing any communications capability. Figure 10.1 illustrates a DB-25 serial connector. The signaling standard for this application is the EIA/TIA-232.

Small Computer Systems Interface Connectors

A small computer systems interface (SCSI, pronounced "scuzzy") connector attaches hard drives, CD-ROM drives, and tape drives to a shared bus. Each device on the bus has an address from 0 to 7 on older standard SCSI buses and addresses 0 to 15 on newer standard SCSI buses. SCSI has evolved greatly since its inception, and you must be able to accurately identify both external and internal connectors. Table 10.1 defines the characteristics of the different SCSI connectors, and Figure 10.2 illustrates them. You can mix and match devices of different speeds, but such a combination will degrade speed and performance. Make sure that you match the speed of the hard drives. You can

Table 10.1 SCSI connectors.

SCSI Bus Type	Maximum Bus Width	Maximum Number of Devices	Speed
SCSI-1	5Mbps	8 bits	8
Fast SCSI	10Mbps	8 bits	8
Fast Wide SCSI	20Mbps	16 bits	16
Ultra SCSI	20Mbps	8 bits	8
Ultra SCSI	20Mbps	8 bits	4
Wide Ultra SCSI	40Mbps	16 bits	16
Wide Ultra SCSI	40Mbps	16 bits	8
Wide Ultra SCSI	40Mbps	16 bits	4
Ultra2 SCSI	40Mbps	8 bits	8
Wide Ultra2 SCSI	80Mbps	16 bits	16

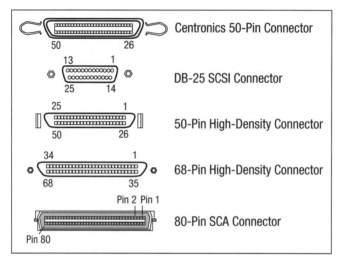

Figure 10.2 SCSI connectors.

assign the tape backup drive to a lower SCSI speed because it is accessed only during backup, and the bus will automatically adjust to the speed of the device.

Centronics 50-Pin Connector

This is the original 5Mbps, 8-bit SCSI bus connector that supports a maximum of eight devices and is used to connect to external SCSI devices. It is a 50-pin connector with holding clips on each side, as illustrated in Figure 10.2. Most SCSI SLOW and some 8-bit Fast computers and host adapters use this connector. This is older technology, and you will find it mainly on legacy equipment.

DB-25 SCSI Connector

This connector looks like a DB-25 parallel printer connector (see Figure 10.2). You will find it mainly on older Macintosh and Sun Microsystems computers, and originally it was installed as an add-on card in IBM-compatible computers. It is a 5Mbps, 8-bit SCSI bus connector that supports a maximum of eight devices.

 Although the DB-25 SCSI connector is not widely used anymore, you need to know that it was one of the original SCSI connector standards.

50-Pin High-Density Connector

This connector has pins 1 through 25 on the top row and pins 26 through 50 on the bottom row, with two metal connector clips at the ends of the external connector, as illustrated in Figure 10.2. This is an external connector that connects external hard drives, optical drives, CD-ROM drives, and tape drives. Although this connector is of older technology, it is still widely used, especially by 8-bit Fast computers and host adapters.

The 50-pin SCSI connector was the standard SCSI connector for several years.

68-Pin High-Density Connector

This connector is also used to connect external SCSI devices. Pins 1 through 34 are located on the top row and pins 35 through 68 are on the bottom row. It has two metal fastening screws at the ends of the external connectors, as Figure 10.2 illustrates. All Fast/Wide SCSI-3 computers and old Digital Equipment Corporation (DEC) single-ended SCSIs use this connector.

Most servers today deploy the 68-pin high-density SCSI connector.

80-Pin Single Connector Attachment Connector

The *single connector attachment (SCA)* connector is an external connector that includes connection pins for the power cables and the data wires. The 80-pin SCA-2 is current technology, and you will most likely see it used on high-end SCSI devices, such as Wide, UltraWide, or Ultra2 Wide external SCSI connections. This connector has pins 1 through 40 on the top row and pins 41 through 80 on the bottom row, as shown in Figure 10.2. It looks similar to a Centronics connector but is denser and a little wider.

Fiber Channel Connector

Fiber channel is a switched technology that allows interconnection of servers, workstations, external drive arrays, printers, mainframes, and LANs in a campus environment. It has data rates of 100 to 800Mbps, depending on the type of media connecting the device to the fiber channel switch. Fiber channel is similar to asynchronous transfer mode (ATM), but it makes a better peripheral technology connection than ATM, making it a better backbone technology. The fiber channel device uses a variety of connectors, including multimode fiber, coaxial cable, and shielded twisted pair cable. The fiber channel interconnect standard was developed by the American National Standards Institute (ANSI) X3T9 committee.

Universal Serial Bus Connector

The *universal serial bus (USB)* connector is a small, flat four-conductor connector that Microsoft and Intel developed, and you will find it installed on most new computers today. It is a relatively new standard and replaces the many connectors located on the back of computers. Manufacturers are equipping all their new machines with the USB connector. Eventually, it will replace the keyboard, mouse, printer, serial, joystick, audio, and many other connectors. It is a bus topology that can achieve data rates of 12Mbps.

RJ-45 Connector

The RJ-45 is the standard connector used for terminating unshielded twisted pair (UTP) cable plants and can be rated for category 5 speeds (the same as the cable is rated). The RJ-45 connector is an eight-wire connector that looks similar to an RJ-11 telephone connector except it is somewhat larger. Refer to the discussion on NICs and Figure 10.3 for an illustration of an RJ-45 connector.

UTP Patch Panel

UTP patch panels come in several standard densities, ranging from 24 ports to 96 ports. The patch panel is designed to be mounted in a standard 19-inch-wide equipment cabinet. It is located in the main distribution facility (MDF) or the intermediate distribution facility (IDF) and is where the UTP cable between the computer and cabinet terminates. The panel is a female receptacle that receives an RJ-45 connector. A patch cable is connected between the patch panel and the network device, such as a hub or a switch.

Type 1 Connector And Cable

IBM token ring networks commonly use type 1 cable. It is a thick, shielded cable with a 9-pin connector on one end and a type 1 connector on the other. Category 5 UTP cable has replaced type 1 as the preferred cable type.

Devices

A network device is a piece of equipment that is attached to the physical cable plant. It accepts a communications signal that conforms to a standard, such as Ethernet, and retransmits it with the intent of delivering it to the desired destination. Some network devices are more intelligent than others, allowing them to autosense and dynamically change their configuration.

Network Interface Card

The network interface card (NIC) is a layer 1 device and is the only device on the network that is actually installed inside the machine. Workstations, servers,

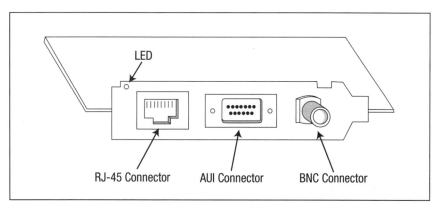

Figure 10.3 A network interface combo card.

print servers, and gateways all have NICs. NICs provide the connection point to a network, and each type of NIC is specifically designed for different types of networks, such as Ethernet, token ring, FDDI, and ARCNET.

Newer NICs usually have RJ-45 connectors on them, as shown in Figure 10.3. However, some legacy systems might have several types of connectors on them. A combo card was popular during the transition from AUI and BNC networks to the RJ-45 networks that are common today.

When you purchase a network card, make sure that it is for the correct topology and signal standard and that it matches the type of bus your computer supports. For example, a standard NIC would be a 10/100 Mbps PCI Ethernet card with an RJ-45 connector. Windows 95/98 will autodetect most NICs, so make sure that you have the latest driver installed on the machine before you install the card.

Hub

A hub is a layer 1 device that repeats a signal to all the hub ports that can connect to network segments or devices (see Figure 10.4). Hubs can have as few as 4 ports, but are usually either 12- or 24-port models. The unit has female RJ-45 connectors on the front that attach directly to a computer by means of a category 5 cable, or it can attach to a patch panel with an RJ-45 patch cable. The front panel of the hub has a link light that indicates connectivity with another device. You need to make sure that the hub supports the signal standard deployed throughout your network. One popular hub is a 10/100 autosensing Ethernet hub, which supports legacy systems and provides growth for faster speed. Repeating hubs require almost no configuration, if any at all. When you connect two hubs using ports on the front panel, you must use a crossover cable or crossover port.

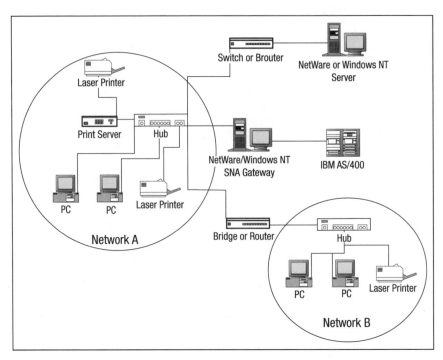

Figure 10.4 Network devices.

Switch

A switch is a layer 2 device that separates a network into segments, as illustrated in Figure 10.4. It is essential for large Ethernet networks because it eliminates the collisions that are frequent with shared networks. Switches support hierarchical network designs and can connect different architectures.

A switch is similar in appearance and function to a hub, but, unlike a hub, each port is more like a network segment unto itself. A switch repeats data only to the recipient/port specified by the MAC address, whereas a hub repeats data to all ports. Although you can configure a routing switch to do IP routing, the MAC address is the most basic means of addressing, and it is easier to configure the switch to handle MAC address switching rather than IP routing.

A switch will usually have a 9-pin, out-of-boundary management port on it. The management port is for the initial configuration of the device and requires a null modem connection between it and a computer. After the initial configuration, you should manage the device across the network by means of a Telnet connection. A switch has RJ-45 female connectors, and each connector has a link integrity light above it.

Brouter

A brouter (bridging router) is a device that works at layers 2 and 3 of the Open Systems Interconnect (OSI) model. As a bridge, it is protocol independent and can filter LAN traffic; as a router, it can forward network packets based on the network destination. Brouters can both bridge multiple protocols and provide routing for those protocols, if the protocols are routable. Most routers have bridging functions but are not considered brouters. Most networks today employ layer 3 switches instead of brouters. Figure 10.4 illustrates the placement of a brouter in a network.

> Remember that a brouter can work as both a layer 2 and a layer 3 device.

Gateway

A gateway works across layers 5, 6, and 7 of the OSI model. This device translates between two networks or segments that do not use the same protocols or the same data formatting. The System Network Architecture (SNA) gateway is a common gateway that translates a LAN protocol, such as TCP/IP, IPX, or NetBEUI, to the SNA protocol to communicate with an IBM mainframe or minicomputer. Microsoft Windows NT and Novell NetWare servers usually have gateways. Figure 10.4 illustrates the placement of a gateway in a network.

Bridge

A bridge is a layer 2 device with two or more ports that forwards frames from one LAN segment to another (see Figure 10.4). It is similar to a switch but usually connects two or more dissimilar networks, such as Ethernet and token ring, or Ethernet or token ring and a wide area network (WAN) connection. A bridge commonly segments coaxial networks when they are the primary types of network.

Network Operating System Server

Although the network operating system (NOS) is not a physical device, the server on which the NOS is installed is a device. Each NOS has its own characteristics and configures the server uniquely. Figure 10.4 illustrates the placement of a server in a network. The two most popular NOS servers are Windows NT and NetWare. They are installed as nodes on a network, and the workstations connect to them for file and print sharing. Many of the servers provide advanced functions, such as email servers, Web servers, gateways between diverse systems, database servers, and network management servers. Both

Novell and Microsoft provide extensive training to install and set up each of these advanced functions.

Router

A router will have one or more serial ports with a Channel Service Unit/Data Service Unit (CSU/DSU) connected to it and one or more LAN ports connected to a switch or hub. The identifying characteristic is the serial port for the CSU/DSU. The router is used to connect to remote offices or the Internet and is installed as a device on the network, as illustrated in Figure 10.4. An Internet router is usually the gateway address in the TCP/IP protocol parameters. It is an OSI layer 3 device that routes packets to the proper destination on the basis of the destination network address in the packet. A router is configured with the local subnet address information and the address information of the router to which it is connected on the WAN port. Cisco, Bay Networks, and other router manufacturers offer classes that teach you how to install and set up their routers.

Print Server

A print server is a device that shares a printer on a LAN and has a queue to temporarily store print jobs until they are printed. A print server connects to both the LAN and the printer, as illustrated in Figure 10.4. The printer connection can be parallel or serial. Some print servers are internal to the printer and are easy to spot because the LAN is connected directly to the printer. Both Windows NT and NetWare provide print queue and print server services. The basic design of a shared printing environment is to have a queue temporarily store the print jobs and a defined path between the queue and the printer. The defined path can be a network card address or the direct connection between the printer and the computer's local parallel printer port.

Staging The System

To begin setting up the network and all its components, you must have all the pieces in one place, called a *staging area*. You should stage the system at least one week prior to the actual, on-site installation so that you can fix anything that is not working and order any missing components.

In the staging area, you will assemble the system components, configure and test the equipment to make sure that all the hardware components function properly when installed, and ensure that all the necessary parts, including cables, are available. You should also ensure that any add-on cards or devices are properly configured. Your next step, loading the software, entails making sure that you have the latest version of the software (including patches) and activating any snap-in utilities.

After you have determined that the system is functioning, you need to compile and load a list of system users, test accounts, administrative accounts, and password defaults. The usernames should conform to a corporate standard, such as the first initial followed by the last name. The password standard should be a minimum of seven characters and include letters, numbers, and special characters.

Next, you have to design the IP network configuration and IP address scheme. In this phase, you need to consider whether the IP addresses are to be statically or dynamically assigned, whether those addresses will be real or fictitious, and whether multiple subnetworks will be used.

Cabling Scenarios

The physical media of a network is the highway that the information travels on to reach its destination. Any highway system has roads that are rated for different speeds, and the same is true for network cabling—different types of network cables are rated for different speeds. The highest-rated network cable is fiber-optic cable, which carries most of the load of data traffic around the country. Category 5 UTP cable carries most of the load of LAN traffic for businesses and organizations. Many organizations have digital telephone systems and digital network connections distributed throughout their offices.

A common problem is connecting analog modems to the digital telephone system or a network connection. This can result in damaging the telephone system, the network device, or the modem.

 Make sure that all the wall plates are clearly marked and that the telephone and network connections can be easily distinguished.

Many connectivity applications use RJ-45 connectors, which are the most commonly used connectors in networking. When you purchase RJ-45 connectors, make sure that they are rated for the speed of the network. The wiring pin-out for category 3 UTP is pins 1 and 2 for transmit and pins 3 and 6 for receive.

The maximum distance for UTP cable is 328 feet (100) meters in an Ethernet environment. The distance should be measured from patch cable to patch cable through the cable plant. The cable should be tested with a 100MHz or greater signal interjected throughout the cable to determine the length, crosstalk, continuity, electrical noise, attenuation, and capacitance.

100 meters is the maximum length of a UTP network cable from a network device such as an Ethernet hub or switch.

Implementing The Network

The following checklist is a basic outline to use before starting a network implementation. One of the most important aspects of upgrading or replacing equipment in a network is planning. Make sure that you have addressed every aspect of the implementation. Most network implementations fail or suffer greatly because of poor planning.

Implementation Checklist

Once you are ready to begin installing the network or upgrade on-site, you need a checklist to make sure that you have covered all the bases. The following list is a guideline to help you get ready to implement an integration project:

➤ Make a baseline of your initial configuration.

➤ Make sure that you have installed all the components for the networking equipment (such as cards and interfaces) and that they are operating correctly.

➤ Make sure that all the hardware for the server is installed and working properly.

➤ Have the entire set of manufacturers' installation and driver disks available.

➤ Flash the networking hardware and server with the latest flash revision or update the firmware code.

➤ Have all the service packs and hot fixes available for installation.

➤ Be familiar with the installation and configuration instructions.

➤ Refer to the installation and configuration instructions during the install, as products are changed between revisions.

➤ Have the technical support numbers and hours of operation available during the installation.

➤ Reference any available technical databases to see whether any known issues exist that you need to avoid.

➤ Have a recovery or backup plan ready if the implementation fails.

Installing The Network   **197**

Practice Questions

Question 1

> Which of the following connectors are external SCSI connectors? [Choose the three best answers]
> - a. DB-25 connector
> - b. DB-9 connector
> - c. 68-pin high-density connector
> - d. 50-pin Centronics connector
> - e. RJ-45 connector

The correct answers are a, c, and d. Answer b is incorrect because the DB-9 connector is a serial connector. Answer e is incorrect because the RJ-45 connector is used for LAN connections.

Question 2

> What physical evidence tells you which layer of the OSI model a device sits on? [Choose the two best answers]
> - a. The number of ports that it has
> - b. The type of connectors that it uses
> - c. The protocols that it handles
> - d. You cannot tell by looking at it
> - e. By its function and placement on the network

The correct answers are d and e. Although you can identify a device by its physical characteristics and know what that device does, you cannot assess which layer the device operates on by looking at it. The number of ports that it has is not significant because most network devices generally use RJ-45 connectors, and all RJ-45 connectors are the same. Therefore, answers a and b are incorrect. You cannot tell by looking at a device which protocols it handles. Therefore, answer c is also incorrect.

Question 3

> When is the best time to schedule a total or partial network installation or upgrade? [Choose the three best answers]
>
> ❏ a. During the business day
> ❏ b. Over a holiday
> ❏ c. During your lunch hour
> ❏ d. Over the weekend
> ❏ e. After hours

The correct answers are b, d, and e. Ideally, you want to introduce new equipment into the network when user demand is minimal. Answer a is incorrect because you want to avoid network upgrades or equipment installation while users are online. Answer c is incorrect because your lunch hour is not long enough to do an implementation, everyone takes lunch at different times, and many people work through their lunch hours.

Question 4

> An RJ-45 connector is similar in structure to what more familiar connector?
>
> ○ a. BNC connector
> ○ b. DB-25 serial connector
> ○ c. RJ-11 connector
> ○ d. USB connector

The correct answer is c. RJ-45 connectors are similar in structure to the RJ-11 connector that you find at the end of your telephone cable. Answers a, b, and d are incorrect, because they bear no semblance to an RJ-45 connector.

Question 5

Which connector was the original SCSI connector that supported most SCSI SLOW buses?

- a. 80-pin SCA connector
- b. Centronics 50-pin connector
- c. 50-pin high-density connector
- d. DB-25 SCSI connector

The correct answer is b. The Centronics 50-pin connector was the original 5Mbps, 8-bit connector that was used to connect SCSI SLOW devices. The other selections were introduced later, so choices a, c, and d are incorrect.

Question 6

What type of connector does this figure illustrate?

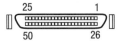

- a. RJ-45 connector
- b. 80-pin SCA connector
- c. Centronics 50-pin connector
- d. 50-pin high-density connector

The correct answer is d. The illustrated connector is a 50-pin high-density SCSI connector. An RJ-45 connector is an 8-pin connector. Therefore, answer a is incorrect. An 80-pin SCA connector has 80 pins. Therefore, answer b is incorrect. The Centronics 50-pin connector is larger and differently constructed than the 50-pin high-density connector. Therefore, answer c is incorrect.

Question 7

> Which SCSI adapter uses the 68-pin high-density connector? [Choose the two best answers]
>
> ❑ a. Fast/Wide SCSI-3 adapters
> ❑ b. Original Sun Microsystems computers
> ❑ c. Most new personal computers
> ❑ d. DEC single-ended SCSI

The correct answers are a and d. All Fast/Wide SCSI-3 adapters and the old DEC single-ended SCSI use the 68-pin high-density connector. Answer b is incorrect because the original Sun Microsystems computer used a 25-pin SCSI connector. Answer c is incorrect because most personal computers come with IDE connectors.

Question 8

> What was the original SCSI connector standard installed in Macintosh computers?
>
> ○ a. 50-pin high-density connector
> ○ b. Centronics 50-pin connector
> ○ c. DB-25 connector
> ○ d. 68-pin high-density connector

The correct answer is c. The DB-25 SCSI connector was the first connector to be a SCSI standard, so you will find it on older Macintosh and Sun computers. It also was originally installed as an add-on card in IBM-compatible computers. The Centronics connector was the first SCSI connector but was not an acclaimed standard. Therefore, answer b is incorrect. The 68-pin and 50-pin high-density connectors are newer technologies. Therefore, answers a and d incorrect.

Question 9

> What is the only layer 1 device that is located inside the computer?
>
> ○ a. Motherboard
>
> ○ b. SCSI bus
>
> ○ c. DB-25 SCSI card
>
> ○ d. NIC

The correct answer is d. The network interface card (NIC) is the only layer 1 device that is installed inside the computer. All other network devices are located outside the computer or are self-contained. Answers a and b are incorrect because although the motherboard and the SCSI bus are located inside the computer, they are not layer 1 devices. Answer c is incorrect because the DB-25 SCSI card was initially an add-on card for IBM compatibles and is not a layer 1 device.

Question 10

> Which network device works at OSI layers 2 and 3?
>
> ○ a. Router
>
> ○ b. Switch
>
> ○ c. Brouter
>
> ○ d. Bridge

The correct answer is c. A brouter accomplishes, in a limited fashion, the tasks of both a router (layer 3) and a bridge (layer 2). As a bridge, it is protocol independent and can filter LAN traffic; as a router, it can forward network packets on the basis of the network destination. A router works at the Network layer (layer 3) of the OSI model. Therefore, answer a is incorrect. A bridge and switch work at the Data Link layer (layer 2) of the OSI model. Therefore, answers b and d are incorrect.

Question 11

> Why is it important to stage the system? [Choose the five best answers]
> - ❏ a. To make sure that all the parts are there
> - ❏ b. To configure all the system components
> - ❏ c. To keep it out of the way until it needs to be deployed
> - ❏ d. To test the network equipment
> - ❏ e. To install any add-on devices
> - ❏ f. To load the software

Answers a, b, d, e, and f are correct. Your goal in staging is to bring the network to full operation before you integrate it with the existing network. Knowing that all the new equipment is working before you integrate it will minimize the problems that you will encounter after you do integrate it. Keeping it out of the way is a storage issue not a staging issue. Therefore, answer c is incorrect.

Question 12

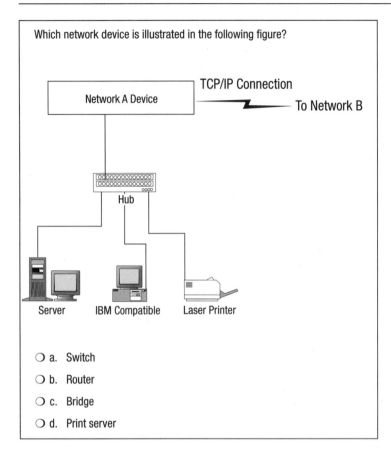

- ○ a. Switch
- ○ b. Router
- ○ c. Bridge
- ○ d. Print server

The correct answer is b. A router is a WAN device that connects remote buildings via a TCP/IP connection. A switch and a print server are LAN devices. Therefore, answers a and d are incorrect. A bridge can also connect two networks, but not over a TCP/IP connection. Therefore, answer c is also incorrect.

Need To Know More?

Mazda, Fraidoon, ed.: *Telecommunications Engineer's Reference Book*. Reed Educational and Professional Publishing Ltd., Woburn, MA,1998. ISBN 0-240-51491-2. An excellent reference book explaining the intricacies of telecommunications in great detail.

Sheldon, Tom: *Encyclopedia of Networking, Electronic Edition*. Osborne McGraw-Hill, New York, 1998. ISBN 0-07-882333-1. A good overview of general networking terms and networking characteristics. Covers everything from A to Z.

www.3com.com is a good source of information on NICs, switches, routers, and the OSI model.

www.baynetworks.com also publishes information on switches, routers, and the OSI model.

www.cisco.com publishes information on switches, routers, and the OSI model.

www.microsoft.com has extensive information on its advanced server products, such as SNA Gateway, SMS Server, and Internet products.

www.novell.com has detailed information on all its advanced server products for LANs and WANs.

Standard Operating Procedures

Terms you'll need to understand:

✓ Standard operating procedure (SOP)
✓ Bandwidth control
✓ Packet prioritization
✓ Flash BIOS
✓ Baseline
✓ Benchmark testing

Techniques you'll need to master:

✓ Understanding the Open Systems Interconnect (OSI) model
✓ Establishing a network baseline
✓ Effecting an escalation procedure
✓ Implementing disaster recovery plans
✓ Familiarizing yourself with Y2K compliance programs

Once you have installed the network or upgrade, you need to establish some standard operating procedures. These will include procedures for normal operation, for maintenance operations, and for emergency operations and disaster recovery.

Every effective network should have a *standard operating procedure (SOP)* manual. The SOP manual should cover all the policies and procedures for network operation. You should ensure that all users know the user policies so that they will know what to expect. The SOP manual should define allowable data storage, email storage, email content, Internet usage, and security. The procedures portion of the manual should also discuss procedures for adding, deleting, and modifying users as well as for adding peripherals, adding hardware, and modifying the server and network as a whole. The SOP manual should be a comprehensive reference book for the network administrators.

Cabling Configuration

When you set out to design the cabling plant, you should design it with future growth in mind. Any modifications that you make to the network or cabling configuration should serve to improve both bandwidth and data flow. One way that you can achieve greater bandwidth is by installing a high-bandwidth medium, such as fiber-optic cable, as the main backbone. Fiber-optic cable will also allow you to have greater distances between repeaters than the copper medium available for network cabling. You should also consider designing cable plants that support data, voice, and video on the same cable instead of maintaining three separate cabling systems. Implement priority packet delivery so that the network can route realtime data to its destination in a timely fashion.

Whenever you make a modification to the cabling plant, you should also update the cabling plant diagrams. If you are implementing a network upgrade, you most likely will not redraw the entire cabling plant. However, you will want to make sure that you draw your new cable additions or changes to existing cabling and store them with the main drawings. Ensure that your drawings reflect the location of each cable run, the wall outlet number, the patch panel location and number, the cable number, and the cable type.

 Multimode fiber-optic cable can transmit an Ethernet signal approximately 2 kilometers before it needs to be repeated.

Client Configuration

You should deploy a basic, consistent configuration to every client throughout the entire network. Keep the client configuration as standard as possible and try to use the same network cards and desktop setups on all the machines. The profiles function in both Windows NT and NetWare lets you set user desktop profiles. If the network interface cards (NICs) and profiles are the same for all the machines, performing upgrades or maintenance on those machines is easier because you will not have to struggle with separate configurations and any conflicts that they create.

Server Configuration

Although some people might refer to a server as being the "network," servers (and access to those servers) really belong in layers 5 to 7 of the Open Systems Interconnect (OSI) model. A server is a computer (host) that connects to a network and has a network operating system (NOS) installed on it. File and print sharing is the NOS's basic function, but most NOSs can perform many other functions, such as email, Web, Internet, and database services. You should install the latest flash BIOS and patches on the server and the NOS. If the organization has multiple servers, all servers should have the same release and patch revision.

You should make sure that you install the servers with the latest BIOS flash and that you patch all the servers to the same revision level.

Peripherals Setup

Some of the peripherals that you might find on a network are printers, scanners, plotters, shared tape backups, CD-ROM towers, and optical jukeboxes. The NOS security on the local area network (LAN) and the user rights/profiles control access to these devices. You should implement a standard naming convention that identifies the type of device and the device location.

Printers are the most common peripheral on a network. You can set up printers locally or as shared network printers. Before you set up a shared peripheral, you need to consider the physical location, connectivity, and NOS sharing/security. The following sections discuss each of these considerations.

Physical Location

Locate shared devices in a common area that users can easily access. Ideally, you should place printers so that they are centrally located near all the primary users. Other shared devices might require a location near the server. The server usually contains the tape backups for the network/server, and the workstation contains a backup agent for workstation backup. In most cases, you will store a CD-ROM tower with the server, and the IS department will control it. You must determine the location of peripheral devices on a case-by-case basis.

The physical location of a printer should be as close as possible to the user or department that is the primary user of that printer.

Connectivity

Many devices require a connection to the network or a direct connection to the computer that is going to share it. Shared devices often connect to a server to increase access to the server, but it also decreases the physical security of the server. In this case, you might want to consider a server just to support the shared device.

NOS Sharing And Security

Most devices give you procedures for installing them on a Windows NT or NetWare server. The procedures will normally include instructions on setting up the device on the NOS and activating the associated drivers. The procedures should also describe how to share the device and how to set up security on the device. The NOSs provide basic sharing and security for most devices, but the third-party software solution that comes with the device will often provide more functionality. A prime example is tape backup software: Windows NT and NetWare have a built-in backup solution, but most people choose to purchase a third-party backup solution instead because it provides more functionality.

Network Setup

For the purpose of this discussion, we assume that the network itself comprises the layer 1, 2, and 3 components (the cables, hubs, bridges, switches, and routers). You should always maintain a map of where these devices are located and what connects to them. If these devices have configuration files, print them out or save them in a master location on the database. Bridges, switches, and routers usually have firmware that you can program to provide enhancements over the default functions. Before you change these configurations, set up a test scenario and run it before you implement the changes on the network.

The network should have several advanced function options available, such as bandwidth control, packet prioritization features, and VLAN segmentation. Many routers and switches give you the ability to program them to accommodate different prioritization schemes within a network.

Remote Access

Remote access provides a way for users that are not on the LAN to gain access to network resources, such as when they are at home or away on a business trip.

Initially, the need to provide network access to on-the-road employees was the impetus for many remote access installations. Remote access also facilitates the ever-increasing telecommuting movement.

While you are determining which remote access solution you need to install, you should focus mainly on the applications that the users need most. The amount of information sent across the remote connection and the applications that the client will be using are the factors that determine the type of remote access that you need to install. You can choose from several types of remote access solutions, each having different functionality but still providing remote access to network resources. The following sections discuss the most prevalent types of remote access.

Shared Modem Pool

Shared modem pools give users access to the resources on the network by means of a connection that is similar to a LAN connection, except that it operates at modem speeds instead of LAN speeds. When you specify this type of connection, one of your major considerations will be how much information will be sent across the connection. A shared modem pool connection is not good for graphics-intensive applications, remote execution of applications, or high-volume data transfer. However, it is good for email, host connectivity (such as AS400 or Unix), or accessing a database when the application is loaded locally and points to the database on the server.

Remote Control And Virtual PC Sessions

Remote control of a PC on a LAN provides screen, keyboard, and mouse updates across the remote access connection. Some manufacturers produce servers that provide virtual PC sessions for terminals, local PCs, and remote PCs. A virtual PC session is similar to a remote control session in that the terminal or PC receives screen, keyboard, and mouse updates. However, it differs from a remote control session in the capabilities that it provides for corporate users. This type of remote connection is efficient for graphics- and data-intensive applications that would be too slow across a standard modem connection. A shared LAN modem pool or local modems on these devices can provide access to a virtual PC session.

Virtual Private Network

A virtual private network (VPN) is a Point-to-Point Protocol (PPP) connection to a local Internet Service Provider (ISP), and through that connection you can gain access to your organization's network. Windows NT supports Point-to-Point Tunneling Protocol (PPTP) connections to provide a secure tunnel (VPN) through the Internet. The VPN connection can access a standard NOS server or a virtual PC server. The VPN is a method to reduce long-distance telephone costs while providing a secure connection to corporate resources.

 Most remote access solutions use the asynchronous PPP connection as the transport between the remote user and the modem pool.

Security

Your security policy determines the access level that each user has on the network. You should pay special attention to this policy when you are establishing it, and you should maintain it regularly. The security policy should have a basic access level for all the servers, applications, the Internet, and any other resources. Set up each user with the basic security policy and then modify it as necessary to meet the needs of specific users.

External protection of corporate resources often receives the most attention, but it should not be the only emphasis of your information security practices. Sensitive corporate data needs protection from internal users as well as external users. Often, companies focus on data protection from hackers on the Internet; although this is an important practice, it should not be done to the exclusion of internal protection. Internal security is often overlooked because employees are considered trusted users. Weak internal security is a major source of security leaks.

User Accounts

Your organization should adopt a standard naming convention for user accounts, and all user accounts should adhere to that convention. The username should be descriptive of the individual user to whom you are assigning it, such as first initial and last name (for example, sreeves). All the user accounts should be set up the same way. You should also assign them to a home directory on the server and to the appropriate groups, and their local printers should be set up as well. In addition, set up the users for the necessary general applications (software that everyone gets, such as Word and Excel) and specific applications (job-specific software, such as an accounting package). Set up the general applications according to a standard operating procedure for all employees. Specific applications might need customization according to the user's corporate responsibilities. In all cases, you should develop and adhere to a set standard and address the exceptions on a case-by-case basis.

Establishing A Baseline

Once you get the network running and stabilized, it is vital that you make a baseline of all the components in the network, including measuring and documenting the level of traffic on each network segment. Network management packages can monitor this type of traffic activity and provide a history of the activity. The NOSs have utilities built into them that provide a baseline measurement on many of the components that constitute the NOS. The NOS can monitor hardware and operating system parameters and report on the utilization of many of these parameters. The workstation has some basic utilities that will provide a baseline measurement of the system. It is always a good idea to do a periodic capture of some of the more important components of a network and operating system. Windows 95 provides a utility called System Monitor, which allows the review of critical components of a system. One of the more critical components is memory, the lack of which can cause sporadic problems.

A baseline is the yardstick against which you measure any network changes. It is important to establish a baseline and then refer to that baseline periodically (for instance, during the preventive maintenance rotation) or when a user complains about network performance.

Benchmark Testing

The best way to test the throughput of a network is to perform benchmark testing, for which software is available to monitor the network and report the results. NetPIPE is one of those packages. You should perform benchmark testing under normal network utilization.

NetPIPE is a protocol-independent performance tool that visually represents the network performance under a variety of conditions. By taking the end-to-end application view of a network, NetPIPE displays the overhead associated with different protocol layers. NetPIPE answers the following questions:

➤ How soon will a given data block of a certain size arrive at its destination?

➤ Which network and protocol will transmit certain sizes of blocks the fastest?

➤ What is the maximum throughput and saturation level for a given network?

➤ What is the optimum block size for maximum throughput?

➤ How much communication overhead is due to the network communication protocol layer(s)?

➤ How quickly does a small (less than 1K) control message arrive, and which network and protocol will be best for this purpose?

Data Backups

At a minimum, the SOP should indicate a daily backup for corporate data. As a precaution, you should verify the backup logs daily to ensure that the server is actually backing up all the important data. In addition, you should review the backup set periodically to ensure that the backup program is selecting all the important data. You also need to periodically back up all the corporate data and then verify that the data is on the tape. A standard operating procedure for tape backups would be as follows:

➤ Check the backup set to ensure that the backup program has selected all the corporate data.

➤ Check the backup logs daily for errors during the backup.

➤ Keep a tape backup log with the status of each backup.

➤ Clean the tape drive weekly.

➤ Store backup tapes offsite.

➤ Check the offsite tapes periodically to ensure data corruption is not happening at the offsite location.

Remember that tape backup is the most common type of offline storage and that offsite storage of the backup tapes is recommended.

Emergency Response

If you wait until the height of an emergency to start thinking about what you are supposed to do in that emergency, you will be forced to make a snap decision, and decisions that are not based on preplanning can spell disaster. You cannot possibly think of every disaster scenario and prepare for it, but you can alleviate the repercussions of many disasters and rebound faster if you have formulated a plan beforehand. Your emergency response scenarios should at least include the following considerations:

➤ What to do when the server goes down

➤ What to do when the network goes down

➤ What to do in case of a fire

➤ What to do in case of a flood

➤ What to do in case the server gets stolen (it has been known to happen!)

- What to do in case of vandalism
- What to do if your network integrity (security) has been breached

Once an emergency occurs, you need to implement your emergency procedures immediately to get control of the situation. You will need to address the preceding scenarios and any others that you can think of and then formulate your emergency plan around them.

Emergency Response Team

In the event of an emergency, your organization should have an emergency response team that will respond to any network security issue, whether informational or physical. Initially, the emergency response team will assess the damage, including how much physical damage the perpetrator inflicted on the network or how much information was compromised.

Next, the team should try to bring the system back online, if possible. This might entail installing spare equipment to replace the missing or damaged equipment or restoring the system from the most recent tape backup. In a simpler scenario, the system might simply need to be restarted. In the case of a network security compromise, a temporary stopgap measure might be needed, such as disconnecting the network from outside access.

After that, the team should determine how the problems occurred and then rectify the problem immediately, or define a course of action to rectify the problem in the near future if they cannot implement the solution right away. For example, if an employee vandalized the network equipment, the proposed solution would be to put the network equipment in a locked room or locked cabinet. The emergency response team could not implement these solutions immediately, but they could put together a plan to present to management. Then the company could implement the solution as soon as it was feasible. In addition, the emergency response team will initiate the escalation procedures.

Escalation Procedures

Every organization should have an escalation procedure that informs management of network outages. The escalation procedure should include criteria for the following:

- The time the network went down
- The cause of the network outage
- The expected resolution to the problem
- The projected time until the network is back online

As stated previously, the emergency response team will determine most of these aspects. The procedure should progress through the management chain as the length of the outage progresses. Downtime involves lost revenue, and management should always be involved whenever revenue is being lost. Many times when management is included in the entire chain of events, they appreciate the complexity of the problems and are willing to make the investment to implement redundancy.

> *Note: The CEO of a major network equipment manufacturer has an escalation policy in which he must be informed when a customer's wide area network (WAN) has been down for more than 24 hours.*

Your escalation procedures should be unique to your server environment and corporate structure. Whatever you decide, the entire IS department should know what the escalation procedure is and understand its importance. Here is an example of how you might set up your escalation procedure for a medium-size business:

Problem: The server is corrupted and needs to be restored.

1. Network engineer learns of the situation and calls in the emergency response team (hour 1)
2. Operations manager notified (within hour 1)
3. IS director notified (hour 3)
4. Plant/site manager notified (hour 4)
5. Corporate IS notified (hour 6)
6. CEO notified (hour 8)

Disaster Recovery

You must implement a disaster recovery plan for all the main components of the network (such as bridges, switches, and routers). You can implement disaster recovery to varying degrees, depending on the situation and the degree of network failure. In case of a device failure, you might need to bypass that device. This would require reprogramming the device as discussed in the vendor manual for that piece of equipment. You would also have to implement a degree of network reconfiguration to compensate for the failed device.

Servers

The disaster recovery plan for your servers should detail the events that occur at certain intervals in a specified order. If a critical server is going to be down for an extended period of time, you need to configure a temporary replacement to assume the responsibilities of the downed server. Reinstalling and configuring a server to replace one that is down can be a time-consuming process if the server you are replacing did more than basic file and print sharing. The server should have a 24-hour parts-replacement guarantee at a minimum and a 4-hour guarantee for critical components. If the server must not be allowed to go down, redundancy servers can take over without interrupting network service. Keep in mind that you can almost always alleviate server downtime, but sometimes it comes with a price tag.

Workstations

A workstation disaster is probably the easiest on which to perform disaster recovery. Users can share workstations until you repair or replace the workstation. The only aspect that you might have to change is the specific user's profile.

Y2K

Y2K disaster recovery has become an important part of the computer industry. Many organizations have implemented Y2K compliance programs but have not implemented disaster recovery programs to compensate for device failure due to Y2K or to oversights in their Y2K compliance programs.

> *Note: The time to design and test a disaster recovery plan is not while it is happening. It should be a well-thought-out plan that is affordable and that can be implemented easily during a disaster.*

Emergency Scenario

Let's put all the pieces discussed previously (emergency response team, escalation procedures, and disaster recovery) into some sort of sequence. The following illustrates chronologically the problems, resolutions, and escalation procedures in an emergency scenario.

Company X has multiple locations. It has a primary site that has an AS400, multiple Windows NT servers, Internet connectivity, email, a domain name server (DNS), Dynamic Host Configuration Protocol (DHCP), and Windows Internet Name Service (WINS). The primary site has WAN connectivity to the secondary site, which has a Windows NT backup domain controller (BDC), local DHCP, local WINS, and email.

The network engineer was upgrading the secondary site and experienced problems seeing some, but not all, of the devices located at the primary site. He then took remote control of the primary domain controller (PDC) at the primary site by way of the WAN and ran a utility on the PDC that corrupted the PDC's Registry and crashed the server.

As soon as the network engineer realized that he could not get the server back up, he notified the operations manager of the problem (hour 1, 6:00 P.M., day 1). In turn, the operations manager called in the emergency response team, who came in, assessed the situation, and formulated a restoration plan.

First, the team tried to restore from tape backup, but the tape backup was corrupted. Then, they installed an alternate copy of Windows NT Server and tried to save the data. However, they encountered intermittent errors on every attempt. Next, they deleted the boot partition and installed a new copy of Windows NT Server without deleting the data partition. The system went into a state of "no boot partitions available."

The emergency response team tried to call hardware tech support, but the server manufacturer did not provide tech support after normal business hours. The operations manager was called again at hour 11 and told that the system (comprising the mail system, primary DNS, and primary WINS system) was still not up.

At hour 14, the operations manager escalated the downed server to the corporate IS director, explaining the problem, how it happened, what they had done to fix the problem (including failed attempts), and the proposed plan of action. The IS director informed the CEO at hour 15. The boot partition was restored at hour 24, and the system was brought back online, but with configuration errors. Thirty-six hours later, the system was operational with no configuration errors, and the escalation process was downgraded.

> *Note: Keep in mind that the timeline for this escalation was unique to this server configuration and corporate structure. Your escalation procedure should also be unique to your network environment and corporate structure.*

System Change And Upgrade Approvals

Why do you need to have an SOP that covers system changes and upgrade approvals? If your network is large enough to have several network engineers, you should have change control procedures in place. Whenever you propose a change or an upgrade to your system, you need approval from senior management. The following are some of the points that you need to cover before approaching management with your upgrade or change proposal:

- What are the known problems that the system change or upgrade will cause?

- Have you researched the technical bulletins from the equipment manufacturer(s) regarding the system change or upgrade?

- Have you researched the technical bulletins from the software vendor(s) regarding the system change or upgrade?

- Have you researched the technical bulletins from the operating system vendor regarding the system change or upgrade?

- Do you have a disaster recovery procedure in place in case the system change or upgrade fails?

Growth And Capacity Planning

After your network has been up and running for several years, you might experience noticeable growth through the addition of users, devices, and larger applications. This might cause the original network capacity to be insufficient. You should monitor the network capacity on a monthly basis and generate plans to upgrade the system before it reaches the saturation point. When you present management with your proposed system change or upgrade, you need to have the original baseline statistics and the results of your recent monitoring to give a clear picture of where you were, where you are, and where you need to go in terms of your network.

Practice Questions

Question 1

> Which type of network medium can transmit an Ethernet signal the farthest before needing to repeat it?
>
> ○ a. Multimode fiber-optic cable
>
> ○ b. Ribbon cable
>
> ○ c. UTP cable
>
> ○ d. Coaxial cable

The correct answer is a. Fiber-optic cable can transmit an Ethernet signal approximately 2 kilometers before a repeater is needed. Ribbon cable is not used for Ethernet. Therefore, answer b is incorrect. UTP cable can transmit an Ethernet signal only 100 meters before needing to repeat it. Therefore, answer c is incorrect. 10Base5 coaxial cable can transmit an Ethernet signal only 500 meters before needing to repeat it, and 10Base2 coaxial cable can transmit a signal just 200 meters before needing to repeat it. Therefore, answer d is incorrect.

Question 2

> Where should high-use network peripherals, such as printers, be physically located?
>
> ○ a. Next to the server and network equipment
>
> ○ b. Centrally located as near to the users as possible
>
> ○ c. In a room designed for all network peripherals
>
> ○ d. As close to the boss's office as possible

The correct answer is b. The network peripheral should be centrally located near the primary users of that device. Answer a is incorrect because high-use peripherals should never be located next to servers and network equipment. High traffic flow is an invitation for users to tamper with vital network components. Answer c is incorrect because although a room designed for network peripherals in a small organization might meet the requirement of being centrally located, this would not be the case in a large organization. Answer d is incorrect because all peripherals should not be next to the boss's office.

Question 3

What is the most common type of asynchronous protocol in use today?
- ○ a. TCP/IP
- ○ b. PPP
- ○ c. IPX
- ○ d. SLIP
- ○ e. NetBEUI

The correct answer is b. PPP has error-correcting and speed-negotiating features built into it and has become the most widely supported asynchronous protocol on the market. TCP/IP is not an asynchronous protocol but is encapsulated inside of PPP. Therefore, answer a is incorrect. IPX is also not an asynchronous protocol but is encapsulated inside of PPP. Therefore, answer c is incorrect. SLIP is an asynchronous protocol that is limited in many ways, the most prevalent of which is that it can encapsulate only IP and therefore has not gained market share. Therefore, answer d is incorrect. NetBEUI is not an asynchronous protocol but is encapsulated inside of PPP. Therefore, answer d is incorrect.

Question 4

Why should you have a network baseline? [Choose the two best answers]
- ❑ a. To have a reference of network performance at a given time
- ❑ b. To determine whether the network has a break in the cable
- ❑ c. To determine whether the network has become saturated
- ❑ d. To determine whether the cable termination has degraded over time

The correct answers are a and c. The network needs a baseline as a reference to determine whether the traffic levels have increased to the point of saturation. Answers b and d are incorrect because a break in the cable and cable termination would be checked by using a cable tester.

Question 5

> Why should you have SOPs for data backups? [Choose the three best answers]
>
> ❏ a. To make sure that the guidelines for backing up the necessary data are documented
>
> ❏ b. To be able to hold a person accountable for any mistakes
>
> ❏ c. To be able to review the current backup procedures and modify them accordingly
>
> ❏ d. To have a place to document any problems recorded in the backup logs

The correct answers are a, c, and d. The corporate data that is backed up is often the only place to restore data from after a disaster occurs. You must have SOP in place to regulate when and how tape backups are made, how they are verified, and where they are stored. These steps will all help safeguard corporate data by providing a reliable backup system. Answer b is incorrect because holding people accountable for mistakes is not a reason for having an SOP.

Question 6

> Why should you have a progressive escalation procedure that informs management when a network has been down for a specific length of time?
>
> ○ a. One of the managers might eventually be able to fix the problem.
>
> ○ b. Managers can apply more pressure, which will make the network engineers work harder.
>
> ○ c. Management needs to be informed of problems that affect productivity, and a reporting mechanism should be in place that keeps them informed.
>
> ○ d. An escalation procedure would only add to the already tense situation; therefore, no escalation procedure is necessary.

The correct answer is c. Management needs to be kept informed of problems. Answers a and b are incorrect because they might have some validity but are not good reasons for having an escalation procedure. Answer d is incorrect because you should have an escalation procedure.

Question 7

> Which statements apply to disaster recovery? [Choose the two best answers]
>
> ❏ a. The best disaster recovery plans are formulated at the height of any disaster.
>
> ❏ b. A disaster recovery plan needs to be planned and tested before any disaster occurs.
>
> ❏ c. A disaster recovery plan needs to be affordable and able to be implemented in a timely fashion.
>
> ❏ d. Disaster recovery plans are a waste of valuable resources.

The correct answers are b and c. Disaster recovery needs to be planned and tested before a disaster occurs. Answers a and d are incorrect because formulating a plan during a crisis is not a good idea, and having such a plan is not a waste of resources.

Need To Know More?

 Mazda, Fraidoon, ed.: *Telecommunications Engineer's Reference Book*. Reed Educational and Professional Publishing Ltd., Woburn, MA, 1998. ISBN 0-240-51491-2. An excellent reference book explaining the intricacies of telecommunications in great detail.

 Sheldon, Tom: *Encyclopedia of Networking, Electronic Edition*. Osborne McGraw-Hill, New York, 1998. ISBN 0-07-882333-1. A good overview of general networking terms and networking characteristics. Covers everything from A to Z.

 Microsoft has a CD subscription called TechNet that is an invaluable resource when setting up SOPs. Perform a search on baseline, tape backup, and operating procedures.

 www.cisco.com has white papers concerning fault tolerance and disaster recovery for WANs and switched networks.

 www.microsoft.com has a knowledge base that explains in detail the specifics of setting up standards when installing a network.

 www.novell.com has a knowledge base of its entire product and associated services. It provides detailed and current information about SOPs for many of its products.

Change Control System

Terms you'll need to understand:

√ Baseline

√ Universal naming convention (UNC)

√ User rights

√ User profiles

Techniques you'll need to master:

√ Making a network baseline

√ Understanding the network administrator's duties

√ Assigning access rights

√ Developing a contingency plan

√ Effecting network changes

√ Implementing security system changes

√ Doing general housekeeping on the network

√ Mapping a drive

√ Capturing a printer

It is reasonable to expect that any network will have a foreseeable life expectancy and at some time in the future will require an upgrade or replacement. Although you might be aware of the procedures required to implement changes, you need a checklist that addresses each step of the procedure. An effective change control policy will ensure that any changes, additions, or upgrades to your network will be correctly planned, approved, implemented, and documented. You should keep the change control policies along with the standard operating procedures.

Document Network Baseline

As discussed in Chapter 11, it is important that you have a baseline of all the components in the network once the network is running and stabilized. Although we discussed this previously, we will reiterate the information in the light of developing a standard operating procedure for network baselines. Network management packages can monitor this type of traffic activity and provide a history of that activity. Network operating systems (NOSs) have utilities built into them that provide a baseline measurement on many of the components that constitute the NOS. The NOS can monitor hardware and operating system parameters and report on the utilization of many of these parameters. It is always a good idea to do a periodic capture of some of the more important components of a network and operating system.

The whole purpose of a baseline is to make sure that during an upgrade or change you will not reach the point of no return. A baseline provides you with a safety net. If the change or upgrade does not work, the most that you will need to do is return to the previous configuration. Before you add a new NOS or network device, you should perform a new baseline to determine the network traffic levels and NOS performance statistics. Once you add and stabilize the new device, you need to perform another baseline for the network and the NOS. You then need to reference the new baselines against the previous ones to see whether the NOS or network performance has degraded or improved.

We cannot put enough emphasis on documenting everything about your network. Your documentation should include your baseline, tape backups, and as many aspects of your network configuration as you can print out. Although most work today is done on computers, occasions might arise when you simply need a comprehensive print-out of what your network looks like and how it is configured.

Contingency Plan

When preparing an upgrade to a network, server, or workstation, it is imperative that you have a recovery plan in place to restore the system to its original state. In the following sections, we discuss several system components and provide some suggestions for contingency plans.

Workstations

A contingency plan for restoring a workstation to its original configuration is to back it up before any upgrade takes place. A portable backup device works well, and a central backup device on a server can also back up workstations. Some utilities can keep a master image of a hard drive on a server that can be restored across the network.

Servers

A centralized backup is the best contingency plan for a server. The backup utilities shipped with most NOSs will perform backups of the system and data files. Third-party backup software will often have more features than the NOS's backup software.

Network Equipment

It is possible to store the configuration for many network devices on a Trivial File Transfer Protocol (TFTP) server. Most network equipment that can be programmed has this capability. Some devices have flash memory cards on which you can store the configuration. It is always a good idea to print out the configuration and keep it in a safe location. A further precaution is to store the configuration on a central TFTP server, if you can.

Network Changes

In this section we define some network elements that are associated with Windows NT and NetWare. These elements consist of administrative utilities that affect server administration and some that affect the user workstation.

As mentioned in Chapter 11, the network should have a policies and procedures manual that covers all aspects of the network operation. You should communicate to all users the content of the user policies so that they will know what to expect. The policies and procedures manual should define allowable data storage, email storage, email content, Internet usage, and security. The procedures portion of the manual should also discuss procedures for adding, deleting, and modifying users as well as procedures for adding peripherals and hardware and modifying the network and server as a whole. It should be the reference book for network administrators. All network changes are the responsibility of the network administrator, who has an exclusive account for managing the users, devices, security, and all other aspects of the network.

You must have administrator rights and privileges to manage any phase of an NOS. In Windows NT, that account is *Administrator*, and in NetWare 5 and intraNetWare, it is *Admin*. In Unix, it is the *root* or *su* user, and in OS/2 it is the *administrator*.

NOS Changes And Server Upgrades

You should definitely seek senior management's approval before you make any changes to the NOS or server. These changes can affect the entire company, and management should be prepared just in case the server or network crashes because of your change.

Before you upgrade or change the production NOS, you should test the change on a nonproduction NOS server that is configured as close to the production server as possible. Access to the production server(s) should be restricted, and the policy manual should state that any proposed changes must undergo performance testing prior to implementation on a production server. In addition, before you make a change, you should perform a server and data backup and then verify that data. This will safeguard you against making irreversible changes to the NOS or server configuration. If the new change or upgrade fails or corrupts the server, you can bring the server back to the original hardware configuration with the backup.

User Software Changes

Before changing or upgrading the software, you need to back it up just in case the change or upgrade fails, and you need to restore it to the original configuration. As with NOS or server changes, you need to test the change or upgrade on a nonproduction system first and document any problems that you encounter. You must then resolve these problems before you implement the change to an operational system. It is foolhardy to implement the change with known problems and simply hope for the best. That way of thinking will put your entire network in jeopardy. Although changing or upgrading the software will not usually affect senior management greatly, you should still present your change proposal to them for approval. Their primary consideration will be for those applications by which the company as a whole could be affected, such as payroll or production applications. Software, like that used for word processing, is usually not a matter of serious concern if the user is provided with increased capability and training on the new software.

Security System Changes

Before changing system security, you must exercise extreme caution. Your network security is your company's first line of defense against hostile penetration,

Change Control System   227

and a security breach is an open door to data compromise. You must completely document your proposed changes, and senior management must approve them. To ensure that you are making the best choices for security changes, you need to let a knowledgeable peer review the changes before you present them to senior management.

Next, you need to have a fail-safe plan. If for any reason someone breaches your new security configuration after you implement it, you will want to return immediately to the old security configuration until you figure out how the network was breached.

You need to look at the little things as well. One of the main mistakes that many administrators make is granting access rights to the group "Everyone." Although this might seem to be an efficient measure, it sometimes results in file and directory security compromises.

If your system connects to the Internet, you need to pay special attention to changing anything that relates to security access. The NOS manufacturers release bulletins and technical papers that provide step-by-step instructions on how to secure their systems. Review these instructions before changing the system security and make sure that you implement any recommendations that they give.

Passwords are another security breach because so many users pick easy passwords. Ensure that the network users have a defined standard for their passwords. Ideally, your change control procedure should recommend passwords that are about seven characters long and that contain letters, numbers, and special characters. Caution users about using passwords that are the same as their name, their children's or wife's name, or their hobbies. Also, caution them against writing their passwords down. A password should not be composed of just a word because a dictionary attack could easily compromise a user's password.

The change control should also set a regular schedule for mandatory password changes. For individual users, once per month is acceptable. However, for network logon passwords that implement the same password for all network users, you should change that password every time an employee leaves the company.

User Changes

The changes that you make to individual users are generally limited to adding or deleting users or changing their privileges. You will normally effect user changes on the request of a department manager to accommodate new users or tailor an existing user's rights and privileges. User changes do not usually require senior management's involvement.

Adding/Deleting/Modifying Users
User Manager for Domains is the utility used for Windows NT domain administration, and the NWAdmin utility is for NetWare NDS administration. Before adding users, it is important to define all the system access that the users will need to accomplish their jobs. This includes information such as home directory, shared directories, local printers, applications, and Internet access.

User Profiles
User profiles can be stored on the local workstation or on the server. The profiles can be mandatory profiles, which all users get, or they can be roaming profiles, which are user-specific profiles that are stored on the server and implemented by the user's logon name and password. The profile determines the workstation desktop display and the type of desktop functions the user has access to.

Access Rights
User rights are defined by the network administrator and include access rights to files and directories. User rights also include group rights to files and directories, provided that the user is a member of that group. You can give specific access to network printers, but printers usually are open to all users on the network. However, you will want to set access restrictions for specialized network devices.

Housekeeping
Housekeeping is a necessary function of any system to ensure that it is performing optimally and that all unnecessary files are purged from the system. The users need to perform housekeeping on their home directories and email accounts. The administrator needs to make sure that old revisions of software, drivers, and utilities are archived to tape backup and purged from the system. You should keep the archive for a predetermined length of time before you delete it. Archived data is more important to keep around because it is more difficult to reproduce than commercial software.

Selecting The Appropriate Backup Technique
The appropriate backup type for an organization depends on the following factors:

➤ The amount of data that needs to be backed up

➤ The type of data that needs to be backed up

- How far back one needs to go to retrieve the data
- Whether the backup type can be offline, near-line, or online storage

Some organizations might choose a combination of all three, depending on the need to access the data. Chapter 5 discusses the different types of backups in depth.

Removing Outdated/Unused Drivers And Properties

When you are upgrading a system, it is a good idea to make a backup copy of all the data that will be affected. Make sure that you have the data stored on an offline storage device, such as a backup tape. If you have space available on the hard drives, it is a good idea to make an online backup of the data. Online data backups resulting from an upgrade can be a problem mainly because you never seem to go back and erase them in a timely fashion. Storing the data online for several weeks should be sufficient time to determine whether a problem exists with the upgrade.

Drive Mapping

The *universal naming convention (UNC)* is an industry-standard way to redirect a drive letter to a shared area on a server or network workstation. The UNC is identified with two backslashes, the name of the server or workstation, and the shared hard drive area. The DOS command used by NetWare is **map**, and the DOS command used by Windows 95/98 and Windows NT is **net use**. The Windows Explorer pull-down menu command is Tools|Map Network Drive. Each of these ways to redirect a drive letter to a shared network resource uses the UNC to identify the server and shared hard drive area. The NetWare command is **map h:=\\servername\users\home**. The DOS command for Windows 95/98 and Windows NT is **net use h:\\servername\sharename**. The Tools|Map Network Drive pull-down menu used with the Explorer utility requires that you enter only the UNC name.

Printer Port Capturing

The UNC is also an industry-standard way to redirect a printer port to a shared printer on a network, server, or workstation. The UNC is identified with two backslashes, the name of the server or workstation, and the shared printer. The NetWare command is **CAPTURE [P=printername | Q=queuename] [L=LPT#] [options]**. The Windows 95/98 and Windows NT command is **net use lpt1:\\servername\prtsharename**.

Practice Questions

Question 1

> What is a contingency plan? [Choose the two best answers]
> - a. A plan to upgrade a system
> - b. An alternate plan if the first plan does not work
> - c. The original configuration plan
> - d. A recovery plan in case something goes wrong

The correct answers are b and d. You must have a contingency plan in place before doing any type of system change or upgrade in case the system or upgrade fails. It is not an upgrade plan or the original configuration plan. Therefore, answers a and c are incorrect.

Question 2

> If you are going to upgrade a workstation, which contingency plans should you perform in case the upgrade fails? [Choose the two best answers]
> - a. Make a tape backup of the system before the upgrade and restore it if the upgrade fails.
> - b. Make an image of the hard disk, store it on a central server before the upgrade, and restore it if the upgrade fails.
> - c. Make a backup of the system after the upgrade and reinstall the operating system.
> - d. Make an image of the hard disk, store it on a central server after the upgrade, and reinstall the operating system.

The correct answers are a and b. You would want a backup of the system to restore from if the upgrade failed. Answers c and d are incorrect because a backup of the system after the upgrade would not help restore the system.

Question 3

If you are going to upgrade a server, which contingency plan should you perform in case the upgrade fails?

- ○ a. A tape backup of the system before the upgrade
- ○ b. An image of the hard drive stored on a local workstation before the upgrade
- ○ c. An FTP server backup of all the data before the upgrade
- ○ d. A TFTP server backup of all the data before the upgrade

The correct answer is a. The only reliable contingency plan is a tape backup of the system before the upgrade. Although you could store a hard drive image of the server on a workstation, it would not be the preferred method. Therefore, answer b is incorrect. It is unlikely that an FTP or a TFTP server could back up a server to the point where it could be restored after a catastrophic failure. Therefore, answers c and d are incorrect.

Question 4

If you are going to upgrade a router, which contingency plans should you perform in case the upgrade fails? [Choose the two best answers]

- ❑ a. Use TFTP to retrieve the original configuration before uploading the new configuration and reload the original configuration if the upgrade fails.
- ❑ b. Copy the configuration to the local hard drive of the nearest network node and reload it if the upgrade fails.
- ❑ c. Make a local tape backup of the configuration before the upgrade and reload it if the upgrade fails.
- ❑ d. Use a flash memory card, if one is installed, to store the original configuration before upgrading the router and reload the original configuration if the upgrade fails.

The correct answers are a and d. Some routers use TFTP servers to store their configuration on, whereas others use a flash memory card. You would want to make a backup of the original router configuration in case something goes wrong. Storing the configuration on the nearest node does not have any merit. Therefore, answer b is incorrect. Routers do not have tape backup units. Therefore, answer c is incorrect.

Question 5

What is the administrator's account for Windows NT?

○ a. AdminNT

○ b. root

○ c. su

○ d. Administrator

○ e. Admin

The correct answer is d. The network administrator's account in Windows NT is Administrator. Answer a is incorrect because no such account exists. Answers b and c are incorrect because both are the Unix administrator's accounts. Answer e is incorrect because Admin is the NetWare and intraNetWare administrator's account.

Question 6

What essential steps should you take before you implement a security system change? [Choose the two best answers]

❑ a. Shut down your Internet access.

❑ b. Have a knowledgeable peer review your recommended changes.

❑ c. Read the NOS manufacturer's bulletins and technical papers beforehand.

❑ d. Hire a hacker to test it out.

The correct answers are b and c. You should have a separate, knowledgeable set of eyes other than your own look at your proposed security changes for problems that you might have overlooked. The NOS manufacturers usually release bulletins and technical papers that provide detailed instructions on how to secure their NOSs. Answer a is incorrect because you do not need to shut down Internet access simply to make a decision on whether a change is feasible. Answer d is incorrect because at no time do you ever want to give someone with hostile intentions an open door to your network.

Question 7

On which considerations does the choice of backup technique rest? [Choose the three best answers]

❑ a. How much storage room you have in the server room
❑ b. The amount and type of data that you need to back up
❑ c. How far back you need to go to retrieve the data
❑ d. Whether the backup will be offline, near-line, or online storage
❑ e. How many changes have been made to the data

The correct answers are b, c, and d. Your choice for backup type depends on the amount and type of data that you need to back up, how far back you need to go to retrieve the data, and what kind of storage you choose. If you have never backed up your system and you have had it a couple of years, your backup type will need to be more data intensive and reliable than if you are simply expanding your current backup abilities. In addition, graphics-intensive applications will require much more room on the backup media than will straight data. You will also need to decide whether your backup will be offline (tape backup, which requires that you find the tape and then restore the data), near-line (rewritable optical carousel, which is available within minutes and can hold gigabytes of information), or online (redundant disks, which provide almost immediate availability).

Answer a is incorrect because storage room is irrelevant to the backup style that you choose. Answer e is incorrect because data and configuration changes are the whole reason behind performing backup procedures.

Question 8

What is the importance of a change control system? [Choose the two best answers]

❑ a. So that no one can make any changes to the system
❑ b. So that it takes longer to make changes to the system
❑ c. So that all changes and upgrades are correctly planned, approved, implemented, and documented
❑ d. To make sure that each step of the implementation is executed properly

The correct answers are c and d. A change control procedure establishes a standard whereby all changes and upgrades are planned and implemented in a consistent fashion; it lets change take place quickly, efficiently, and in a well-thought-out manner. Answer a is incorrect because every network has growth potential that needs to be met. Answer b is incorrect because as growth needs arise, you need to implement changes quickly.

Question 9

What is the ideal password configuration?
- a. Four characters, all numbers
- b. Seven characters, comprising numbers, letters, and special characters
- c. Six characters, comprising letters and special characters
- d. Seven characters, all letters
- e. Nine characters, comprising numbers and letters

The correct answer is b. Ideally, a user's password should be about seven (no less) characters in length and should be a mixture of numbers, letters, and special characters. Answers a and c are incorrect because the password should contain more than four or six characters. Answer d is incorrect because the password does not contain numbers or special characters and could be subject to a dictionary attack. Answer e is incorrect because it does not contain any special characters.

Question 10

Which of the following are accurate ways to map a drive? [Choose the three best answers]
- a. map h:=\\servername\users\home
- b. net use h:\\servername\sharename
- c. Through the Tools|Map Network Drive menu in the Explorer utility
- d. c:\programname\filename

Change Control System

The correct answers are a, b, and c. The NetWare command is **map h:=\\server-name\users\home**, the Windows 95/98 and Windows NT command is **net use h:\\servername\sharename**, and the Tools|Map Network Drive menu simplifies the mapping procedure by requiring that you enter only the UNC name. Answer d is incorrect because that is not a UNC name, so you cannot use it to map a drive.

Question 11

Which commands do you use to redirect (capture) a printer port to a shared printer on the network? [Choose the two best answers]

❑ a. CAPTURE [P=printername | Q=queuename] [L=LPT#] [options]
❑ b. GOTO printer1
❑ c. c:\uselpt1\servername
❑ d. net use lpt1:\\servername\prtsharename

The correct answers are a and d. **CAPTURE [P=printername | Q=queuename] [L=LPT#] [options]** is the NetWare command, and **net use lpt1:\\servername\prtsharename** is the Windows 95/98 and Windows NT command. Answers b and c are incorrect because you cannot use either to capture a printer.

Need To Know More?

 Microsoft has a CD subscription called TechNet that is an invaluable resource for making sure you have a contingency plan in place before doing an upgrade. Search on updating, changing, and deleting.

 www.cisco.com has white papers concerning TFTP and flash memory cards.

 www.microsoft.com has a knowledge base that explains in detail the need for a verified tape backup of all data in case of a catastrophic failure or problem.

 www.novell.com has a knowledge base on its entire product line and associated services and covers contingency planning for many of its products.

Network Support And Preventive Maintenance

13

Terms you'll need to understand:

- √ Preventive maintenance
- √ Patches
- √ Upgrades
- √ Flashes
- √ Fixes

Techniques you'll need to master:

- √ Developing a maintenance schedule
- √ Monitoring server and network function
- √ Performing a visual inspection of the network
- √ Applying patches and upgrades

Preventive maintenance (PM) and network support must be factored into the design of any network system. What is preventive maintenance? It is all the little things that you do to keep the network up and running; the same little things that, if left unattended, would make for much larger problems in the future. Preventive maintenance lets you identify and correct problem areas long before they become serious network failures. Some organizations often neglect preventive maintenance in their overall network plans, leaving a substantial amount of corrective maintenance (CM) when the system malfunctions. Just as a car needs a maintenance schedule, your network also needs a maintenance schedule. In this chapter, we discuss preventive measures that you can take to keep your network in good health.

Developing A Maintenance Schedule

In reality, preventive maintenance is an ongoing task, but you should do a complete network checkup at least once every six months. As an alternative, you can set up your schedule so that you address different network components at different times, so you don't have to do the whole network at once. In addition to the six-month standard, you should check out the network whenever you change the hardware or software configuration.

Maintenance should include every piece of hardware and software in the network because all are capable of malfunctioning. You should also document your maintenance schedule, including every application and device that is affected. In addition, you should make a complete checklist every time you begin a new maintenance rotation so that you will know which line items you have addressed and which you have not. The following sections discuss some of the major considerations for preventive maintenance and give a recommended schedule for each.

Preventive Maintenance

What should be included in the PM rotation? Everything that is associated with the network, including operating system and applications software, connectivity to the network, security, the backup system, and the equipment environment.

However, the following are a few aspects that you should not address:

➤ You should not open any of the computers or devices to inspect any internal components unless you have specifically identified a problem with that computer or device and are effecting corrective maintenance.

► Do not tamper with the electrical service either inside or outside the building. If you perceive any problem with electrical service, inform your site engineer, who can then deal with the problem.

The first part of your PM rotation will be a physical walk-through, during which you will check the following:

► **Computers and devices** You will want to visually check all the devices and ensure that they are running properly. Look for indications such as connectivity lights and disk activity lights. Even simple signs, such as people using the computers, will let you know that the equipment is functioning. Test any device or computer that does not seem to be working properly.

► **Connectors and cables** Check all devices, servers, and computers to make sure that they are properly connected to the network. Look for loose or broken connectors and visually inspect cables for wear, excessive kinking, or cuts. However, this does not mean that you need to crawl up into the ceiling or under the floor to look at the cables, as such cables are not subject to wear. If the visual inspection passes and you still suspect the cable, get a cable tester and test the cable.

► **Network environment** This means simply making sure that the server and network environment is within the tolerances of the equipment. We discuss this in more detail later in this chapter.

After you accomplish the physical inspection, you need to turn your attention to the inner workings of the network, as discussed in the following sections.

Server And Workstation Backup

You need to back up the server nightly and store the media in a safe place or offsite. Chapter 5 discusses backup options and other backup considerations. Server backup usually receives the most attention, whereas workstation backup is often neglected in the backup schedule. Users can store data on their workstations as well as on the server, and you need to back up workstation data to have a completely reliable network. As a rule, back up the workstation data nightly along with the server data. However, if a corporate server is available, users should store corporate data on the server and not on the workstation.

In addition to regular backups, you should perform a full backup of your system data and configuration before you implement any changes to the network. This will provide you with a safety net just in case you need to restore the network to its original configuration.

Antivirus Software

After you install antivirus software onto your system, you need to update it at least once every three months, but once a month is preferable. Some antivirus vendors provide automatic downloads of virus updates that occur whenever they have a new virus signature. Other vendors have updates, but you need to go to their Web sites to get them. Chapter 7 provides complete details on antivirus software and updates.

You need to update your antivirus software virus signatures once a month. New viruses appear often, and if you do not update regularly, you are leaving your system open to virus infection.

After you download the virus signature update to the network, you need to have a way to automatically distribute the signature files to the workstations. In a workstation and server environment, you can set up the server to distribute the signature files to the workstations automatically. The server's antivirus software maintains the safety of the server against a virus attack, especially from across the Internet. The workstation's antivirus software protects the workstations from viruses on contaminated diskettes or locally loaded software.

Some antivirus software vendors have a product called an antivirus total defense package that protects workstations, servers, email, and the Internet.

Patches And Upgrades

Most intelligent network devices, workstation operating systems, and network operating systems (NOSs) require patches, fixes, and upgrades. You need to perform patches, operating system upgrades, application upgrades, and hardware flash upgrades on a periodic schedule that is based on the release of the patch or upgrade. You can download patches and upgrades from your vendor's Web site. Remember to thoroughly test the patch or upgrade before you implement it on a wide scale.

Before applying a patch or performing an upgrade to an operational system, make a verified backup of the entire system. Also, make sure that you read the release notes associated with the patch or upgrade and address any precautions before you proceed.

If you are patching or upgrading network hardware, once you address the release notes and precautions, you can begin the procedure. However, if you are upgrading or patching an operating system that is on a computer (for example, Windows NT on a Compaq server), contact the computer manufacturer to see whether any known problems exist with the patch or upgrade. If you are upgrading or patching a laptop operating system, you need to check with the laptop manufacturer as well. Laptops use drivers that might not work with a patch or upgrade that is intended for a server or a desktop computer.

Perform a limited-scale trial run on any computers or devices that could conceivably have problems during the patch or upgrade. Before you apply the patch or upgrade, address any foreseen problems beforehand and formulate a contingency plan. In all cases, you should exercise caution when you are performing any procedure that modifies the operating system code.

Remember to patch all the servers and workstations to the same revision level. Servers do a significant amount of background synchronization, and sporadic errors can occur if they are not at the same patch or operating system level.

It is very important that you patch all the network servers to the same revision level.

Patches And Fixes

Vendors design patches to fix specific problems with the firmware or operating system after it has been released on the market. As a rule, vendors identify problems when customers call for technical support for the product in question. As vendors become aware of a particular problem, they create a remedy for that specific problem, usually in the form of software.

Sometimes, but not always, the vendor will apprise a product's customers of the remedy (fix) by email or letter. To implement that fix, you visit the vendor's Web site and download the applicable fix. A patch is a grouping of all the fixes and enhancements for a particular product over a given amount of time. You can safely schedule patches and fixes for once every six months.

You should exercise caution when you apply a patch or an upgrade to an operational system. A patch to a device or an operating system is designed to fix specific problems. Before applying a patch to your system, you should read the README file, paying special attention to any mention of whether the patch will fix your problems. Often, you will have to apply a major patch to an operating system because other software and devices depend on that patch.

Upgrades

You should perform upgrades regularly to keep the existing system current and not let it fall behind in revisions and current technology. Initially, your organization made an investment to purchase the system on the basis of its current and future needs. If the network is not upgraded and it does not receive new enhancements, system performance will slowly erode over time. This limits the system's ability to fulfill its projected performance requirements.

Although you might not opt to upgrade the software, you need to review your network and workstation operating systems and applications software during every six-month maintenance rotation. However, you will not want to upgrade your operating systems or applications more than once a year, nor will you want to upgrade every time the vendor puts a new release on the market. During your assessment, you should be informed of any new releases and the enhancements that they provide. If you determine that the new operating system or application software provides functionality that the old one does not and it is something that the network users need, you will want to consider upgrading the software. In addition, if the vendor determines that it will no longer support your current software, you should upgrade. You can usually purchase the upgrade software through your normal vendors or resellers. If you decide to upgrade, remember to keep the configuration consistent throughout the entire network; that is, if you upgrade one server, update all the servers.

Make sure that all the servers are at the same operating system version. Also make sure that the workstations are at the same operating system version and the same software application level.

Hardware Flash Updates

Hardware flash updates take care of hardware problems and provide code for new product releases. Many servers use SCSI hard drives and RAID controllers. An older server might need a hardware flash update before it recognizes the new controller. Hardware flash updates are found on manufacturers' Web sites and are usually product specific. To upgrade a server, the flash program makes a bootable diskette with the flash code on it. You need only boot the diskette and answer some questions, then the hardware flash program performs the update. Some routers have removable flash memory cards on which they store the boot files, but most are updated by a Trivial File Transfer Protocol (TFTP) program that stores the files in nonremovable flash memory. As a recovery option, you should always have a backup copy of the version of the flash program that is installed on the hardware before upgrading to the latest version.

Monitoring Network And Server Health

You should constantly monitor your network, including all the devices and software, to make sure that it is consistently operating at peak efficiency. Monitoring your network lets you assess the current state of the system, identify potential problems, and make the necessary adjustments, such as load balancing, to prevent the problems from occurring. System monitoring also lets you assess the relationship between the users and the system to determine whether the network is meeting user demand.

Monitoring The Network

Network monitoring tools are different than the server's monitoring tools. The vendors of hubs, bridges, switches, and routers usually provide a basic set of tools (log files) to monitor the network device's health, but the Simple Network Management Protocol (SNMP) monitors and manages larger networks. The network devices can have an SNMP agent loaded on them that points to an SNMP management station. You can assign thresholds for all the parameters that the SNMP agent monitors. When the device parameter reaches that threshold, the device sends a message (trap) to the SNMP management station.

> The SNMP is a tool through which you can monitor and manage network faults on large networks.

Monitoring The Server

You can monitor the server's health from a set of tools that comes with the NOS. Both Windows NT and NetWare have extensive error-logging capabilities. Whenever an error occurs, you should first look in the error logs. Novell and Microsoft make utilities that manage the workstations and servers in local area network (LAN) and wide area network (WAN) environments. The Microsoft tool is called Systems Management Server (SMS), and the Novell utility is called Zero Effort Networks (Z.E.N.works). Some third-party software packages also provide the same capability. Workstations can be monitored by the same tools that are used to monitor the server.

Monitoring The Equipment Environment

Occasionally, you will need to walk through your equipment areas to ensure that the environment is consistent with what it was during the installation. The following sections outline some things you should look for.

Data Interference

During cold weather, do a walk-through of the work areas to make sure that employees are not plugging in space heaters too close to network equipment or cable runs. Also, check to see whether the network equipment or cable runs are exposed to heavy industrial equipment that might not have been present during the installation.

 Space heaters can cause circuit overloads and data interference.

Ensure that employees are not storing diskettes on top of their monitors. The magnetic field from the monitor will corrupt the data on the diskettes.

Temperature

Make sure that the equipment area is well ventilated and does not get too hot. If the ventilation system is malfunctioning, this could be serious because overheating is a major factor in electronic component failure.

Humidity

Check to see whether any network equipment, including workstations, has been moved near a water source, such as a faucet or eyewash station. You will also want to make sure that employees are not hanging plants above or on top of their computers, as water from the plants might drip down.

Air Quality

Occasionally check the exhaust fans in the hardware for excessive dust and dirt. This will indicate how dirty the air in the equipment area is. Sometimes the cause will be a limited event—for example, electricians were working in the ceiling and the dust in the ceiling contaminated the room air. However, if the fans are excessively dirty on a consistent basis, you will need to determine the cause of the airborne debris and eliminate it or move your equipment.

Scheduled Testing

To ensure that your network equipment is operating at peak efficiency, you need to occasionally run diagnostic tests on the equipment. You need to test device operation, connectivity to the network, and network response time.

Testing Equipment

As part of your routine diagnostics, you will need several tools to help you do the job. Although these tools are used in corrective maintenance as well, they will help you assess the integrity of the network and its components.

Loop-Back Connector

A loop-back connector crosses the transmit and receive pins on an RJ-45 connector. This device lets you fully test the transmit and receive functions of a network interface card (NIC). You will normally purchase a loop-back connector in the same way that you would any other cable. You should not be required to make one. You install the loop-back connector in the network patch-cable connection and then begin the NIC diagnostics.

A loop-back connector is used to test a NIC's transmit and receive functionality.

Cable Tester

A cable tester checks the tolerances of a specified type of cable and records the results. If a cable is out of tolerance, the cable tester will identify it, and then the network engineer will be responsible for fixing the problem. All new cable runs should be tested to make sure that they are within tolerance. If a cable is installed and working, it is usually not the first thing to check when a connectivity problem arises. Occasionally, you will find that an existing cable is damaged and needs to be replaced.

A cable tester checks to see whether a cable is within the specified tolerance.

Network Management Console

A network management console is the device where all the SNMP traps are sent so they can be recorded. An SNMP trap is a message that indicates that a managed device has recorded an event that has surpassed a predefined threshold. Some of the more common thresholds are device failure, network saturation, port malfunction, temperature, packet loss, and excessive packet collisions. The management console records these events in a database that can identify trends and problems.

Testing Network Security

You must check and maintain the integrity of your network's security at all times. System logs need to be checked daily. Software applications are available that you can load onto the server to check the server's security integrity. These will test for weak passwords and excessive user rights, among several other security concerns. In addition, some network applications will test the integrity of network-accessible systems.

Upgrades

After a few years in operation, your network might begin to experience distinct signs that the hardware or software needs to be upgraded. However, you will probably not need to upgrade your entire network all at once. The following sections explain the indications appropriate to the different parts of the network.

Network Upgrades

Over time, your network might begin to show signs that you need to consider an upgrade. Your best tool to diagnose overall network performance is a network management package, such as HP OpenView, Bay Networks Optivity Network Management package, or 3Com Transcend. The following are some signs that you will want to look for to indicate that you might need to upgrade your network:

➤ Network latency

➤ Packets that take too long to arrive at their destination

➤ An increased frequency of slowdowns or time-outs

In addition, you will want to consider a network upgrade if you are installing a new application that has network requirements that you do not meet, including the following:

➤ Greater data transmission speed

➤ More processing power

➤ Larger data storage

➤ Better video resolution

➤ Better print resolution

➤ External (WAN) access if you do not currently have it

Software Upgrades

The primary indicator that you need to upgrade your application software is that your current software does not meet the needs of the users. You never want to let the software get too far behind the current revision because the manufacturer will stop supporting it after it reaches a certain version.

Hardware Upgrades

The signs that you need to upgrade your hardware are more diverse than those associated with upgrading your software. Here are some reasons that you might need to upgrade some of your hardware or devices:

- To increase hard disk capacity.
- To increase memory.
- To provide more processing power.
- To comply with changing standards (for example, the Y2K-compliance requirement).
- To prevent older equipment from becoming obsolete because you have added new equipment to the network.
- To comply with external changes that affect your corporate network. For example, if one of your business trading partners requires that you report transactions via electronic data interchange (EDI), you might have to upgrade your internal network or system to continue doing business with them.

Unfortunately, to resolve all these indications, you must purchase new equipment. A hardware flash upgrade cannot fix any of these problems. A device can work only within the limits of its design.

Practice Questions

Question 1

> Which components of the network should you include in the PM rotation? [Choose the four best answers]
> - a. Electrical service to the building
> - b. Network devices and other hardware
> - c. Operating system and applications software
> - d. The entire cabling plant
> - e. The cards installed inside the machines
> - f. Exposed cables and connectors
> - g. The backup system

The correct answers are b, c, f, and g. Everything that is associated with the network, whether software, hardware, or firmware, is checked during the PM rotation. Answer a is incorrect because you should never tamper with the electrical service to the building. If you perceive a problem with the service, call the site engineer or the supplier. Answer d is incorrect because you do not need to visually inspect every inch of the system's cabling, only the sections that are subject to wear. Answer e is incorrect because you should not check the internals of any machine during the PM rotation.

Question 2

> What is the optimum time frame for downloading a virus signature update?
> - a. Once every six months
> - b. Once every three months
> - c. Once a year
> - d. Once a month

The correct answer is d. You should download a virus signature file update once a month. Answers a, b, and c are incorrect because updating the virus signatures at six months, three months, or a year is too long a time. New viruses hit the scene almost weekly. If you go too long between updates, you are leaving your system wide open for infection.

Question 3

> Which steps do you need to take before you implement a patch or upgrade on a desktop computer? [Choose the three best answers]
> - a. Make a verified backup of the entire system.
> - b. Test the patch/upgrade.
> - c. Read the release notes.
> - d. Restore the system.
> - e. Call the manufacturer.

The correct answers are a, b, and c. You want to make a verified backup of the system so that you can restore it in case anything goes wrong. In addition, you should always read the release notes before you do anything with the upgrade or patch and perform a test against any procedure that modifies the operating system code. Answer d is incorrect because you should not have to restore the system before you make any changes to it. Answer e is incorrect because the manufacturer provides all the information that you need in the release notes. However, if you are loading an upgrade or patch for a full-size computer onto a laptop, you do want to call the manufacturer if such a condition is not discussed in the release notes.

Question 4

> Why is it important to apply upgrades, patches, and fixes to the network components? [Choose the three best answers]
> - a. If you do not, your network will not live up to its projected potential.
> - b. If you do not, you will not have the latest technology on your network.
> - c. Because they fix known problems with the software or device.
> - d. Because manufacturers might stop supporting the release that you have.

The correct answers are a, c, and d. Manufacturers create upgrade, patches, and fixes to address known problems with their devices or software. In addition, upgrades give your network components new functionality without requiring you to buy new equipment or a new application. Some manufacturers have also been known to stop supporting old releases after a certain period, meaning that if you want them to give you technical support, you need to keep abreast of their changes and upgrades. Answer b is incorrect because having the "latest and greatest" is not always a benefit. You should always analyze upgrades carefully and make your decision to upgrade on sound reasoning, such as user need or a lack of technical support.

Question 5

> What are some indications that you might need to upgrade your network? [Choose the three best answers]
>
> ❑ a. You cannot print.
> ❑ b. You are experiencing network latency.
> ❑ c. You cannot log on to the computer.
> ❑ d. Packets take too long to arrive at their destination.
> ❑ e. You are installing an application that has certain network requirements that you do not meet.

The correct answers are b, d, and e. All these are signs that you might want to consider upgrading the network. You can further determine this by performing benchmark testing. Answers a and c are incorrect because neither has to do with network performance.

Question 6

> What indication would you look for to determine that you need to upgrade your software application?
>
> ○ a. Your software does not meet the needs of the users.
> ○ b. The users have too much data on their workstations.
> ○ c. It is not the "latest and greatest."
> ○ d. The hardware will not support the application; therefore, you must upgrade the application.

The correct answer is a. The main reason for upgrading your software is that it does not meet the needs of the users. The storage requirements usually increase when an application is upgraded. Therefore, answer b is incorrect. Although some people may think that answer c is correct, it is not the main reason to upgrade an application. You usually have to upgrade the hardware when you upgrade an application, not vice versa. Therefore, answer d is incorrect.

Question 7

> What are some indications that you need to upgrade your hardware? [Choose the three best answers]
> - a. You need to comply with changing standards.
> - b. The manufacturer just released a newer model.
> - c. The specifications call for more processing power.
> - d. You have added new equipment that causes older equipment to become obsolete.
> - e. The person in the next cubicle just got a new system.

The correct answers are a, c, and d. The reason to upgrade your hardware should be a business decision. Changing standards, more processing power, and obsolete equipment are all viable reasons to upgrade hardware. Answers b and e are incorrect because these are not valid business reasons to upgrade.

Question 8

> How can you upgrade your hardware? [Choose the two best answers]
> - a. Buy new equipment.
> - b. Buy new software for the hardware.
> - c. Distribute the processing power by connecting it to a network.
> - d. Use hardware flash upgrades.

The correct answers are a and d. Buying new hardware gives you the latest hardware available. A flash upgrade will incorporate code for new equipment, thus extending the life of old equipment. Purchasing new software does not upgrade the hardware. Therefore, answer b is incorrect. Processing power is not distributed by the computer's being connected to the network. Therefore, answer c is incorrect.

Need To Know More?

 Mazda, Fraidoon, ed.: *Telecommunications Engineer's Reference Book*. Reed Educational and Professional Publishing Ltd., Woburn, MA, 1998. ISBN 0-240-51491-2. An excellent reference book explaining the intricacies of telecommunications in great detail.

 Sheldon, Tom: *Encyclopedia of Networking, Electronic Edition*. Osborne McGraw-Hill, New York, 1998. ISBN 0-07-882333-1. A good overview of general networking terms and networking characteristics. Covers everything from A to Z.

 www.3com.com publishes information on network support and preventive maintenance. Visit the 3COM site and select the Service and Support link to find the latest information on maintaining you 3COM equipment.

 www.baynetworks.com publishes information on network support and preventive maintenance. If you have Bay Networks equipment, visit the Customer Support section of their Web site for maintenance procedures.

 www.cisco.com publishes information on network support and preventive maintenance. If you have Cisco equipment, you will want to visit their site and review the Service and Support section for tips on maintaining your network.

 www.microsoft.com has extensive information on its advanced server products and covers network support and preventive maintenance.

 www.novell.com has exhaustive information on network support and preventive maintenance.

Troubleshooting And Corrective Maintenance

14

Terms you'll need to understand:

√ Corrective maintenance (CM)
√ Technical bulletins
√ Knowledge base
√ Technical support
√ Trouble calls
√ Troubleshooting
√ Diagnostics

Techniques you'll need to master:

√ Maintaining a maintenance history
√ Identifying problems
√ Prioritizing problems
√ Troubleshooting a network fault
√ Using vendor diagnostics to isolate a network fault
√ Using command utilities to isolate a communications fault

Although you might have diligently exercised a thorough preventive maintenance (PM) schedule since your system was new, your network will still experience problems. Equipment gets old or overused, sometimes it is damaged, and sometimes you do not have any idea why it is experiencing problems. Now we move from preventive maintenance and enter the field of troubleshooting and *corrective maintenance (CM)*.

To have an effective CM program, you must be organized and have developed a solid approach to CM before you ever receive the first trouble call. When you receive that first call, it is much too late to think about how you will handle the maintenance process. When users make that call, usually they are already frustrated with the problem and likely will take that frustration out on whoever responds to the call. Before you can effect your maintenance program, you must know your network and your resources, and, most importantly, you must be prepared. If you are prepared, you will not feel pressured into making snap decisions and will be more likely to appease the frustrated customer, if by nothing more than your confidence that you know what you are doing.

Preparation

Many resources are available to help you troubleshoot problems, but the resources provided by the vendor of the hardware, software, or operating system are the best place to start. The vendor is the focal point for problem resolution on its own products and will have comprehensive databases of a myriad of problems and their resolutions.

You should always keep a binder that lists all your resources, as shown in Table 14.1. However, this is only a suggested format. If you decide to format your resource book another way, it should still contain the same information. You should list every type of equipment that you have in your network, including the model numbers, the manufacturer, and the location of all maintenance resources.

Table 14.1 Resource ledger.

Device	Switch
Manufacturer	Switches, Inc.
Model No.	12345-67
Quantity	4
Tech Support	888-888-8888, 9-5 EST
Web Site	www.theirsite.com
Knowledge Base	Yes—disk/online
Diagnostic Software	No

Vendor Documentation

Most vendors supply a sufficient quantity of documentation and technical updates to keep you abreast of not only the initial configuration of your machine but also any suggested changes or resolutions to common problems.

Equipment Documentation

These are the books that you receive with your equipment and should be your first stop in resolving a hardware or software problem. They will give you specifics on installing, operating, and maintaining the network components. Often, manufacturers will also send out supplements or updates to the original documentation. You should keep all your vendor manuals and their updates in a central location, preferably in the IS department.

Technical Bulletins

These contain important information about a specific hardware model or software version. Often, a hardware manufacturer will post technical bulletins on its Web site for all the equipment it manufactures. Technical bulletins address problems that the vendor has identified since the release of the product and provide solutions to fix the problems. You should address technical bulletins according to their impact on your network hardware or software and implement the resolution if that course of action is appropriate.

Manufacturer Web Sites

After you have consulted the vendor manuals, you should go to the manufacturer's Web site. These are excellent places to look for information on software and hardware errors that the vendor knows about. They can also provide you with up-to-date information on your network components, including known bugs or faults with the component. Your resource book should contain the Internet address for each manufacturer.

Vendor Knowledge Bases

Many vendors provide a knowledge base that has detailed information on their products. Microsoft has a CD-ROM knowledge base called TechNet, which provides all kinds of information for most Microsoft products and documents many of the known glitches with those products. Novell also has a CD-ROM knowledge base called Support Connection. You can purchase the CD-ROM knowledge bases from an authorized distributor of the manufacturer's products. If a CD-ROM knowledge base is not available, the manufacturer will most likely offer a knowledge base as a component of its Web site.

Vendor Diagnostic Software

Many vendors provide diagnostic software for their products (discussed later in this chapter). Vendors especially tailor their diagnostic programs to diagnose their own products. Your resource book should reflect any vendor diagnostic software that is available for each product and its location.

Technical Support

When you have availed yourself of all the information that is accessible to you and still cannot resolve a problem, it is time to call technical support. The manufacturer's tech support staff has a complete database of all their products and is familiar with them. This is your very best source of information. Make sure that your resource book lists the tech support numbers for all your network hardware and software and their office/support hours.

Sometimes a product will experience a fault because of a logical setup error. This is a gray area in the technical support arena. Technical support personnel can help identify a logical configuration error but can provide only limited help in correcting logical errors. You can efficiently avoid this type of error through proper planning before you implement a network or upgrade.

Other References

In addition to the manufacturer's documentation, you should also have a solid collection of professional networking reference manuals. They can often provide answers to common questions and provide insight to the extremely varied field of networking.

Trouble Calls

Now that you have all your resources compiled into one, easily accessible location, let's talk about what you should do when you receive a trouble call. You need to log the problem as you receive the call. After you resolve the problem, you should also document the solution that you implemented. Keeping an accurate maintenance history of the devices and software will help you when you have to fix that same problem again. Table 14.2 gives you an idea of how to set up a maintenance trouble-tracking system (maintenance history).

If you do not implement and enforce a trouble-tracking system with a priority scheme, several technical support issues will arise. One of the most common of these problems is that IS department resources get misallocated. To almost all users, their problem is a number one priority, and all too often their approach to receiving tech support is to "scream the loudest." Unless you have a trouble-tracking system that prioritizes problems and ensures a timely response, users

Table 14.2 Maintenance history.

Device	Printer
Manufacturer	Printerco, Inc.
Model No.	12345-67
Location	Administration
Call Day/Time	16 Mar 99/1400
Priority	4
Problem	Can't use department printer
Response Day/Time	17 Mar 99/0800
Solution	Reconnected the cable between the print server and the department printer

will find their own methods for resolving the problem (such as grabbing the IS person out of the hall). Your IS people need to know the priority of the problem and the maintenance history of that particular machine. If they feel compelled to respond to a user's "urgent" request and can't research that material, it may result in misallocated resources and wasted time.

An accurate assessment of the technical support needs cannot be determined if a trouble-tracking system is not in place. A trouble-tracking system should contain all the information that the IS manager needs to determine to whom they will assign the problem. The tracking system should provide details on the number of calls received, the length of time to respond and correct the problem, and any outstanding issues.

Identifying The Problem

Your organization will generally have two knowledge levels of technical support. The first level is the less experienced networking professionals, who will generally handle all the incoming calls. If possible, they will give the user a solution over the telephone. If a telephone response is inappropriate, they may visit the trouble site and effect repairs. The first level of support will exhaust all their resources to rectify the problem. If they cannot solve the problem, or if it is too technically advanced, they will pass the problem on to the second level. The second level will handle all the problems that the first level cannot. These will normally be problems that require a greater knowledge and experience that comes only with time in the field. In addition, the second level of support reserves the right to call the manufacturer's technical support number.

Prioritizing Problems

Next, you must assign the problem a priority. If you have only one trouble call in, it gets priority one, and you take care of it right away. However, if you have several trouble calls in at nearly the same time, you need to determine which tasks take priority. Two aspects of the problem you will want to assess are the seriousness of the problem and how much and what portion of the network is affected. (Keep in mind the political reality that the executive management staff get a high priority.)

In any network environment, you must set a priority system for resolving problems. Certain components of a network are more critical to the operation of the network than others. Shared resources are a critical component in any network environment. When a shared network component is offline, it affects multiple people's ability to work.

Serious problems are the ones that affect the entire network and bring productivity to a halt. If a failed network device is critical to the operation of the network, such as a server, router, switch, or hub, you should give it priority and the resources (people) to resolve the problem. These problems affect a majority of the users, and you must address and implement a resolution quickly. Table 14.3 provides a relative prioritization scheme.

However, you cannot completely forget about the client workstations on the network. Do not allow network problems to always shift the end users down the priority chain so that you wind up neglecting them for a prolonged period. Although a malfunction in a workstation does not affect the entire network,

Table 14.3 Prioritization scheme.

Priority	Type Of Problem
1	Most Important: Affects everyone on the network or affects crucial operations, such as production and payroll. Usually indicates that the entire network or a crucial portion of the network is down.
2	Very Important: Affects everyone on the network and inhibits work, but the network is still up.
3	Important: Affects a group of people, such as an entire department, and inhibits work.
4	Somewhat Important: Affects a group of people, such as a department or a limited user group. Affects some work applications but does not inhibit operations of that group as a whole.
5	Nuisance Problem: Affects a limited number of people and does not inhibit work.

the workstation is the user's interface to the network, and without them users cannot perform network tasks. Certain departments will always get a higher priority when their PCs are down. A department such as Order Entry would take priority over a department like R&D. You must maintain a balance while directing the available resources to the appropriate task.

Duplicating The Error

When you attend to a trouble call, you must first try to duplicate the problem. If you can duplicate it, it is a consistent error, not a one-time incident. You will find it very difficult to resolve a problem if you cannot duplicate it by repeating a certain function or action.

If the error is resident on a workstation, have the operator duplicate the problem and look for obvious errors, such as procedural, input, command, or keystroke errors. If the error is procedural, you may need to recommend that the user get formal training. You also need to watch for any error messages that appear. If the error is not on the workstation, but on another type of network device (such as a switch or hub), you will probably be operating it; watch the LEDs for indications that a device is not working.

If the problem does not generate an error code that identifies the problem and you cannot duplicate it at will, you are looking at a long process of trial-and-error attempts before you resolve the problem. If you can duplicate the problem, you have a starting point for isolating the cause of the problem.

Troubleshooting

After you receive a trouble call, troubleshooting is your very first step to identify where the true problem exists. Troubleshooting a network problem and all the components that make up a network is an essential part of being a systems engineer. Unless you know the network devices, computer hardware, and operating systems that your network comprises, you will be unable to perform comprehensive diagnostics to isolate network problems.

Good documentation and a comprehensive network map are basic requirements for effective problem resolution. How all the components interact is a little tougher to understand but is something you need to know should sporadic network problems occur. To resolve any problem, always look for the obvious and try the simple solution first. Sometimes you have to determine what is not the problem so that you can narrow down the choices of what could be causing the problem.

In addition, it always helps if you document the problem and what does and does not work, and have a plan to either isolate the problem further or solve the problem. Keep notes of what you have tried so that you can put the system back to its original configuration. When you are attempting to troubleshoot a problem, you might try so many things that you cause more problems than you are trying to solve. The following are several important steps to keep you organized and help you achieve effective troubleshooting:

1. Identify the problem.
2. Re-create the problem.
3. Isolate the cause of the problem.
4. Decide on a corrective measure.
5. Implement the correction.
6. Test the corrective measure.
7. Document the problem and the solution.

Before you can begin troubleshooting, you need to develop a mindset that is logical and organized. If you do not have a sound troubleshooting philosophy, you can wind up chasing your tail around in circles.

Troubleshooting Philosophy

The most important aspect of troubleshooting a problem with the network is developing a sound troubleshooting philosophy. First, be familiar with the network components. You have to know how each component of the network functions, then you have to know how the components interact and interface with one another. This knowledge will allow you to eliminate all the components that are not causing a problem.

When you become aware of a problem, look at the most obvious source. For example, if a workstation is not powering up, do not automatically assume that the power supply has failed. Instead, make sure that the power cord is plugged into the power outlet. Then, if the machine is still not powering up, consider the power supply. If you're working with a user on the phone and the symptoms keep pointing back to a certain problem, re-verify the information that the user has given you; this may result in a personal visit to the user.

If you are troubleshooting the entire network, you always need to take a bottom-up approach instead of a top-down approach so that you can narrow down the affected areas. If you are troubleshooting a specific device or equipment, you want to think up to eliminate widespread problems and then think down if it is not widespread. Most errors have a point of manifestation, although that point might not be the source of the error. Figure 14.1 illustrates an example of this.

Troubleshooting And Corrective Maintenance

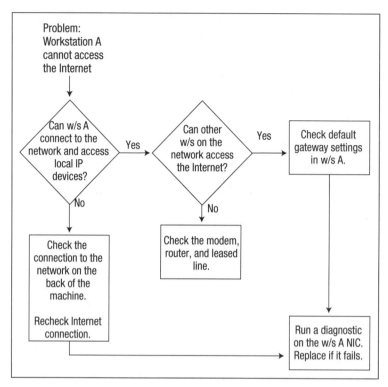

Figure 14.1 Point of manifestation.

The workstation was manifesting a problem, and although the workstation was showing an error, that does not necessarily mean that the workstation had the problem; it could have been a network-wide problem. However, after you eliminate network-wide problems (thinking up), you think down to the workstation components. You will also notice that the first thing that you should have checked was the connection to the network. In this case, the user was already using the workstation, so checking the power input was not a consideration. You simply have to think the problem through and not assume that the problem lies with the major devices until you think the problem up that far.

Isolating The Problem

Initially, you will have to eliminate those things that are not problems to isolate the real source of the problem. When you are isolating a problem, you should document every method and process that you used. Then you can relate to technical support what you have tried, what has failed, and what has succeeded. This will give them better insight and an accurate starting point to solving the problem.

Before you begin to isolate the problem, you need to know a certain degree of machine/system history. You should first refer to the maintenance history and determine whether that system component has had problems in the past and what solution rectified those problems. After you have established a maintenance history, you should ask these important questions:

- Was the system working normally before the problem manifested?
- How long had the system been working without any problems?
- Has anything been added, deleted, or changed?
- Specifically, what were you doing when the problem manifested?
- Have you tried anything to fix the problem?

All these questions will help you establish system/machine status and give you a basis for beginning troubleshooting. Before you begin troubleshooting, you need to have as many variables as possible eliminated from consideration.

When you are isolating a problem, it is important that you have a defined method to test the system/machine to eliminate possible causes. When you change parameters, change only one thing at a time, then test that change to determine whether you have isolated the problem. Also, remember to document the changes so that you can restore the system to its original configuration.

Identifying User Problems

The two aspects of problem isolation that you must address are hardware or software errors and user errors. User-caused problems will generally be isolated to the software, workstation, printer, or any other user devices. Only the network administrator can access most network devices. Although network administrators might cause errors, they usually know what they did to cause them and can effect repairs. However, you will find that most users have no idea of what they did to cause a problem with their machines, and that is where you enter the picture.

When you respond to a user's trouble call, you will have already asked them the questions to begin the isolation process. Next, you need to identify whether the problem is attributable to the operator or to the system. To eliminate user problems from the troubleshooting scenario, take these three steps:

1. Have the user duplicate the error. This will let you see any error messages that appear. It will also let you identify whether the user is performing the task properly. If he or she is not, that might be the cause of the error. If the user can duplicate the error, go to Step 2. If they cannot duplicate the error, then the user may have incorrectly performed the task initially.

2. Log in on the problem workstation and perform the same task yourself. If you can perform the task, you want to make sure that the operator is performing the task properly. It might also indicate that the user is trying to perform a task that is outside of those defined by his or her user rights and privileges. If the workstation still exhibits the same problem, go to Step 3. If it does not exhibit the same problem, then the user either did not perform the task properly, or they were trying to operate outside of their user privileges.

3. Perform the same task on an equivalent workstation. This will help you determine whether it is consistent across all workstations or is limited to the locally loaded software or the workstation in question. It will also help you determine whether the problem lies with the server-loaded software. If all workstations exhibit the same problem, you have a network problem. If the error is limited to the original workstation, you need to troubleshoot that machine.

Identifying Network Problems

If the problem is not resident in a workstation but might be resident in another device on the network, you need to look for visible indications that a machine might have a problem. These indications include link lights or power lights that are not on and error displays on the machines that have them. Other invaluable sources of troubleshooting information are the system (event) logs, network performance monitors, and the Simple Network Management Protocol (SNMP) management console:

➤ **System logs** The administrator's login provides you with access to all the system logs. The system logs record significant events on the system, including hardware errors and messages, security attempts (login), and application errors. If you suspect a network error, you need to check the system logs first.

➤ **Network performance monitors** Several types of network performance monitors are on the market. They monitor the traffic levels, collisions, broadcasts, errors, and top network talkers. You can capture data over a defined period and do trend analysis.

➤ **SNMP management console** SNMP can be configured on network devices to send a message to a management console when a device reaches a predefined threshold. Some types of information that the SNMP console monitors are errors, packets, collisions, broadcasts, and hardware failure.

If you determine that a problem is not limited to an individual device, you must determine how widespread the problem really is. You need to ask yourself these two questions:

- Does the problem exist across the network?
- Is the problem exhibited in a workstation, a workgroup, the local area network (LAN), or the wide area network (WAN)?

You should document all the symptoms and determine (by troubleshooting) how far-reaching the problem is. Remember that the more widespread the problem is and the more people it affects, the higher priority it receives.

Network Troubleshooting

When you become aware of a network problem, your first task is that of localizing the problem. Your starting point depends greatly on how and where the problem is manifesting itself. If the problem is manifesting itself in a server, then that will be your starting point. Table 14.4 gives you some general starting points. As you can see, almost any problem can have one of several causes.

User Errors

The user errors that we're referring to here are not exclusively those that a user makes; rather, they are more the errors that affect a user.

Table 14.4   Troubleshooting starting points.

Symptom	Possible Cause
Data errors	Communications and media
	Configuration
	Software/virus
	Hardware
	User errors
Software errors	Configuration
	Software setup
	Virus
	Hardware
Hardware errors	Communications and media
	Hardware components
	Software/virus
Power errors	Communications and media
	Hardware faults

Login Errors

If the user is getting a login prompt but cannot log in, you should immediately check the user's login name and password to ensure that they are correct. Then check the expiration on the password. If the password is still current, see how many times the user tried to log in with that password and failed. The system logs will have this information. The user might have been locked out of the system.

Always check the username and password to make sure that the user entered them correctly. Make sure that the password has not expired and that the user is not locked out of the system.

User And Group Rights Errors

Quite often, users will experience what they believe to be system errors when in fact the user does not have the rights to accomplish the desired task. In addition to individual user rights, you can also assign rights to the group to which the user belongs. If a user is having a task-oriented problem, you will want to look at his or her assigned rights and group rights to ensure that he or she is within his or her privileges. If you promote a user to an administrator, you need to remember to also give administrator rights. You change a user's rights and profiles though the Administrator utility.

Make sure a user has rights to access data and services. If someone needs administrator rights, be sure to assign them administrator rights. In Windows NT, the administrator account is *Administrator*, and in NetWare and intraNetWare it is *Admin*. In Unix, it is the *root* or *su* user, and in OS/2 it is the *administrator*.

Communications And Media

If your data communications are faulty, you will have either consistent faults or intermittent faults. Sometimes when a piece of equipment is experiencing excessive heat it can have intermittent errors. Other faults occur when a piece of equipment is close to a threshold (such as packets per second), in which case the equipment might exhibit intermittent errors. Intermittent errors are very difficult to pinpoint and resolve because you cannot easily re-create them. Figure 14.2 provides a flowchart to troubleshoot intermittent data errors.

Figure 14.3 provides a flowchart to troubleshoot persistent data errors. As you can see from both figures, the network medium and viruses can manifest themselves as persistent or intermittent problems. Persistent errors can be isolated and resolved much faster than intermittent errors.

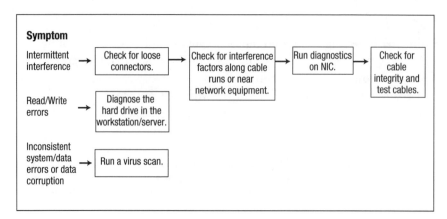

Figure 14.2 Troubleshooting intermittent data errors.

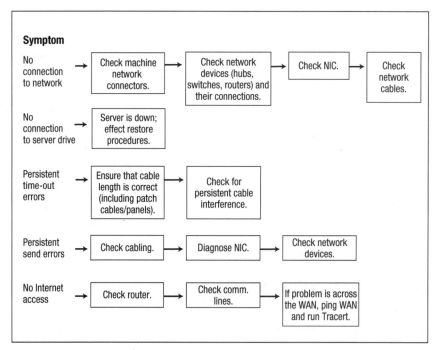

Figure 14.3 Troubleshooting persistent data errors.

Configuration And Addressing Problems

When you first start to set up a computer system, some errors are going to occur. These errors are configuration errors that you must work out during the initial setup. After a system is set up and all the applications are stabilized, if a problem occurs, the first question should be "What has changed?" When you address problems, you should take a systematic approach to eliminate the things that work from those that do not work. The following sections discuss common configuration problems and their resolutions.

Domain Name System

If you are having a problem with the domain name system (DNS) or the DNS server, you will not be able to get to sites by their DNS names. For example, **www.coriolis.com** is a DNS name, but it also has an IP address associated with it, such as 192.168.10.1. If you are not able to reach a site by the DNS name but can reach it by the IP address, you have a DNS problem. If you cannot reach it by either method, you have a connection problem.

Windows Internet Name Service

Windows Internet Name Service (WINS) allows you to resolve NetBIOS names to IP addresses. If you are having a WINS problem on an IP-only network, you will not be able to get to Windows machines for file and print sharing or browsing.

IP Address

If a computer is set up with an IP address and can access local devices but cannot access anything beyond the local subnet, no default IP gateway exists or an incorrect default gateway is specified. You can ping 127.0.0.1 to test the binding of IP on a network interface card (NIC) without the NIC being on a network.

NetWare External Network Numbers

The external network number in a NetWare environment is very similar in functionality to the IP subnetwork number. The NetWare external network number has to be unique on a network, and if the packets are going to communicate with another NetWare server across a router, the NetWare server across the router has to have a different network number. If the two external network numbers across a router are the same, the router will not be able to route packets to the proper network.

Interrupt Request (IRQ) Conflicts

Plug-and-play (PnP) PCI cards installed in a PnP computer will automatically configure themselves with open IRQ, I/O ports, and memory addresses. You need to watch out for non-PnP ISA cards installed in a computer to which you want to add a card. The PnP card might take a value that the non-PnP ISA card is using. If that happens, a conflict will arise, and you will need to resolve it by changing the value in either the PnP or the non-PnP card. Some computer systems will let you reserve the I/O, IRQ, and memory values of non-PnP cards and this allows the PnP cards to consider those values when assigning values.

If you install a NIC and your sound card stops working, you should determine what value is conflicting with the sound card and change it. You can change the value in either card, but it is best to change the value in the new card because none of the applications that are loaded depend on the new card. The existing card might have applications loaded that are looking for the device at the specified values, and changing one of those values could cause the applications to stop working.

Software Errors

If the software is displaying an error, you first need to establish whether the hardware is the cause of the error message. If a specific software package is displaying an error message, refer to the vendor manual for that software. Sometimes the only way to fix a software problem is to reinstall the package. Many software packages are released with bugs, and the software vendor will release fixes between major releases. The best way to troubleshoot a software error is to narrow down the cause or eliminate those things that are not the cause of the problem. For business-critical software packages, it is imperative that you have technical support to resolve the problems.

Viruses

Viruses are very difficult to track down because they can manifest themselves inconsistently as a hardware/system problem, a software problem, or a communications problem, and this can be very frustrating. Although a virus can have physical manifestations, it is still an executable program that you (inadvertently, we hope) load onto your computer.

If you or the user have recently loaded any new programs onto the workstation or server and you soon begin to experience problems of any kind, you should suspect a virus infection. In this case, listen to your intuition. As soon as you suspect a virus, download the latest virus signature update and run the virus scan. After you address the infected device, run the same virus scan against the entire network in case the virus was spread. You need to remember that the most damaging viruses affect the boot sector, master boot sector, and partition table.

 Remember that a boot sector or master boot sector virus will disable the computer and keep it from booting properly, if at all.

Hardware Errors

Most often, hardware will have some sort of error indicator or, at the very least, indicators to let you know that the machine is functioning properly. Visually inspect the device, making sure that you look for abnormal physical conditions, such as lights and indicators that are not functioning or illuminated error lights. You also want to check the connections to the network and make sure that the device appears to be functioning properly.

If you move a server or any other major network component to a new location, and you want to see whether it is working, you do not have to run a complete diagnostic against that component. Instead, simply plug in the machine and see whether it works. In the case of a server, turn it on and have users access files and printers. If they can, it is working. Some indications that the main hardware components are not functioning are discussed in the following sections.

Servers

Most servers are installed with a network operating system (NOS) that has logging capabilities. The logs can identify hardware and software problems. Most of the major server manufacturers have management software that can monitor hardware components for failure and perform prefailure diagnosis. The four ways you can tell whether your server is having a hardware problem are by using the management software, monitoring the NOS logs, if the server reboots, or if the server fails.

Routers

A router is an intelligent device that requires programming before it can function properly. A malfunctioning router could be a software problem or a hardware problem. A hardware problem would require vendor-supplied diagnostic software that checks the hardware components in a router to determine whether a problem exists. The most likely cause of a router malfunction after it is set up and running is a hardware problem.

When the communication lines go down between the two routers, it might appear to be a router problem when it is not. If you have a WAN connected by two routers and the two routers stop communicating, here are the steps to follow to troubleshoot the problem:

1. Check the communication line between the two routers.

2. Inspect the routers for an obvious hardware failure, such as no power or flashing fault indicators.

3. Connect to the routers and run a hardware diagnostic.

4. Determine whether anything changed and check the software settings.

Switches

Most switches come out of the box ready to do media access control (MAC) address switching. Some programming is required for port address grouping and VLAN setup. Here we cover MAC address switching, which is the main function of a switch. If the switch fails, the connected segments will not be able to communicate beyond the switch. A physical inspection of the device will determine whether it has a major problem, such as no power or fault lights illuminated. If one segment is not functioning, move that segment to another port and test the connectivity. Another option is to set the device back to factory default. This option will clear any programmed values and return the switch to a MAC address switch.

Hub

A hub is a simple multiport repeater. It repeats any signal that it receives onto all the ports. If you suspect a faulty hub, the best thing to do is to replace it and see whether that fixes the problem. If you suspect a faulty port, you should move the device to another port and, if that fixes the problem, mark that port as bad. You will need to test the horizontal and patch cables connected to that port to determine whether they are faulty.

Bridges

A bridge is very similar to a switch in functionality. It connects two or more segments and forwards the packets to the proper segment or drops the packets if the destination is on the same network. A bridge is somewhat of a legacy device and is used mainly to connect coaxial and attachment unit interface (AUI) segments together. A bridge works at the Data Link layer of the OSI model and logical configuration errors will not be common. If a bridge is not functioning properly, run the manufacturer-provided diagnostic software or check for error lights on the device. Check the cables attached to each port for signal integrity if a fault is present. In some instances, MAC address filters can be applied to ports, which will restrict access to devices to those ports.

Gateways

A gateway translates from one protocol to another protocol. If you suspect a problem, the first thing to do is to check the log files. If that does not work, try stopping and restarting the gateway. Sometimes the problem is located at the point of origin or at the destination host. You might need to check the configuration at the point of origin and make sure that nothing has changed. If all the users are affected, it is most likely the gateway or the destination host. A systematic troubleshooting approach will narrow down the list of suspect devices and allow you to focus on the remaining possibilities.

Print Servers

A print server is a network device that a printer is connected to. A very popular print server is Hewlett-Packard JetDirect. It can be internal to the printer or external and have a parallel port and a network connection on it. Print queues are usually located on Windows NT or NetWare servers, and they point the queue to the print server. When a printer stops working, the two places to look for the cause are the print server and the print queue. Resetting the print server is usually the first choice, and stopping and starting the print queue is the next choice.

Tape Drives

Tape backup problems can be caused by hardware or software. If you receive a tape drive fault, you should first clean the tape drive, something that you should do on a regular basis according to the manufacturer's recommended schedule. If that does not fix the problem, run a hardware diagnostic test on the tape drive and determine whether it is working properly. If it passes all those tests, call technical support at the backup software vendor and determine whether it is a software problem.

Modems And Modem Cards

Adding external modems is relatively simple: just plug them into the serial ports and configure the software that is going to use them. Adding internal modems can be a little more challenging. It might be necessary to manually configure a modem if you are adding more than one internal modem to a computer. Table 14.5 displays the values of COM1 through COM4.

 COM1 and COM3 share IRQ 4 but do not share the I/O address; COM2 and COM4 share IRQ 3 and also do not share the I/O address.

In a Windows 95/98 computer, you would go to the Control Panel and double-click on the System icon. You would then click on the Device Manager tab and check to see whether any conflicts are displayed for the two modems. If you

Table 14.5 COM port values.

COM Port	IRQ	I/O Address
COM1	4	03F8
COM2	3	02F8
COM3	4	03E8
COM4	3	02E8

have a modem conflict, it is likely that you will not be able to connect to the Internet and research the troubleshooting database provided by the modem manufacturer. Look for a CD-ROM with troubleshooting tips on it or call the technical support personnel at the modem's manufacturer.

Always have the modem's documentation and the technical support number available because if the modem is broken, you cannot access the Web site for technical help.

Diagnostics

After you have performed the troubleshooting techniques and narrowed down the list of suspect devices, you should run the appropriate diagnostics against those devices. This is a furtherance of the isolation methodology, but by the time you run diagnostics, you should be relatively certain that the device in question is causing the problems.

Diagnostic Tools

The following tools are ones that you would commonly use to resolve network equipment problems.

Hardware Loop-Back

This cable crosses the transmit and receive pins in the same connector and allows the diagnostic utility to test the transmit and receive functions without using the entire network to do so. For example, you need to use a loop-back connector to fully test a NIC.

The diagnostic program that the NIC manufacturer provides is the best method to determine whether a NIC is malfunctioning. A loop-back connector is required to test the transmit and receive functions of the card.

Diagnostic Software

The best diagnostic software to use is usually the one provided by the hardware vendor. The primary advantage is that the vendor usually provides it at no cost because it came with the equipment. The hardware vendor also knows the necessary parameters to check to determine whether a hardware malfunction has occurred.

Some third-party diagnostic software packages are available if the hardware vendor does not provide one or it is inadequate. Some network managers employ enterprise management solutions that have diagnostic capabilities built into them.

Cable Tester

You use a cable tester to determine faults in the network cabling. The cable tester should support all the different types of media that you have in your organization. The cable tester also certifies that the cables are within specification.

Communications Diagnostics

If you have determined that the problem rests within the communications between sites, you need to implement one or more of the following tools.

Packet Internet Groper

The Packet Internet Groper (Ping) is a utility that sends an Internet Control Message Protocol (ICMP) echo request message to a host on a TCP/IP network. It waits for a response from the remote host and then registers the time that it takes to respond.

It is a good troubleshooting tool to determine whether a route is available to a remote host. If you are having trouble connecting to a host computer, the ping utility will determine whether the IP stack on the system is working. The IP stack might be working while the service you are trying to connect to is down.

To generate a ping, go to the Windows DOS prompt (C:\WINDOWS>) and enter "ping" followed by the IP address (192.156.136.22) or the DNS name (www.3com.com). It will look like this:

```
C:\WINDOWS>ping 192.156.136.22
```

If you specified a correct IP address and the route to the machine is functioning, you will see a reply message. As a rule, Windows 95/98 and Windows NT machines will send the ping four times before they give up.

In addition to the simple ping command, you can specify several command options (switches) to define the parameters of your ping query and ping response, as shown in Table 14.6. To use these options, put a space after "ping", then enter the IP address. For example, if we used a -k host-list command, the entire command line would look like this:

```
C:\WINDOWS>ping -k host-list 192.156.136.22
```

Table 14.6 Ping command switches.

Switch	Function
-t	Ping the specified host until interrupted.
-a	Resolve address to hostnames.
-n	Number of echo requests to send.
-l size	Send buffer size.
-f	Set Don't Fragment flag in packet.
-i TTL	Time To Live.
-v TOS	Type Of Service.
-r count	Record route for count hops.
-s count	Timestamp for count hops (range is 1–4).
-j host-list	Loose source route along host line.
-k host-list	Strict source route along host line.
-w timeout	Timeout (in milliseconds) to wait for each reply.

Here is an example of the ping command and its results:

```
C:\WINDOWS>ping -a www.3com.com

Pinging www.3com.com [192.156.136.22] with 32 bytes of data

Reply from 192.156.136.22: bytes=32 time=488ms TTL=238
Reply from 192.156.136.22: bytes=32 time=515ms TTL=238
Reply from 192.156.136.22: bytes=32 time=496ms TTL=238
Reply from 192.156.136.22: bytes=32 time=501ms TTL=238

Ping statistics for 192.156.136.22:
Packets: Sent = 4, Received = 4, Lost = 0 (0% loss),
Approximate round trip times in milli-seconds:
Minimum = 488ms, Maximum = 515ms, Average = 500ms
```

Make sure that you know the ping command switches and how they are used.

Telnet

Telnet connects to TCP/IP host computers on port 23. Both computers must support the Telnet protocol for it to work. As two computers use modems to connect through telephone lines with a telephone number, the computers use Telnet to connect through the Internet with an IP address instead. The computer to which you are connecting will prompt you for a username and password, if that organization has implemented security measures. If you are not connecting to a public or general account, you will need to have your own account set up prior to your login.

To run Telnet, you need Telnet software, such as NCSA Telnet or the Telnet program that ships with Windows 95/98/NT. Within the software, select Open Connection (or a similar command) and enter the IP address. With Windows 95/98, go to the Start menu and select Run, then enter the command and the IP address or the DNS name, similar to the following:

```
telnet 166.177.40.38
```

or

```
telnet ftp.novell.com
```

NETSTAT

The NETSTAT command shows the status of all TCP and UDP port activity on a workstation or server. Table 14.7 shows the NETSTAT command switches. If you wanted to see what ports are active on your workstation, you would run this command:

```
C:\>NETSTAT [-a] [-e] [-n] [-s] [-p proto] [-r] [interval]
```

Table 14.7 NETSTAT command switches.

Switch	Function
-rn	Shows the default route for your network.
-p [udp] [tcp]	Shows connections for the protocol specified.
-r	Displays the kernel routing table.
-n	Presents addresses as dotted quad IP numbers rather than the symbolic host and network names (useful when avoiding address lookups over the network to a DNS or NIS server).
-a	Displays all connections and listening ports.
-e	Displays Ethernet statistics.
interval	Displays the length of time to wait (in seconds) before displaying the statistics again.

To reach machines on a local network, you do not need any extra routes. To reach machines outside the local network, define a default route that tells your machine to send all traffic not belonging to your network to this default router. Use the NETSTAT -rn command to ensure that you have the default route properly defined, then ping the default router to be sure that it is alive. Here is an example of NETSTAT command results:

```
C:\WINDOWS>netstat
Active Connections
Proto    Local Address         Foreign Address       State
TCP      scott-reeves:1037     www.msn.com:80        ESTABLISHED
```

NBTSTAT

This command utility displays protocol statistics and current TCP/IP connections using NetBIOS over TCP/IP. NBTSTAT is a great tool for listing local NetBIOS names. Table 14.8 lists the command switches for the NBTSTAT command. At the DOS prompt, enter:

```
C:\>NBTSTAT [-a RemoteName]
```

Table 14.8 NBTSTAT command switches.

Switch	Function
-a	Lists the remote machine's name table, given its name.
-A	Lists the remote machine's name table, given its IP address.
-c	Lists the remote name cache including the IP addresses.
-n	Lists local NetBIOS names.
-r	Lists names resolved by broadcast and by WINS.
-R	Purges and reloads the remote cache name table.
-S	Lists the sessions table with the destination IP addresses.
-s	Lists the sessions table converting destination IP addresses to host names through the HOSTS file.
RemoteName	Shows the remote host machine's name.
IP address	Gives a dotted decimal representation of the IP address.
interval	Redisplays selected statistics, pausing for a specified time period.

The following is an example of the NBTSTAT command and its results:

```
C:\WINDOWS>nbtstat -n

Node IpAddress: [166.177.40.38] Scope Id: []
        NetBIOS Local Name Table

Name                    Type            Status
---------------------------------------------------
SCOTT_REEVES  <00>      UNIQUE          Registered
REEVES        <00>      GROUP           Registered
SCOTT_REEVES  <03>      UNIQUE          Registered
SCOTT_REEVES  <20>      UNIQUE          Registered
REEVES        <1E>      GROUP           Registered
```

Tracert

The Tracert (trace route) utility displays the route to a particular machine. You would use this command to determine whether a problem with a router exists. To use the Tracert command, enter the command and the IP address of the device to which you want to connect. The results will show you the entire path taken to get to the specified server, as shown in the following:

```
C:\WINDOWS>tracert www.coriolis.com
Tracing route to www.coriolis.com [209.140.152.4]
over a maximum of 30 hops

  1   124 ms   123 ms   128 ms  port2.hanover.desupernet.net
                                [208.157.110.3]
  2   128 ms   128 ms   129 ms  ethernet0.hanover.desupernet
                                [208.157.110.1]
  3   152 ms   136 ms   132 ms  serial1-3.chambersburg.desupernet.net
                                [208.157.107.9]
  4   141 ms   134 ms   146 ms  serial2-0.harrisburg.desupernet.net
                                [208.7.254.9]
  5   159 ms   169 ms   162 ms  border3-hssi1-0.WillowSprings.cw.net
                                [204.70.107.5]
  6   163 ms   166 ms   173 ms  core1-fddi-0.WillowSprings.cw.net
                                [204.70.104.17]
  7   203 ms   194 ms   199 ms  core6.Washington.cw.net [204.70.4.113]
  8   207 ms   201 ms   196 ms  204.70.10.182
  9   181 ms   176 ms   174 ms  mae-east.good.net [192.41.177.101]
 10   272 ms   278 ms   273 ms  157.good.net [207.98.190.157]
 11   284 ms   297 ms   292 ms  coriolis.phoenix.good.net
                                [207.98.136.203]
 12   341 ms   294 ms   304 ms  www.coriolis.com [209.140.152.4]

Trace complete.
```

IPCONFIG

IPCONFIG.EXE is a utility that provides the user with diagnostic information related to a workstation's TCP/IP network configuration. IPCONFIG also accepts various Dynamic Host Configuration Protocol (DHCP) commands, allowing a system to update or release its TCP/IP network configuration. IPCONFIG is available on Windows NT Workstation and Windows NT Server:

IPCONFIG [/? | /all | /release [adapter] | /renew [adapter]]

With no parameters, IPCONFIG will display only the IP address, subnet mask, and default gateway for each adapter bound to TCP/IP. Table 14.9 shows the IPCONFIG switches.

You can use the /release and /renew switches only on systems that are configured with DHCP. If you do not specify an adapter name with the /release or /renew switch, the IP address leases for all adapters bound to TCP/IP will be released or renewed.

WINIPCFG

WINIPCFG is used on Windows 95/98 workstations. It tells you about your Windows IP configuration, including all TCP/IP addresses currently assigned to your system, lease information, network card addresses, and DNS information.

The duration of your IP address lease depends on security considerations, overall traffic, and other network-specific circumstances. Most often, the lease is for the duration of the connection when you are dealing with Internet dial-ups. On a TCP/IP-based network, the lease might never expire or might be limited to a few hours, depending on the company needs or the criteria set by the system administrators.

The display will show your computer's name and the DNS that it is configured to call when it needs to find a named resource. It also tells you the IP address

Table 14.9 IPCONFIG switches.

Switch	Function
/?	Display this help message.
/all	Display full configuration information. Displays all the current TCP/IP configuration values, including the IP address, subnet mask, default gateway, WINS configuration, and DNS configuration.
/release	Releases the IP address for the specified adapter.
/renew	Renews the IP address for the specified adapter.

and the subnet mask used to uniquely identify this computer on the Internet. Because it is a dial-up connection, the default gateway is the same as the IP address because it identifies your system as the computer connected to the Net. The gateway for computers that gain Internet access through a network connection will specify which server processes requests for Internet access. DHCP Server identifies the network server that assigns IP addresses to computers logging on to the network.

WINIPCFG provides you with a snapshot of current connections when you are troubleshooting problems. That is why advanced information about WINS proxies and routing are included. You should avoid using the /release and /renew options. Although they are useful in resolving faulty TCP/IP connections, if you release your TCP/IP lease, you might lose access to network resources until you reestablish your logon.

Address Resolution Protocol

IP uses the Address Resolution Protocol (ARP) to map IP network addresses to the MAC addresses used by a data link protocol. ARP operates below the Network layer as a part of the OSI Data Link layer and is used for IP connections over Ethernet.

ARP resolves addresses by sending a piece of information from a client process executing on the local computer to a server process executing on a remote computer. The information that the server receives allows it to uniquely identify the network system for which the address was required and then provide the required address. When the client receives a response from the server, the address is resolved.

ARP can send any of four types of ARP messages, which are identified by four values in the Operation field of an ARP message. The types of message are ARP request, ARP reply, RARP request, and RARP reply. The following is the format of an ARP message used to resolve the remote MAC hardware address (HA):

```
C:\WINDOWS> arp -s inet_addr eth_addr [if_addr]
```

Table 14.10 shows the available switches to the ARP command. To reduce the number of address resolution requests, a client normally caches resolved addresses for a (short) period. The ARP cache is of a finite size; if you allow it to grow unchecked, it will fill with incomplete and obsolete entries for computers that are not in use. Therefore, the ARP cache periodically flushes all entries. This deletes unused entries and frees space in the cache. It also removes any unsuccessful attempts to contact computers that are not currently running.

Table 14.10 ARP command switches.

Switch	Function
-a or -g	Displays the IP address and MAC address and whether it is dynamic or static.
-d	Deletes an entry from the ARP table.
-s	Adds a permanent static entry to the ARP table.
inet_addr	Internet address.
eth_addr	MAC address.
if_addr	Internet address of a specific interface.
-N if_addr	Displays the ARP entries for the interface specified.

Here is an example of the ARP command and its results:

```
C:\WINDOWS>arp -a

Interface: 166.177.40.38 on Interface 2

Internet Address    Physical Address    Type
209.166.163.217     20-53-52-43-00-00   dynamic
```

Corrective Maintenance

After you have isolated the cause of the problem, your normal response is to replace the faulty component if it is confined to hardware. Aside from modem cards and NICs, you will almost never need to open a device to make repairs. However, even modem cards and NICs are replacement-level items; they just happen to be located inside other devices.

You should always have a means to secure a device replacement almost immediately, whether that means having spares on hand or calling your supplier and having them get a replacement to you as quickly as possible. Because network downtime usually means lost revenue, you will certainly want to consider having spares for as many components as you can possibly afford. Before you install the spare onto the network, remember to configure it exactly like the device that it is replacing.

Test The Solution

After you swap out the defective device, always test the network and try to re-create the original problem. If you can re-create the problem, you must return to square one. If the network tests fine, you have solved the problem.

CM Follow-Up

It is important to take time to document the problem and the resolution to the problem so that you will have a maintenance history to which you can refer for similar problems. You should also follow up with the customer to see whether the solution actually resolved the problem and to identify any outstanding issues. Once the problem has been resolved, you should document it in the trouble-tracking system. You should also discuss the problem resolution with the first level of support, so that in the future they will have more of an understanding of that and similar problems before they pass it on to the second-level support team.

Practice Questions

Question 1

> If a user can access local devices on an IP network but cannot access devices on a remote network, what is the cause?
>
> ○ a. Corrupted/incorrect WINS address
> ○ b. Corrupted/incorrect DNS server
> ○ c. Corrupted IP stack
> ○ d. Corrupted/incorrect default IP gateway

The correct answer is d. If the IP packet is destined for a remote network, the system sends it to a default gateway for delivery. WINS is IP-to-NetBIOS name resolution. Therefore, answer a is incorrect. Although the DNS server could affect accessing a remote network, it would also affect the local network. Therefore, answer b is incorrect. A corrupted IP stack would hamper local access as well as remote network access. Therefore, answer c is incorrect.

Question 2

> What would be the result of connecting a workstation to a hub when the horizontal cable run is 93 meters and two patch cables are 10 meters each?
>
> ○ a. You do not count patch cables in the length, and it is within the 100 meters specification.
> ○ b. It is close enough that it should work.
> ○ c. Specifications are always cautious; it should work.
> ○ d. It is longer than the maximum allowed length, and reliable connectivity is not guaranteed.

The correct answer is d. Patch cables are included in the total length, and connectivity cannot be guaranteed when the length exceeds the maximum specified (which is 100 meters). Answer a is incorrect because patch cables are counted in the total length. Answers b and c are incorrect because they represent poor judgment.

Question 3

If you only know the IP address of a remote computer and want to know its MAC address, what utility should you use?

○ a. WINIPCFG

○ b. ARP

○ c. IPCONFIG

○ d. Tracert

The correct answer is b. The ARP utility is used to return the MAC address of a remote workstation. WINIPCFG is used to get the local IP configuration of a Windows 95/98 machine. Therefore, answer a is incorrect. IPCONFIG is used to get the local IP configuration of a Windows NT computer. Therefore, answer c is incorrect. Tracert is used to trace the path a packet takes through a routed network. Therefore, answer d is incorrect.

Question 4

If you move a server to another segment on the network, what should you do to make sure that it is working correctly?

○ a. Reinstall the NIC driver and reload the protocols.

○ b. Reset all the network devices and then connect it to the network.

○ c. Connect it to the network and see whether everything is working as specified; you might not need to do any troubleshooting.

○ d. Connect it to the network, then reset all the network devices.

The correct answer is c. Connect it up and see whether the users can access all the services and that it is working properly. Reinstalling the drivers should not be required. Therefore, answer a is incorrect. Resetting the network device should not be necessary. Therefore, answers b and d are incorrect.

Question 5

> If a home user is having a modem connection problem, where is the best place to go for technical support? [Choose the two best answers]
> - a. Check the manufacturer's Web site
> - b. Call a friend who has a computer
> - c. Call the modem vendor for technical support
> - d. Research hard copy or CD-ROM documentation for troubleshooting methods and try them

The correct answers are c and d. Look for troubleshooting methods in the documentation provided, and if that does not work, call the vendor. Answer a is incorrect because although the manufacturer's Web site is a good choice, if the modem is not working, you cannot browse the Web site. Answer b is incorrect because calling a friend with a computer is probably the last resort.

Question 6

> If your computer will not boot after downloading and executing files from the Internet, what is the first thing you should check?
> - a. Hard drive failure
> - b. Boot sector virus
> - c. Corrupted program file
> - d. Bad power supply

The correct answer is b. The virus signature file should be updated and the system scanned for boot sector viruses. A hard drive failure may exhibit these symptoms but should not be the first thing checked. Therefore, answer a is incorrect. A corrupted program would not stop a computer from booting. Therefore, answer c is incorrect. The entire computer would be dead if the power supply was bad. Therefore, answer d is incorrect.

Question 7

What would be the result of a UTP cable, passing Fast Ethernet, lying on a fluorescent light?

- a. Fluorescent lights do not cause interference to Fast Ethernet.
- b. The fluorescent light would interfere with the Fast Ethernet signal.
- c. Fluorescent lights interfere with fiber-optic signal, not electromagnetic signals.
- d. It would melt the cable.

The correct answer is b. The electromagnetic interference would cause signal instability. Answer a is incorrect on the basis of answer b. Answer c is incorrect because fluorescent lights do not interfere with fiber-optic signals. Answer d is incorrect because fluorescent lights do not get that hot.

Question 8

Which of these two trouble calls would receive the higher priority:

- A user in the accounting department has called you four times in the last hour because he cannot use their local modem to perform an electronic bank transfer.
- The primary corporate application server is down.

The two problems are not related.

- a. The accounting department, because the corporate finances are affected.
- b. The application server, because all the users are affected.
- c. Both, because they are equal in importance.
- d. Do not give either of them a higher priority. Instead, go between the two problems and try to fix them simultaneously.

The correct answer is b. Because all the users are affected, it is a critical operation. Answer a is incorrect because although the user is putting higher pressure on you to repair the problem and corporate finances are at stake, the company is not losing revenue, and minimal users are affected. Answer c is incorrect because the two problems are not equal in importance. Answer d is also incorrect because you would not be effectively addressing either problem, and the application server deserves your full attention.

Question 9

> Assume that you are first-level support and that you are answering the help desk. You receive a trouble call for a problem that you are not familiar with. What should you do? [Choose the three best answers]
>
> ❏ a. Call the manufacturer's technical support number.
> ❏ b. Go to the manufacturer's Web site knowledge base.
> ❏ c. Pass the call on to second-level support personnel.
> ❏ d. Tell the user that you cannot help them.
> ❏ e. Tell the user to call the manufacturer's technical support number.
> ❏ f. Refer to the vendor documentation.
> ❏ g. Go to the user site and run diagnostic software on the device.

The correct answers are b, c, and f. They are all things that you would do to resolve the problem. Answer a is incorrect because the second-level support should call tech support, if required. Answer d is incorrect because helping the user with network problems is your job. Answer e is incorrect because the user should never call the manufacturer's tech support; this is reserved for the IS personnel after they have exhausted all of their knowledge and resources. If you are not familiar with the problem, you will not know which device to run diagnostics on. Therefore, answer g is incorrect.

Question 10

> Which command utility would you use to connect to a router across the network?
>
> ○ a. FTP
> ○ b. Tracert
> ○ c. NBTSTAT
> ○ d. Telnet
> ○ e. NETSTAT

The correct answer is d. Telnet opens a session to a TCP/IP host, and routers support configuration through Telnet. Answers a, b, c, and e are incorrect because they are commands for other functions.

Need To Know More?

 Mazda, Fraidoon, ed.: *Telecommunications Engineer's Reference Book*. Reed Educational and Professional Publishing Ltd., Woburn, MA, 1998. ISBN 0-240-51491-2. An excellent reference book explaining the intricacies of telecommunications in great detail.

 Sheldon, Tom: *Encyclopedia of Networking, Electronic Edition*. Osborne McGraw-Hill, New York. ISBN 0-07-882333-1. A good overview of general networking terms and networking characteristics. Covers everything from A to Z.

 www.3com.com publishes information on troubleshooting NICs, switches, and routers.

 www.baynetworks.com publishes information on troubleshooting switches and routers.

 www.cisco.com publishes information on troubleshooting switches and routers.

 www.microsoft.com has extensive information on troubleshooting its advanced products, such as Windows NT, SNA Gateway, SMS Server, SQL Server, and Internet products.

 www.novell.com has exhaustive information on troubleshooting all its advanced server products for the LAN and the WAN. The products are NetWare, GroupWise, ManageWise, and Z.E.N.works.

Sample Test

In this chapter, we provide pointers to help you develop a successful test-taking strategy, including how to choose proper answers, how to decode ambiguity, how to work within the CompTIA testing framework, how to decide what you need to memorize, and how to prepare for the test. At the end of the chapter, we include 74 questions on subject matter pertinent to the CompTIA Network+ Certification Exam. Good luck!

Questions, Questions, Questions

There should be no doubt in your mind that you are facing a test full of specific and pointed questions. The Network+ exam that you take will include 65 questions, and you will be allotted 90 minutes to complete the exam.

Questions for the Network+ test belong to one of five types:

➤ Multiple choice with a single answer

➤ Multiple choice with multiple answers

➤ Multipart with a single answer

➤ Multipart with multiple answers

➤ Simulations whereby you click a GUI screen capture to pick graphics

Always take the time to read a question at least twice before selecting an answer and always look for an Exhibit button as you examine each question. Exhibits include graphics information related to a question. An *exhibit* is usually a screen capture of program output or GUI information that you must examine to analyze the question's contents and formulate an answer. The Exhibit button brings up graphics and charts used to help explain a question, provide additional data, or illustrate page layout or program behavior.

Not every question has only one answer; many questions require multiple answers. Therefore, you should read each question carefully, determine how many answers are necessary or possible, and look for additional hints or instructions when selecting answers. Such instructions occur in brackets immediately following the question itself.

Picking Proper Answers

Obviously, the only way to pass any exam is to select enough of the right answers to obtain a passing score. However, CompTIA's exams are not standardized, as the SAT and GRE exams are; they are far more diabolical and convoluted. In some cases, questions are strangely worded, and deciphering them can be a real challenge. In such cases, you might need to rely on answer-elimination skills. Almost always, at least one answer for a question can be eliminated immediately because it matches one of these conditions:

➤ The answer does not apply to the situation.

➤ The answer describes a nonexistent issue, an invalid option, or an imaginary state.

➤ The answer can be eliminated because of information in the question itself.

After you eliminate all answers that are obviously wrong, you can apply your retained knowledge to eliminate further answers. Look for items that sound correct but that refer to actions, commands, or features that are not present or not available in the situation that the question describes.

If you're still faced with a blind guess among two or more potentially correct answers, reread the question. Try to picture how each of the remaining answers would alter the situation. Be especially sensitive to terminology; sometimes the choice of words ("remove" instead of "disable") can make the difference between a right answer and a wrong one.

Only when you've exhausted your ability to eliminate answers but remain unclear about which of the remaining possibilities is correct should you guess at an answer. An unanswered question offers you no points, but guessing gives you at least some chance of getting a question right; just don't be too hasty when making a blind guess.

You can wait until the last round of reviewing marked questions (just as you're about to run out of time or out of unanswered questions) before you start making guesses. However, guessing should be a last resort.

Decoding Ambiguity

CompTIA's exams have a reputation for including questions that can be difficult to interpret, confusing, or ambiguous. The only way to beat CompTIA at its own game is to be prepared. You'll discover that many exam questions test your knowledge of things that are not directly related to the issue raised by a question. This means that the answers you must choose from, even incorrect ones, are just as much a part of the skill assessment as the question itself.

Questions often give away their answers, but you have to be Sherlock Holmes to see the clues. Often, subtle hints appear in the question text in such a way that they seem almost irrelevant to the situation. You must realize that each question is a test unto itself and that you need to inspect and successfully navigate each question to pass the exam. Look for small clues, such as a hub does not segment a network, a switch/bridge segments the network using MAC addresses, and a router passes network traffic. Little things such as these can point to the right answer if properly understood; if missed, they can leave you facing a blind guess.

Another common difficulty with certification exams is vocabulary. Be sure to brush up on the key terms presented at the beginning of each chapter. You might also want to read through the Glossary at the end of this book the day before you take the test.

Working Within The Framework

The test questions appear in random order, and many elements or issues that receive mention in one question might also crop up in other questions. It's not uncommon to find that an incorrect answer to one question is the answer to another question and vice versa. Take the time to read every answer to each question, even if you recognize the answer to a question immediately. That extra reading might spark a memory or remind you about a networking feature or function that helps you on another question elsewhere in the exam.

Don't forget, you can revisit any question as many times as you like. If you're uncertain of the answer to a question, check the box that's provided so that you can return to it later. You should also mark questions that you think might offer information that you can use to answer other questions. On previous tests, we have usually marked somewhere between 25 and 50 percent of the questions on the exams we have taken. The testing software is designed to let you mark every question if you choose; use this framework to your advantage. Everything you'll want to see again should be marked; the testing software can then help you return to marked questions quickly and easily.

> We strongly recommend that you first read through the entire test quickly before getting caught up in answering individual questions. This will help jog your memory as you review the potential answers and can help identify questions that you want to mark for easy access to their contents. It will also let you identify and mark the tricky questions for easy return as well. The key is to make a quick pass over the territory to begin with—so that you know what you're up against—and then to survey that territory more thoroughly on a second pass, when you can begin to answer all questions systematically and consistently.

If you see something in a question or one of the answers that jogs your memory on a topic, or that you feel you should record if the topic appears in another question, write it down on your piece of paper.

> Don't be afraid to take notes on what you see in various questions. Sometimes, what you record from one question, especially if it's not as familiar as it should be or if it reminds you of the name or use of some network device, utility, or network interface details, can help you on other questions later on.

Deciding What To Memorize

The amount of memorization you must undertake for an exam depends on how well you remember what you've read and how well you know the material by heart. If you're a visual thinker and can see a network design and how all the components interact with each other in your head, you won't need to memorize as much as someone who's less visually oriented. However, the exam will stretch your abilities to memorize network features and functions, interface details, and troubleshooting.

At a minimum, you'll want to memorize the following kinds of information:

- Basic information about network components
- The OSI model and how network components function within that framework
- The fundamentals of the TCP/IP protocol and the utilities associated with it
- The different types of remote connectivity
- How security works and how to implement it
- Troubleshooting the network

Don't forget that The Cram Sheet at the front of the book is designed to capture the material that's most important to memorize; use this to guide your studies as well.

Preparing For The Test

The best way to prepare for the test—after you've studied—is to take at least one practice exam. We've included one here in this chapter for that reason. The test questions are located in the pages that follow, and, unlike the preceding chapters in this book, the answers don't follow the questions immediately; you'll have to flip to Chapter 16 to review the answers separately.

Give yourself 90 minutes to take the exam, and keep yourself on the honor system—don't look back at the text in the book or jump ahead to the answer key. When your time is up or you've finished the questions, you can check your work in Chapter 16. Pay special attention to the explanations for the incorrect answers; these can also help reinforce your knowledge of the material. Knowing how to recognize correct answers is good, but understanding why incorrect answers are wrong can be equally valuable.

Taking The Test

Relax. Once you're sitting in front of the testing computer, there's nothing more you can do to increase your knowledge or preparation. Take a deep breath, stretch, and start reading that first question.

You don't need to rush, either. You have plenty of time to complete each question and to return to those questions that you skip or mark for return. If you read a question twice and remain clueless, you can mark it. Don't spend more than five minutes on any single question—if it takes you that long to get nowhere, it's time to guess and move on.

You can read through the entire test, and before returning to marked questions for a second visit, you can figure out how much time you've got per question. As you answer each question, remove its mark. Continue to review the remaining marked questions until you run out of time or complete the test.

Set a maximum time limit for questions and watch your time on long or complex questions. If you hit your limit, it's time to guess and move on. Don't deprive yourself of the opportunity to see more questions by taking too long to puzzle over questions, unless you think you can figure out the answer. Otherwise, you're limiting your opportunity to pass.

That's it for pointers. Here are some questions for you to practice on.

Practice Test

Question 1

Which type of network configuration lends itself to all the computers being both workstations and servers?

- a. Client/server
- b. Ethernet
- c. Peer-to-peer
- d. Minicomputer with terminals

Question 2

Which device would you install to protect the network from the Internet while caching the most active Web sites accessed?

- a. Firewall server
- b. Gateway server
- c. Proxy server
- d. Network Address Translation (NAT) server

Question 3

Which OSI Physical layer device is inside a computer?

- a. Memory
- b. Hard drive
- c. NIC
- d. Pentium III chip

Question 4

What are the major network operating systems? [Choose the four best answers]

- ❑ a. DOS
- ❑ b. Windows NT
- ❑ c. NetWare
- ❑ d. OS/2
- ❑ e. Windows
- ❑ f. Unix

Question 5

Which clients can connect a Windows 9x workstation to a NetWare server? [Choose the two best answers]

- ❑ a. NetWare Client32
- ❑ b. Client for Microsoft Networks
- ❑ c. Client for NetWare Networks
- ❑ d. Microsoft Family Logon

Question 6

What is the tree structure for NetWare?

- ○ a. Bindery
- ○ b. NDS
- ○ c. NTDS
- ○ d. Vines

Question 7

Which utility do you use on Windows NT to see the TCP/IP configuration?

- ○ a. WINIPCFG
- ○ b. IPCONFIG
- ○ c. IPCFG
- ○ d. NTIPCFG

Question 8

If an IP host on a local subnet can access devices on the local subnet but cannot access a device beyond the local subnet, what is the problem?

- ○ a. No WINS address or an incorrect WINS address
- ○ b. No default gateway address or an incorrect default gateway address
- ○ c. The DHCP server fails to assign an IP address to all hosts on the local subnet
- ○ d. There could be a corrupted host file on the router

Question 9

How does a NIC get a MAC address?

- ○ a. DHCP server
- ○ b. Entered by user during setup
- ○ c. Dynamic MAC server
- ○ d. NIC vendors

Question 10

If you have two or more hard drives and create a stripe set across them, what RAID level would that be?

- ○ a. RAID 0
- ○ b. RAID 1
- ○ c. RAID 4
- ○ d. RAID 5

Question 11

What is the NNTP port?

- ○ a. 119
- ○ b. 25
- ○ c. 21
- ○ d. 80

Question 12

Where do you configure a Windows 95/98 client to use a proxy server?

- ○ a. The TCP/IP protocol
- ○ b. The security service
- ○ c. The gateway service
- ○ d. The Web browser

Question 13

Which TCP/IP utility would you use to determine whether a bottleneck exists in your network?

- ○ a. Tracert
- ○ b. ARP
- ○ c. Ping
- ○ d. IPCONFIG

Question 14

If you have two hard drive controllers connected to two separate hard drives and you mirror/duplex the drives, what RAID level would that be?

- ○ a. RAID 0
- ○ b. RAID 1
- ○ c. RAID 4
- ○ d. RAID 5

Question 15

What is the most popular asynchronous protocol?

- ○ a. SLIP
- ○ b. SDLC
- ○ c. PPP
- ○ d. TCP/IP

Question 16

What transport does PPTP use?

○ a. SLIP
○ b. PPP
○ c. TCP/IP
○ d. LLC

Question 17

What is the name of the file where static IP addresses are stored in a Windows NT server?

○ a. IPSTAT
○ b. HOSTS
○ c. LMHOSTS
○ d. IPHOSTS

Question 18

What UART chip is capable of speeds greater than 115.2Kbps?

○ a. 8250
○ b. 16550
○ c. 16450
○ d. 17550

Question 19

How can you protect your private network from the Internet? [Choose the two best answers]

❏ a. Firewall
❏ b. Password security
❏ c. MAC port grouping
❏ d. VLAN

Question 20

What are the best password characteristics?

- ○ a. They should contain a minimum of 7 alpha and numeric characters.
- ○ b. They should contain a minimum of 17 alpha, numeric, and special characters.
- ○ c. They should contain a minimum of 7 alpha, numeric, and special characters.
- ○ d. They should contain a minimum of 7 numeric and special characters.

Question 21

What is the maximum length of a 10Base2 network in an Ethernet network?

- ○ a. 100 meters
- ○ b. 185 meters
- ○ c. 500 meters
- ○ d. 2 kilometers
- ○ e. 200 meters

Question 22

What is the maximum length of a UTP category 5 cable segment in an Ethernet network?

- ○ a. 100 meters
- ○ b. 185 meters
- ○ c. 500 meters
- ○ d. 2 kilometers
- ○ e. 200 meters

Question 23

What is the Windows name resolution standard?

- ○ a. DNS
- ○ b. DHCP
- ○ c. WINS
- ○ d. WSIN

Question 24

On a Windows 95/98 workstation, which type of access control to shared resources is controlled from the server?

- ○ a. Share-level access control
- ○ b. User-level access control
- ○ c. Computer-level access control
- ○ d. Host-level access control

Question 25

What is the FTP port?

- ○ a. 80
- ○ b. 21
- ○ c. 25
- ○ d. 23

Question 26

On a Windows 95/98 workstation, which type of access control to shared resources is controlled from the workstation?

- ○ a. Share-level access control
- ○ b. User-level access control
- ○ c. Computer-level access control
- ○ d. Host-level access control

Question 27

What are the different types of external SCSI connectors? [Choose the three best answers]

- ❏ a. 25-pin DB-25 SCSI connector
- ❏ b. 50-pin high-density SCSI connector
- ❏ c. 78-pin high-density SCSI connector
- ❏ d. 68-pin high-density SCSI connector
- ❏ e. 15-pin SCSI connector

Question 28

Which network device does not segment a network?

- ○ a. Bridge
- ○ b. Hub
- ○ c. Switch
- ○ d. Router

Question 29

Which multiport network device can segment a network and forward packets at near-wire speeds to each port simultaneously?

- ○ a. Dual port NIC
- ○ b. Hub
- ○ c. Switch
- ○ d. Router

Question 30

Which network device functions in the Data Link and Network layers of the OSI model?

- ○ a. NIC
- ○ b. Brouter
- ○ c. Bridge
- ○ d. Hub
- ○ e. Gateway

Question 31

What is a multistation access unit (MAU)?

- ○ a. An Ethernet hub
- ○ b. A token ring concentrator
- ○ c. A Fast Ethernet hub
- ○ d. A switch
- ○ e. A router

Question 32

How do you display the current ARP entries? [Choose the two best answers]

- ❏ a. ARP -d
- ❏ b. ARP -a
- ❏ c. ARP -g
- ❏ d. ARP -s

Question 33

Which type of topology has more than one path to a device?

- ○ a. Star
- ○ b. Bus
- ○ c. Backbone
- ○ d. Mesh

Question 34

Which network topology has all the nodes returning to a central hub?

○ a. Star
○ b. Ring
○ c. Bus
○ d. Fully meshed

Question 35

Which network topology has all the nodes connected to one coaxial cable?

○ a. Star
○ b. Ring
○ c. Bus
○ d. Fully meshed

Question 36

What is the Telnet port?

○ a. 23
○ b. 80
○ c. 110
○ d. 25

Question 37

Which network topology has all the nodes connected to the node before it and the node after it in the topology?

○ a. Star
○ b. Ring
○ c. Bus
○ d. Fully meshed

Question 38

Which network devices work at the OSI Data Link layer? [Choose the two best answers]

- ❑ a. Switch
- ❑ b. Hub
- ❑ c. NIC
- ❑ d. Bridge
- ❑ e. Router
- ❑ f. Gateway

Question 39

Which protocol works only at the Data Link layer of the OSI model?

- ○ a. AppleTalk
- ○ b. IPX
- ○ c. NetBEUI
- ○ d. TCP/IP

Question 40

Which network device works at the Network layer of the OSI model?

- ○ a. Router
- ○ b. Hub
- ○ c. Gateway
- ○ d. Switch
- ○ e. Bridge

Question 41

Which protocols work at the Network layer of the OSI model? [Choose the three best answers]

- ❑ a. DLC
- ❑ b. TCP/IP
- ❑ c. IPX
- ❑ d. NetBEUI
- ❑ e. AppleTalk

Question 42

Which protocols are connectionless-oriented protocols? [Choose the three best answers]

- ❑ a. IP
- ❑ b. TCP
- ❑ c. SPX
- ❑ d. IPX
- ❑ e. UDP

Question 43

Which protocols are connection-oriented protocols? [Choose the two best answers]

- ❑ a. UDP
- ❑ b. TCP
- ❑ c. IP
- ❑ d. SPX
- ❑ e. IPX

Question 44

Which protocols work at the Transport layer of the OSI model? [Choose the three best answers]

- ❑ a. IP
- ❑ b. SPX
- ❑ c. TCP
- ❑ d. IPX
- ❑ e. UDP

Question 45

Which layer of the OSI model do the FTP and Telnet programs use?

- ○ a. Application
- ○ b. Physical
- ○ c. Data Link
- ○ d. Network
- ○ e. Transport

Question 46

Which IEEE standard defines a token-passing ring network?

- ○ a. 802.11
- ○ b. 802.2
- ○ c. 802.5
- ○ d. 802.3
- ○ e. 802.12

Question 47

What is the HTTP port?

○ a. 110
○ b. 80
○ c. 21
○ d. 25

Question 48

Which IEEE standard defines an Ethernet network?

○ a. 802.2
○ b. 802.5
○ c. 802.12
○ d. 802.3
○ e. 802.11

Question 49

Which IEEE standard defines the Logical Link Control protocol?

○ a. 802.2
○ b. 802.11
○ c. 802.3
○ d. 802.5
○ e. 802.12

Question 50

Which protocol would you use to do network management?

○ a. SMTP
○ b. SNMP
○ c. SNAP
○ d. SNIFFER

Question 51

Which protocol dynamically assigns TCP/IP addresses?

- ○ a. WINS
- ○ b. DNS
- ○ c. NDS
- ○ d. DHCP
- ○ e. NTDS

Question 52

Which protocols can you use to connect a Windows NT server and a NetWare server? [Choose the two best answers]

- ❑ a. DLC
- ❑ b. TCP/IP
- ❑ c. NetBEUI
- ❑ d. IPX
- ❑ e. RIP

Question 53

Which types of backup reset the archive bit? [Choose the two best answers]

- ❑ a. Differential
- ❑ b. Full
- ❑ c. Incremental
- ❑ d. Folder copy
- ❑ e. Mirror

Question 54

If you receive media errors on all your tapes, what should you do first?

- ○ a. Call technical support
- ○ b. Clean the tapes
- ○ c. Clean the tape drive
- ○ d. Replace the tapes

Question 55

Where should the backup tapes be stored?

- ○ a. Next to the server for convenience.
- ○ b. At an offsite location.
- ○ c. In the building but not in the server room.
- ○ d. The easiest way to do tape backup is to put all the tapes in a seven-cartridge automatic tape loader and never have to manually change the tapes.

Question 56

On the coldest days of winter, you notice that the network seems to be unstable in the office areas. What should you look for as the possible cause of the problem?

- ○ a. A cold air draft near the network equipment
- ○ b. Space heaters causing electrical and network interference
- ○ c. The cable runs on the outside wall getting too cold
- ○ d. Excessive interference caused by the central heating system

Question 57

What would you use a crossover cable for? [Choose the four best answers]

- ❏ a. A hub-to-PC connection
- ❏ b. A PC-to-PC connection
- ❏ c. A switch-to-PC connection
- ❏ d. A hub-to-hub connection
- ❏ e. A hub-to-switch connection
- ❏ f. A switch-to-switch connection

Question 58

How would you determine whether a fault exists in a network cable?

○ a. Replace the cable with a new cable

○ b. Test the cable with a cable tester

○ c. Terminate the ends again

○ d. Inspect the cable for defects

Question 59

What would be the result of connecting a workstation to a hub when the horizontal cable run was 95 meters and two patch cables are 10 meters each?

○ a. It would work fine because patch cables are not counted in the length.

○ b. It is close enough to the maximum length to guarantee reliable connectivity.

○ c. It is longer than the maximum allowed length, and reliable connectivity cannot be guaranteed.

○ d. It might or might not work; you won't know until you put it into production.

Question 60

If you received a file from an external source and loaded it on your system, then the next day your system failed to boot, what is the first thing you should check?

○ a. Motherboard failure

○ b. Trojan horse

○ c. Hard drive failure

○ d. Memory failure

○ e. Boot sector virus

Question 61

How often should the virus signature file be updated?

- ○ a. Daily
- ○ b. Hourly
- ○ c. Weekly
- ○ d. Monthly
- ○ e. Quarterly
- ○ f. Annually

Question 62

What is full duplex in an Ethernet environment?

- ○ a. When data can flow in both directions at the same time in a non-shared collision domain.
- ○ b. When data can flow in both directions at the same time in a shared collision domain.
- ○ c. It is a proprietary link between Ethernet switches.
- ○ d. It is a proprietary link between Ethernet hubs.

Question 63

If you have a network user that wants to print to a network printer several offices over, what is the best way to accomplish that task?

- ○ a. Let the user have access to a computer in that department so they can print
- ○ b. Buy a printer just like it and put it in the user's department
- ○ c. Redirect the local parallel printer port so that it is captured to the queue that services that printer
- ○ d. Take a floppy disk to someone in that department and ask them to print it

Question 64

What is the UNC format for accessing a shared drive on a server?

- ○ a. /servername/sharename
- ○ b. \\servername\sharename
- ○ c. \\sharename
- ○ d. \\sharename\\servername

Question 65

During an initial workstation configuration for dial-up access to an Internet provider, the modems seem to connect to each other, but full communications is never established and the connection is dropped. What could be the problem?

- ○ a. The workstation is set up for PPP when it should be set up for SLIP.
- ○ b. The workstation is set up for SLIP when it should be set up for PPP.
- ○ c. The local modem is defective.
- ○ d. The telephone line is not data quality.

Question 66

What standard does the NetWare 4.x NDS correspond to?

- ○ a. IEEE 802.2
- ○ b. ITU X.400
- ○ c. ITU X.25
- ○ d. ITU X.500

Question 67

If a home user is having a modem connection problem, where is the best place to go to for technical support? [Choose the two best answers]

- ❑ a. The manufacturer's Web site
- ❑ b. Someone you know who has a computer
- ❑ c. Call the modem manufacturer for technical support
- ❑ d. Research the technical literature, hard copy, or CD-ROM for troubleshooting methods and try them

Question 68

Which TCP/IP utility would you use to connect to a Web server on port 80, send it HTTP commands, and interactively monitor the results to determine whether a problem exists?

○ a. FTP

○ b. Telnet

○ c. Tracert

○ d. SNMP

Question 69

If you add an ISA card to a system and one of the PCI cards stops working, how would you fix it?

○ a. Determine whether an IRQ or memory I/O conflict exists and change the value that is conflicting

○ b. Take the card out and forget about adding it

○ c. Send the card back because it is defective

○ d. Get a card from a different manufacturer and try it

Question 70

Which utility displays the NetBIOS over TCP/IP statistics?

○ a. NETSTAT

○ b. WINIPCFG

○ c. IPCONFIG

○ d. NBTSTAT

Question 71

Which utility displays the active OSI Transport layer ports that are open on a workstation or server?

○ a. NETSTAT

○ b. WINIPCFG

○ c. IPCONFIG

○ d. NBTSTAT

Question 72

Which device connects dissimilar protocols?

- ○ a. Switch
- ○ b. Gateway
- ○ c. Hub
- ○ d. Router

Question 73

What types of ports are on the front of an MAU? [Choose the three best answers]

- ❏ a. Ring in
- ❏ b. MAU in
- ❏ c. Ring out
- ❏ d. MAU out
- ❏ e. Token ring port

Question 74

If you have three or more hard drives and create a stripe set with parity data across all the drives, what RAID level would that be?

- ○ a. RAID 0
- ○ b. RAID 1
- ○ c. RAID 4
- ○ d. RAID 5

Answer Key

1. c
2. c
3. c
4. b, c, d, f
5. a, c
6. b
7. b
8. b
9. d
10. a
11. a
12. d
13. a
14. b
15. c
16. c
17. b
18. b
19. a, b
20. c
21. b
22. a
23. c
24. b
25. b
26. a
27. a, b, d
28. b
29. c
30. b
31. b
32. b, c
33. d
34. a
35. c
36. a
37. b
38. a, d
39. c
40. a
41. b, c, e
42. a, d, e
43. b, d
44. b, c, e
45. a
46. c
47. b
48. d
49. a
50. b
51. d
52. b, d
53. b, c
54. c
55. b
56. b
57. b, d, e, f
58. b
59. c
60. e
61. d
62. a
63. c
64. b
65. b
66. d
67. c, d
68. b
69. a
70. d
71. a
72. b
73. a, c, e
74. d

Question 1

The correct answer is c. In a peer-to-peer environment the workstations can share files and printers. A client/server environment has the server as the central point for file and print sharing. Therefore, answer a is incorrect. Ethernet is a type of topology. Therefore, answer b is incorrect. Terminals cannot share resources. Therefore, answer d is incorrect.

Question 2

The correct answer is c. A proxy server will cache the most active Web sites locally, decreasing Internet traffic and increasing Web response time. Answers a, b, and d are incorrect because firewalls, gateways, and NAT servers do not cache Web sites.

Question 3

The correct answer is c. The NIC is an OSI Physical layer device that constructs the packets for release on the physical medium. Answers a, b, and d are incorrect because memory, hard drive, and Pentium III chips are computer devices, not network devices.

Question 4

The correct answers are b, c, d, and f. Windows NT, NetWare, OS/2, and Unix all have basic file and print sharing along with security for multiple users. Answers a and e are incorrect because DOS and Windows are personal workstation operating systems and do not include the basic NOS functionality.

Question 5

The correct answers are a and c. NetWare Client32 is a third-party client provided by Novell, and Client for NetWare Networks is provided with Windows 95/98. Answers b and d are incorrect because Client for Microsoft Networks and the Microsoft Family Logon provide connectivity to Windows networks.

Question 6

The correct answer is b. NetWare NDS is a tree structure that contains objects for all users and devices in a NetWare LAN and WAN. Answer a is incorrect because the Bindery was the original NetWare database and was not designed in a tree fashion. Answer c is incorrect because NTDS is the directory services database for Windows NT. Answer d is incorrect because Vines is the directory services database for Banyan.

Question 7

The correct answer is b. IPCONFIG is used to display the IP configuration on a Windows NT workstation and server. Answer a is incorrect because WINIPCFG is used to display the configuration on Windows 95/98 workstations. Answers c and d are incorrect because they are fictitious.

Question 8

The correct answer is b. The default gateway is a usually a router, and without a correct default gateway specified in the TCP/IP parameters, a TCP/IP host cannot communicate beyond the local subnet. WINS is the Windows Internet Name Service. Therefore, answer a is incorrect. A DHCP server failing to assign an IP address would prohibit access to the local subnet. Therefore, answer c is incorrect. A host file on a router is irrelevant. Therefore, answer d is incorrect.

Question 9

The correct answer is d. NIC manufacturers are assigned a block of MAC addresses to assign a unique address to each NIC. A DHCP server assigns IP addresses to workstations. Therefore, answer a is incorrect. The MAC address is assigned during manufacturing. Therefore, answer b is incorrect. A MAC server does not exist. Therefore, answer c is incorrect.

Question 10

The correct answer is a. RAID 0 requires a minimum of two hard drives and is disk striping without parity. RAID 1 is mirroring/duplexing of two separate hard drives. Therefore, answer b is incorrect. RAID 4 requires a minimum of three drives, and one physical drive is the parity drive. Therefore, answer c is incorrect. RAID 5 requires a minimum of three drives, and the parity data is striped across all the drives. Therefore, answer d is incorrect.

Question 11

The correct answer is a. The NNTP TCP port is 119. SMTP is port 25. Therefore, answer b is incorrect. FTP is port 21. Therefore, answer c is incorrect. HTTP is port 80. Therefore, answer d is incorrect.

Question 12

The correct answer is d. A proxy server is set up in the Web browser. Answer a is incorrect because TCP/IP does not have a tab for proxy server setup. Answers b and c are incorrect because the security service and gateway service do not exist in Windows 95/98.

Question 13

The correct answer is a. The Tracert utility will display each router and the time it takes to communicate between each hop. ARP returns the MAC address for an IP address. Therefore, answer b is incorrect. Ping determines whether a node is reachable. Therefore, answer c is incorrect. IPCONFIG shows the IP configuration of a Windows NT workstation/server. Therefore, answer d is incorrect.

Question 14

The correct answer is b. RAID 1 is mirroring/duplexing. RAID 0 is disk striping without parity. Therefore, answer a is incorrect. RAID 4 requires a minimum of three drives, and one physical drive is the parity drive. Therefore, answer c is incorrect. RAID 5 requires a minimum of three drives, and the parity data is striped across all the drives. Therefore, answer d is incorrect.

Question 15

The correct answer is c. PPP has error-correcting and autonegotiating features and can encapsulate a variety of protocols. SLIP cannot perform autonegotiating and only encapsulates IP. Therefore, answer a is incorrect. SDLC and TCP/IP are not asynchronous protocols. Therefore, answers b and d are incorrect.

Question 16

The correct answer is c. PPTP uses the TCP/IP protocol as the transportation protocol between the ends of the tunnel. SLIP does not support PPTP. Therefore, answer a is incorrect. PPP encapsulates PPTP packets when one end of the tunnel is an asynchronous connection. Therefore, answer b is incorrect. The LLC is part of the OSI Data Link layer that controls access to the network medium. Therefore, answer d is incorrect.

Question 17

The correct answer is b. Static IP addresses are stored in the HOSTS file. Answer c is incorrect because LMHOSTS is the static database for the WINS information. Answers a and d are incorrect because they are fictitious.

Question 18

The correct answer is b. The 16550 UART chip can attain speeds of 256Kbps. The 8250 and 16450 chips cannot achieve speeds greater that 115.2Kbps. Therefore, answers a and c are incorrect. Answer d is incorrect because it is fictitious.

Question 19

The correct answers are a and b. A firewall opens the necessary ports to internal host computers, and password security will deter a hacker from easily gaining access. MAC port grouping and VLANs are ways to secure a LAN. Therefore, answers c and d are incorrect.

Question 20

The correct answer is c. A secure password should contain alpha, numeric, and special characters and be a minimum of seven characters long. Answer a is incorrect because it does not contain special characters. Answer b is incorrect because it contains too many characters. Answer d is incorrect because it does not contain alpha characters.

Question 21

The correct answer is b. The maximum length of a 10Base2 network segment is 185 meters. 100 meters is the maximum length of a 10BaseT/100BaseT network segment. Therefore, answer a is incorrect. 500 meters is the maximum length of a 10Base5 network segment. Therefore, answer c is incorrect. 2 kilometers is the maximum length of a 10BaseF/100BaseFL network segment. Therefore, answer d is incorrect. Answer e is incorrect because it is 15 meters longer than the maximum length allowed.

Question 22

The correct answer is a. The maximum length of a 10BaseT/100BaseT network segment is 100 meters. 185 meters is the maximum length of 10Base2 network. Therefore, answer b is incorrect. 500 meters is the maximum length of a 10Base5 network segment. Therefore, answer c is incorrect. 2 kilometers is the maximum length of a 10BaseF/100BaseFL network segment. Therefore, answer d is incorrect. Answer e is incorrect because it is 100 meters longer than the maximum length allowed.

Question 23

The correct answer is c. WINS associates an IP address to a NetBIOS name. DNS provides TCP/IP name resolution. Therefore, answer a is incorrect. DHCP dynamically assigns IP addresses. Therefore, answer b is incorrect. WSIN is fictitious. Therefore, answer d is incorrect.

Question 24

The correct answer is b. The Network Properties page has an Access Control tab that allows you to set up user-level access control. User-level access controls security from the server. Share-level access control is controlled from the workstation. Therefore, answer a is incorrect. Answers c and d are incorrect because they are fictitious.

Question 25

The correct answer is b. The FTP TCP port is 21. HTTP is port 80. Therefore, answer a is incorrect. SMTP is port 25. Therefore, answer c is incorrect. Telnet is port 23. Therefore, answer d is incorrect.

Question 26

The correct answer is a. The Network Properties page has an Access Control tab that allows you to set up share-level access control. Share-level access controls security from the workstation. User-level access controls security from the server. Therefore, answer b is incorrect. Answers c and d are incorrect because they are fictitious.

Question 27

The correct answers are a, b, and d. You can find each of those connectors on SCSI cards. Answers c and e are incorrect because they are fictitious.

Question 28

The correct answer is b. A hub repeats a signal on all ports. Answer a, c, and d are incorrect because a bridge, switch, and router are used to segment networks.

Question 29

The correct answer is c. A switch can segment a network into multiple segments and forward traffic between the ports at near wire speeds. A NIC and a hub do not segment networks. Therefore, answers a and b are incorrect. A router can segment a network, but that is not its primary function, and it cannot do it at wire speeds. Therefore, answer d is incorrect.

Question 30

The correct answer is b. A brouter has bridging and routing functions. A NIC connects a computer to the physical medium. Therefore, answer a is incorrect. A bridge segments two or more networks and forwards packets on the basis of the MAC address. Therefore, answer c is incorrect. A hub is a Physical layer device. Therefore, answer d is incorrect. A gateway works at layers 5 through 7 of the OSI model. Therefore, answer e is incorrect.

Question 31

The correct answer is b. An MAU is a device to which token ring stations connect. It is a concentrator with a ring inside it. The ring-in and ring-out ports allow for connection to other MAUs and increase the size of the ring. Answers a and c are incorrect because Ethernet and Fast Ethernet hubs are concentrators for an Ethernet network. Answers d and e are incorrect because a switch and a router can work in Ethernet, token ring, and many other types of networks, and they can segment a network.

Question 32

The correct answers are b and c. ARP -a and ARP -g display the IP address, MAC address, and whether it is dynamic or static. ARP -d deletes an entry from the ARP table. Therefore, answer a is incorrect. ARP -s adds a permanent static entry to the ARP table, Therefore, answer d is incorrect.

Question 33

The correct answer is d. A fully meshed network has redundant connections between routers. A star topology concentrates all the connections to one point, and the connections to a hub are in a star configuration. Therefore, answer a is incorrect. A basic bus topology is a coaxial Thinnet network. Therefore, answer b is correct. A backbone is usually the fastest part of a network and is where the servers are located. Therefore, answer c is incorrect.

Question 34

The correct answer is a. A star topology has all the connections returning to a central point that is usually a hub. A ring topology makes a connection from computer to computer. Therefore, answer b is incorrect. A basic bus topology is a Thinnet or Thicknet coaxial network. Therefore, answer c is incorrect. A fully meshed network is usually composed of a routed network. Therefore, answer d is incorrect.

Question 35

The correct answer is c. A bus topology has all the nodes connected to a coaxial cable. A star topology has all the nodes connected to a central hub. Therefore, answer a is incorrect. A ring topology makes connections from computer to computer. Therefore, answer b is incorrect. A fully meshed network is a routed network such as the Internet. Therefore, answer d is incorrect.

Question 36

The correct answer is a. The Telnet TCP port is 23. HTTP is port 80. Therefore, answer b is incorrect. POP3 is port 110. Therefore, answer c is incorrect. SMTP is port 25. Therefore, answer d is incorrect.

Question 37

The correct answer is b. A ring topology makes a connection from computer to computer and passes an access token around the network. A star topology has all the nodes connected to a central hub. Therefore, answer a is incorrect. A bus topology has all the nodes connected to a coaxial cable. Therefore, answer c is incorrect. A fully meshed network is a routed network such as the Internet. Therefore, answer d is incorrect.

Question 38

The correct answers are a and d. The characteristic of a device that works at the Data Link layer is that it uses the MAC address to forward packets to the proper destination. A hub and NIC work at the Physical layer of the OSI model. Therefore, answers b and c are incorrect. A router works at the Network layer of the OSI model. Therefore, answer e is incorrect. A gateway works at layers 5 through 7 of the OSI model. Therefore, answer f is incorrect.

Question 39

The correct answer is c. The NetBEUI protocol does not have a source and destination network address and therefore is nonroutable. It has to be bridged or switched if it is to be forwarded beyond its own segment. Answers a, b, and d are incorrect because AppleTalk, IPX, and TCP/IP are all routable protocols.

Question 40

The correct answer is a. A router looks at the source and destination network addresses and forwards the packet to the destination. A hub repeats the packet on all the ports. Therefore, answer b is incorrect. A gateway works at layers 5 through 7 of the OSI model. Therefore, answer c is incorrect. A switch and a bridge work at layer 2 of the OSI model. Therefore, answers d and e are incorrect.

Question 41

The correct answers are b, c, and e. TCP/IP, IPX, and AppleTalk have a source and destination network address that is required to route a packet. Answers a and d are incorrect because DLC and NetBEUI are not routable protocols.

Question 42

The correct answers are a, d, and e. IP, IPX, and UDP are connectionless-oriented protocols. Answers b and c are incorrect because TCP and SPX are connection-oriented protocols.

Question 43

The correct answers are b and d. TCP and SPX are connection-oriented protocols. Answers a, c, and e are incorrect because UDP is a connectionless-oriented protocol at the Data Link layer, and IP and IPX are connectionless-oriented protocols at the Network layer of the OSI model.

Question 44

The correct answers are b, c, and e. SPX, TCP, and UDP all work at the Transport layer of the OSI model. Answers a and d are incorrect because IP and IPX work at the Network layer of the OSI model.

Question 45

The correct answer is a. FTP and Telnet work at the Application layer (layer 7) of the OSI model. Answers b, c, d, and e are incorrect because the Physical, Data Link, Network, and Transport layers are layers 1 through 4 of the OSI model.

Question 46

The correct answer is c. IEEE 802.5 defines the standard for token-passing ring networks. IEEE 802.11 is the wireless network standard. Therefore, answer a is incorrect. 802.2 is the Logical Link Control. Therefore, answer b is incorrect. 802.3 defines the CSMA/CD standard. Therefore, answer d is incorrect. 802.12, 100VGAnyLan, defines the standard for demand priority access. Therefore, answer e is incorrect.

Question 47

The correct answer is b. The HTTP TCP port is 80. POP3 is port 110. Therefore, answer a is incorrect. FTP is port 21. Therefore, answer c is incorrect. SMTP is port 25. Therefore, answer d is incorrect.

Question 48

The correct answer is d. IEEE 802.3 defines the standard for Ethernet (CSMA/CD). 802.2 defines the standard for the Logical Link Control. Therefore, answer a is incorrect. 802.5 defines the token-passing ring standard.

Therefore, answer b is incorrect. 802.12, 100VGAnyLan, defines the standard for demand priority access. Therefore, answer c is incorrect. 802.11 defines the wireless network standard. Therefore, answer e is incorrect.

Question 49

The correct answer is a. IEEE 802.2 defines the standard for Logical Link Control. 802.11 defines the standard for wireless networks. Therefore, answer b is incorrect. 802.3 defines the standard for Ethernet networks. Therefore, answer c is incorrect. 802.5 defines the standard for token-passing ring networks. Therefore, answer d is incorrect. 802.12 defines the standard for demand priority access. Therefore, answer e is incorrect.

Question 50

The correct answer is b. SNMP is a Simple Network Management Protocol that monitors devices on a network, a server, or a workstation and reports the results to a management station. Answer a is incorrect because SMTP is a mail transfer protocol. Answers c and d are incorrect because SNAP and SNIFFER are fictitious protocols.

Question 51

The correct answer is d. DHCP dynamically assigns IP addresses for a network. WINS is the IP-to-Windows name resolution standard. Therefore, answer a is incorrect. DNS is the IP name standard. Therefore, answer b is incorrect. NDS is the Novell directory services standard. Therefore, answer c is incorrect. NTDS is the Windows NT domain directory standard. Therefore, answer e is incorrect.

Question 52

The correct answers are b and d. Both TCP/IP and IPX are supported on NetWare and Windows NT for connecting the two operating systems. DLC is a data link protocol. Therefore, answer a is incorrect. NetBEUI is supported by Windows NT but not by NetWare. Therefore, answer c is incorrect. RIP is a protocol used by routers to update their routing tables. Therefore, answer e is incorrect.

Question 53

The correct answers are b and c. Full and incremental backups reset the archive bit of each file that was backed up. Answers a and d are incorrect because differential and folder copy backups do not reset the archive bit. Answer e is incorrect because it is fictitious.

Question 54

The correct answer is c. Clean the tape drive with a cleaning tape. Answers a and d are incorrect because although they are options, they should not be exercised first. Answer b is incorrect because it is not a viable option.

Question 55

The correct answer is b. The backup tapes should be stored at an offsite location in case a disaster occurs where the server is located. Answers a, c, and d are incorrect because they suggest storing the tapes in the same building, and that is never a good idea, as fire could destroy the tapes.

Question 56

The correct answer is b. Too many space heaters can cause electrical and network interference. Answer a is incorrect because heat, not cold, is usually a killer of electrical equipment. Answer c is incorrect because it is not a realistic answer. Answer d is incorrect because although the central heating system could interfere with the network, it is usually better grounded and not in close proximity to network resources.

Question 57

The correct answers are b, d, e, and f. You would use a crossover cable to connect a PC to a PC, a hub to a hub, a hub to a switch, and a switch to a switch. Answers a and c are incorrect because hub-to-PC and switch-to-PC connections use a straight-through cable.

Question 58

The correct answer is b. All the answers are options to try when you suspect a bad cable, but a cable tester is the only option that does a through-test of the cable.

Question 59

The correct answer is c. Horizontal cable runs and patch cables are counted in the total length of a UTP cable run. Answer a is incorrect because patch cables are counted in the total length of the cable. Answers b and d are incorrect because you should never deploy a system when you know that the combined cable lengths exceed the maximum length.

Question 60

The correct answer is e. A boot sector virus will cause your system to fail to boot. Answers a, c, and d are incorrect because motherboard failure, hard drive failure, and memory failure can cause a system to fail, but you should check for a boot sector virus first. Answer b is incorrect because a Trojan horse usually collects passwords and other data and forwards it to a specified location.

Question 61

The correct answer is d. The maximum length of time between virus signature file updates should be monthly. Answers a, b, and c are incorrect because daily, hourly, and weekly are too often, unless a virus is detected between virus signature file updates. Answers e and f are incorrect because quarterly and annually are too long between virus signature file updates.

Question 62

The correct answer is a. Full duplex cannot work in a shared collision domain, and the data flows in both direction at the same time. Answer b is incorrect because full duplex cannot work in a shared collision domain. Answers c and d are incorrect because they are fictitious.

Question 63

The correct answer is c. Redirect the local printer port by capturing it to a shared print queue. Answers a, b, and d are incorrect because although they are possible solutions, they are not the best ones.

Question 64

The correct answer is b. The UNC format specifies two backslashes, the server name, one backslash, and the shared device name. Answers a, c, and d are incorrect because they are not in the correct format.

Question 65

The correct answer is b. Most Internet providers support PPP because it has more functionality than SLIP. Answer a is incorrect because if the connection were set up for PPP, it would not be a problem. Answers c and d are incorrect because although they could be the cause, the more likely cause would be an incorrectly specified protocol.

Question 66

The correct answer is d. The ITU X.500 is a directory service standard on which Novell based its NDS product. IEEE 802.2 sets the standard for Physical and Data Link layers in the OSI model. Therefore, answer a is incorrect. The ITU X.400 is a message delivery standard. Therefore, answer b is incorrect. The ITU X.25 is a packet-switching standard. Therefore, answer c is incorrect.

Question 67

The correct answers are c and d. Call technical support and review the product literature that was provided with the modem for troubleshooting tips. Going to the manufacturer's Web site is a great idea, but if you are having modem connection problems it is unlikely that you will be able to access it to get help. Therefore, answer a is incorrect. Calling someone who has a computer is not the best idea. Therefore, answer b is incorrect.

Question 68

The correct answer is b. The Telnet utility can open a TCP session on any specified port, commands can be sent to it, and the results can be monitored for troubleshooting purposes. Answer a, c, and d are incorrect because FTP, Tracert, and SNMP do not have this capability.

Question 69

The correct answer is a. Change the value in the card that is conflicting with the original card. Answers b, c, and d are incorrect because they are last-resort options.

Question 70

The correct answer is d. NBTSTAT display the statistics for NetBIOS over TCP/IP. NETSTAT displays the TCP ports that are active on a computer. Therefore, answer a is incorrect. WINIPCFG displays the IP configuration for a Windows 95/98 workstation. Therefore, answer b is incorrect. IPCONFIG displays the IP configuration for a Windows NT workstation or Windows NT server. Therefore, answer c is incorrect.

Question 71

The correct answer is a. NETSTAT displays the TCP ports that are active on a computer. WINIPCFG displays the IP configuration for a Windows 95/98 workstation. Therefore, answer b is incorrect. IPCONFIG displays the IP configuration for a Windows NT workstation or Windows NT server. Therefore, answer c is incorrect. NBTSTAT displays the statistics for NetBIOS over TCP/IP. Therefore, answer d is incorrect.

Question 72

The correct answer is b. A very popular gateway is an IPX-to-SNA gateway. It converts the IPX packet to an SNA packet and vice versa. A switch forwards packets on the basis of the MAC address. Therefore, answer a is incorrect. A hub repeats the signal on all ports. Therefore, answer c is incorrect. A router forwards packets of the same protocol to their intended destination. Therefore, answer d is incorrect.

Question 73

The correct answers are a, c, and e. An MAU has a ring-in, ring-out, and ports to connect token ring workstations. Answers b and d are incorrect because they are fictitious.

Question 74

The correct answer is d. RAID 5 requires a minimum of three hard drives, and the parity data is striped across all the hard drives in the RAID set. RAID 0 is disk striping without parity. Therefore, answer a is incorrect. RAID 1 is mirroring/duplexing of two hard drives. Therefore, answer b is incorrect. RAID 4 requires a minimum of three hard drives, with one of the hard drives storing the parity data. Therefore, answer c is incorrect.

Glossary

Address Resolution Protocol (ARP)—A protocol used to correlate MAC addresses with IP addresses.

Application layer—Layer 7 of the OSI model, which provides distributed information services and is the layer at which users access the OSI model.

Asynchronous Transfer Mode (ATM)—A cell-based protocol for transmitting/switching voice, data, and video traffic.

ATM adaptation layer (AAL)—A protocol that enables an ATM network to provide a variety of services.

backbone—A backbone network is used to tie diverse networks together. It is also where the main network services reside.

backup domain controller (BDC)—A server in a Windows NT network that is configured to provide auxiliary authentication services in case the primary domain controller goes down.

bandwidth—Refers to the difference between the highest and lowest frequencies of a transmission channel. It often defines the information-carrying capacity of a channel.

baseband—A baseband network is a digital network. Voltage is applied to the medium that represents a one or a zero.

baseline—The initial speed and performance configuration of a network.

Basic Rate ISDN (BRI)—A version of ISDN that comprises two B channels and a D channel and uses existing copper wire to provide digital voice and data communications.

bridge—A device that connects two LANs together and where no protocol conversion is needed. It operates at layer 2 of the OSI model.

broadband—Any communication channel that can carry services with bandwidth exceeding that for voice, such as high-speed data and video transmissions. Cable television uses broadband technology.

Broadband ISDN (B-ISDN)—Refers to advanced versions of ISDN, such as ATM, providing speeds of 155Mbps and greater. Provides high-capacity, high-performance voice, video, data, and integrated multimedia services.

cabling plant—The comprehensive cabling layout of your facility.

carrier sense multiple access/collision detection (CSMA/CD)—A LAN access technique that allows a NIC to sense the medium, transmit a packet, and then detect collisions on the line.

Challenge Handshake Authentication Protocol (CHAP)—A secure challenge and response security mechanism for verifying the identity of a user.

change control system—A system of controlling the types of changes made to the network and how they are implemented.

channel service unit (CSU)—A device that connects with the digital communication line and provides a termination for the digital signal. Usually used with a DSU.

client/server networking—A network in which a server (or set of servers) act as the authentication and access point to all the devices and directories on a network.

clustering—The server fault tolerance method that is implemented in Windows NT networks to provide seamless failover in case of a server failure. It requires two servers with similar hardware that are connected to a shared external hard drive cabinet.

coaxial cable—A stranded or solid copper wire used for transmissions at frequencies below 1GHz.

connection-oriented protocol—A protocol, such as SPX and TCP, that does guarantee the delivery of data packets.

connectionless-oriented protocol—A protocol, such as UDP, IP, or IPX, that does not guarantee the delivery of data packets.

corrective maintenance (CM)—The process of repairing faults with devices in the network.

crossover cable—Usually a category 5 cable that is used to connect two network devices, such as two hubs, two computers without a hub, two switches, or a switch and a hub. It is called a crossover cable because pins 1 and 3 are switched and pins 2 and 6 are switched.

data communication equipment (DCE)—Any device that can communicate with the appropriate DTE and provide access to the appropriate line type. In analog communications, it usually refers to a modem that is used in conjunction with a computer as the DTE. In digital communications, it refers to a DSU/CSU.

data encryption—The coding of a signal so that it cannot be read by an unauthorized receiver without a decoder.

Data Link layer—Layer 2 of the OSI model, which establishes, maintains, and releases the data connection between two elements in a network.

data service unit (DSU)—A device that is necessary in transmitting digital data over a hardware channel. It converts signals from bridges, routers, and multiplexers into digital signals. Usually used with a CSU.

data terminal equipment (DTE)—In telecommunications, a computer that can communicate with a DCE.

datagram—A message consisting of a short packet that is sent through the network, usually without first setting up a path.

diagnostics—Usually, software designed to verify the functioning of a specific piece of hardware or a software package.

dial-in—Also called remote connectivity. Dial-in allows a user to access a LAN or a WAN through a remote workstation. This access can be through the Internet or a direct IP connection.

disk duplexing—A fault tolerance method similar to disk mirroring, except that the second drive uses its own controller.

disk mirroring—A fault tolerance method in which the system makes an exact copy of all the data on one drive and writes it to a second drive of equal or greater size. Both drives use the same controller.

DoD model—A four-layer networking model that produced the structure for the Internet. It separates network functions into four layers—the Network Access, Internet, Host-to-Host, and Process layers—as compared to the OSI model, which separates them into seven layers.

Domain Name System (DNS)—A hierarchical routing structure that links domain names to IP addresses.

Dynamic Host Configuration Protocol (DHCP)—A protocol that allows you to dynamically configure TCP/IP nodes and manage them from a central location. It automatically assigns IP addresses and other TCP/IP host addresses, such as DNS, WINS servers, and default gateways.

encapsulation—The process used to send data across a network where the network is not able to recognize the protocol used. The data is encapsulated in its entirety so that the network does not need to decode it. The device at the receiving end strips out the encapsulation before interpreting the data.

Ethernet—A shared-media network architecture that is currently the most widely used architecture for LANs. It operates at the Physical and Data Link layers of the OSI model, uses a bus topology, operates at speeds up to 10Mbps, and uses CSMA/CD.

Fiber Distributed Data Interface (FDDI)—A network architecture that is designed to use fiber-optic lines at very high speeds. It uses a ring topology, can support up to 1,000 nodes on the network, and can support a network span of up to 100 kilometers.

fiber optics—Refers to a communications cable type that uses photon energy along glass fibers instead of electrical impulses along copper wire to transmit signals.

File Transfer Protocol (FTP)—A TCP/IP service that runs on a host computer that allows files to be uploaded or downloaded. It is also the default file transfer protocol for Unix.

firewall—A network component that provides data security between networks, network segments, or LANs and WANs. Usually works in conjunction with gateways.

fix—A vendor-supplied solution to a problem, usually design based, with a network device or software that was discovered only after release of the product.

full duplex—A communications channel that can transmit data in both directions simultaneously.

fully qualified domain name (FQDN)—The complete name for a machine on the network, comprising the hostname and the domain name.

gateway—A default route for all TCP/IP packets that are not destined for the local subnet.

half duplex—A communications channel that can transmit data in both directions, but only one direction at a time.

host—A workstation or server on a TCP/IP network.

HOSTS file—A static database through which static IP addresses are correlated to domain names. It has been replaced by DNS servers, which correlate IP addresses dynamically.

hub—The device that is normally at the center of a star topology network and to which other devices in the network connect. Hubs are essentially repeaters.

Hypertext Transfer Protocol (HTTP)—The protocol that forms a connection between the workstation Web browser and the Web server. Its secure versions are S-HTTP and SSL.

Integrated Services Digital Network (ISDN)—A technique for the simultaneous transmission of a range of services, such as voice, data, and video, over telephone lines.

intermediate distribution facility (IDF)—An intermediate location for routing network cabling in a building. It is connected to the users at one end and to the MDF at the other.

Internet—A giant internetwork originally created to link various research, defense, and corporate networks together.

Internet Information Server (IIS)—The Web server component that is included with Microsoft Windows NT.

Internet Protocol (IP)—A connectionless-oriented protocol that serves as the framework protocol for the Internet and other TCP/IP networks, providing the structure to link subnets into a larger internetwork.

Internet service provider (ISP)—The local, regional, national, or global organizations that provide Internet connection services to both private and enterprise entities.

Internetwork Packet Exchange (IPX)—A protocol based on the Xerox Network System protocol. It is a connectionless-oriented internetworking protocol that provides datagram services. Several NOSs and most desktop operating systems support IPX. It is widely used in NetWare 3.x and 4.x environments.

IP address—A 32-bit number that comprises the host network address and the host node address on the network.

IPCONFIG—A command that displays the TCP/IP settings of a Windows NT computer.

knowledge base—Either a CD-ROM or a component of a manufacturer's Web site that provides comprehensive information on its products/services.

legacy equipment—Older equipment in a network that is functioning with newer equipment.

Lightweight Directory Access Protocol (LDAP)—An IP-based, X.500-based directory service database used in NetWare 4 and higher, through which you can display information about a network and its resources.

Link Control Protocol (LCP)—A component of PPP that configures and tests the data link and negotiates the highest reliable transmission speed before the transmission occurs.

local area network (LAN)—A geographically centralized grouping of network equipment (hubs, bridges, switches, and routers), usually governed by a main server or servers and accessed by user workstations.

loopback—A system/device test method that sends a signal to the device being tested; the signal is returned to the transmitter for comparison with the original transmission.

main distribution facility (MDF)—The central distribution point for the network cabling to a building. The cabling from the MDF can connect to either an IDF or the end users. The MDF can also serve to connect a LAN to a WAN.

maintenance history—A document that contains a history of all the trouble calls and their resolution.

media access control (MAC)—Together with the logical link control, provides higher-level protocols with access to the physical network medium. The MAC address is a unique value that is assigned to NICs by the manufacturer and identifies a specific machine on a network.

megabits per second (Mbps or Mb/s)—A unit of measurement for data transmission speed.

megahertz (MHz)—A unit of measurement for line frequency.

multistation access unit (MAU)—A token ring concentrator that forms an internal ring while the cable terminates to a central location.

NBTSTAT—A command utility for troubleshooting NetBIOS name resolution problems that can correct or remove preloaded NetBIOS entries.

NetBEUI Frame (NBF)—A transport driver that implements the NetBEUI 3 specification and exceeds the 254-session barrier of NetBEUI.

NetBIOS Extended User Interface (NetBEUI)—An IBM/MS proprietary, nonroutable protocol that is best used on small LANs of less than 50 people. It provides a fast transport, has low memory requirements, and does not need configuring.

NETSTAT—A command utility that shows the status of all TCP and UDP port activity on a workstation or server.

Network Control Protocol (NCP)—A component of PPP that establishes a connection with and configures the one or more Network layer protocols that PPP encapsulates and transports.

network interface card (NIC)—A card installed inside network devices that allows the device to connect to the network. It operates on layer 1 of the OSI model.

Network layer—Layer 3 of the OSI model responsible for connecting networks in a LAN or a WAN environment and routing data on a network-wide basis.

network model—The most basic of network formations that is either peer-to-peer based or client/server based.

network operating system (NOS)—A central control software that manages all aspects of a network's hardware and application software.

network topology—The physical or logical arrangement of nodes located on a network, such as star, tree, bus, and mesh.

networking medium—Refers to the network cabling used for signal transmission, including patch panels, patch cables, and crossover cables. It can be fiber, copper, or free space.

Novell Directory Services (NDS)—An X.500-based directory structure that configures the network in a tree structure. It also provides contextless login to allow users to authenticate from any point on the network.

NT Directory Services (NTDS)—A directory structure that provides all the directory services and the security database for all Windows NT domains. It stores all the security information in a PDC and replicates it to the BDCs within the domain.

Open Systems Interconnect (OSI) model—Defined by the International Organization for Standardization (ISO) in which functions are broken into seven layers, each layer providing clearly defined services to adjacent layers to effect network communication.

Packet Internet Groper (Ping)—A command utility that sends an Internet Control Message Protocol echo request message to a host on a TCP/IP network to test network connectivity, and then registers the time it took for a response.

patch—A compilation of hardware or software fixes from the manufacturer.

patch cable—Cables that can connect computers to UTP faceplates or connect a patch panel to a network device, such as a hub or a switch.

patch panel—Used to provide flexibility within the structured cabling system. Can be used for either horizontal patching, which reroutes service between desks, or vertical patching, which reroutes service between floors.

peer-to-peer networking—A networking system in which devices that perform the same function (usually workstations) communicate directly with one another. In a peer-to-peer environment, each workstation functions as both server and client.

Physical layer—Layer 1 of the OSI model that is responsible for the electrical, mechanical, and interface aspects of transmitted data.

plain old telephone service (POTS)—Refers to ordinary, analog, voice telephone service that uses twisted-pair cable to connect homes and businesses to a central office.

plug-and-play (PnP)—Any device that dynamically configures when it is installed in a computer.

Point-to-Point Protocol (PPP)—A Data Link layer protocol that encapsulates other Network layer protocols, such as TCP/IP and IPX, for transmission on synchronous and asynchronous communication lines. It can encapsulate multiple protocols in a given session.

Point-to-Point Tunneling Protocol (PPTP)—A networking protocol that supports multiprotocol, virtual private networks that enable remote users to access corporate networks securely across the Internet through TCP/IP networks. It encapsulates and compresses the PPP packets into IP datagrams and routes them over the Internet.

Post Office Protocol 3 (POP3)—The TCP/IP mail server protocol that delivers mail to clients on a TCP/IP network.

preemptive multitasking—An NOS tasking scheme in which tasks of higher priority preempt those of a lower priority.

Presentation layer—Layer 6 of the OSI model that enables the Application layer to interpret the data being exchanged between two systems.

preventive maintenance (PM)—Scheduled maintenance to ensure against network outages due to equipment wear, environmental variances and interference, and other preventable causes.

primary domain controller (PDC)—A server in a Windows NT network that provides primary authentication, network access, and device/directory structure. Should the PDC fail, a BDC is promoted to perform these functions.

Primary Rate ISDN (PRI)—A circuit-switched network consisting of 23 B channels, which can be strapped together for greater bandwidth, and one D channel.

private branch exchange (PBX)—A telephone switch that usually connects telephones and other communications devices within a company to an outside line.

protocol—Communication rules that define and carry out a specific function, such as exchange of information between two systems, synchronization, and error checking.

proxy server—A device that takes a request from a user on a trusted network, repackages the request, and sends it to an untrusted network.

redundant array of inexpensive disks (RAID)—Refers to a computer storage and fault tolerance system that uses several disk drives in a redundant configuration.

Remote Access Service (RAS)—Provides communication services for remote dial-up users.

router—A layer 3 device that can choose the routes along which it can send data in a network, depending on protocol and IP address.

segment—An Ethernet collision domain.

Sequenced Packet Exchange (SPX)—A connection-oriented protocol that resides in the Transport layer of the OSI model to provide transport services similar to TCP. It is widely used in NetWare 3.x and 4.x environments.

Serial Line Internet Protocol (SLIP)—The popular encapsulation protocol before PPP. It connects one TCP/IP system with another over a modem link and then encapsulates the IP packets into the Data Link layer and transmits them between the modems. SLIP can encapsulate only IP packets, as compared with PPP, which can encapsulate several different protocols.

server—A computer that has an NOS installed on it to provide file and print sharing functions.

server fault tolerance (SFT)—A fault tolerance method implemented in NetWare networks. It is composed of two identical servers with the same hardware configuration. The servers are connected with a mirrored server link to provide seamless takeover.

Session layer—Layer 5 of the OSI model, which is responsible for setting up and breaking links between communicating elements.

shielded twisted pair (STP)—Copper twisted-pair cable that is surrounded by a wire gauze shield.

Simple Mail Transfer Protocol (SMTP)—The protocol that transfers mail between mail servers on a TCP/IP network. It can be set up as a mail relay server or can deliver to a virtual post office.

Simple Network Management Protocol (SNMP)—A network management protocol that collects statistics from devices on a TCP/IP network. It loads an agent that collects information and forwards it to a network management console.

small computer systems interface (SCSI)—Refers to a communications bus that allows up to seven peripheral devices to connect to the computer.

standard operating procedures (SOP)—Operational guidelines set forth by the IS department to standardize both normal and emergency operating procedures.

subnet mask—A way to break down an IP address into more network addresses and less nodes if the default is not used.

symmetric multiprocessing (SMP)—An NOS design in which system resources are shared by all the processors in the system so that the workload is distributed evenly.

Synchronous Optical Network (SONET)—Refers to a synchronous optical transmission system.

Systems Network Architecture (SNA)—An IBM protocol for connecting to mainframes.

Telnet—Provides a terminal emulation window through which you can access remote routers and Unix systems on a TCP/IP network. It is used to modify router commands and run host applications in Unix systems.

Thicknet—A solid-core coaxial cable type also known as 10Base5. It has a communication speed of 10Mbps and is limited to a length of 500 meters per segment.

Thinnet—A coaxial cable type comprised of strands of copper wire and commonly known as 10Base2. It has a communication speed of 10Mbps and is limited to a length of 185 meters per segment.

total cost of ownership (TCO)—The comprehensive cost of purchasing, installing, and maintaining a network.

Tracert—A command utility that traces the route of a packet between two locations and displays the router hops taken to get there.

Transmission Control Protocol/Internet Protocol (TCP/IP)—The TCP connection-oriented delivery service that uses IP as the transport to deliver information across the network. TCP/IP is the protocol of the Internet.

Transport layer—Layer 4 of the OSI model, which is responsible for guaranteed delivery of data.

trouble call—A request for maintenance, usually initiated by a user.

troubleshooting—The process of isolating a system fault.

universal asynchronous receiver/transmitter (UART)—An integrated circuit for transmission of asynchronous data. The UART is used in serial cards for PCs.

universal naming convention (UNC)—A standard syntax to gain access to shared resources on an NOS regardless of the NOS vendor.

universal resource locator (URL)—The addressing scheme used to identify resources on the Internet.

unshielded twisted pair (UTP)—A cable type that has four twisted pairs of wires to eliminate crosstalk. It is the preferred cable type for LANs.

User Datagram Protocol (UDP)—A connectionless-oriented, Transport layer component that provides unreliable data delivery for time-sensitive data. Because it does not have the overhead of TCP, it can send data much faster between locations.

user profiles—Administrator-defined description of what the user's desktop looks like and what functions users have from the desktop.

user rights—Administrator-defined description of the devices and directories on the network that a user has access to.

virtual private network (VPN)—A private, secure network between a remote client and an enterprise network created by a PPP tunnel through the Internet.

virus—Any maliciously created program that infects a network or workstation at its most basic level in order to destroy data. The most destructive of these are boot sector, master boot sector, and partition table viruses.

wide area network (WAN)—Based on the principle of LANs but meant to provide communications and data transfer between geographically separated locations.

Windows Internet Name Service (WINS)—A database that correlates IP addresses to NetBIOS computer names in a Windows-only networking environment. It provides an avenue to deploy TCP/IP-only Windows NT networks without losing any of the functionality provided by NetBIOS names.

WINIPCFG—A graphical representation of all the TCP/IP configurations in a Windows 95/98 workstation. It performs relatively the same function as the IPCONFIG command, but on a different platform.

workstation—The user interface to a network that comprises, at a minimum, a monitor, a CPU, and a keyboard.

X.500—A standard developed by the ITU and ISO that acts as the foundational structure for directory structures.

Index

Bold page numbers indicate sample exam questions.

10Base2. *See* Thinnet.
10Base5. *See* Thicknet.
10BaseFX cable, **30**
10BaseT, 16–17
10-tape rotation method, 92
100BaseT4, 17
100BaseX, 17
100VGAnyLan cable scheme, 17
16550 UART chip, 109, **112**, **299**
3Com Transcend, 246
50-pin high-density connector, 188–189, **199**, 302
68-pin high-density connector, 189, **200**, **302**
80-pin single connector attachment, 189

A

A+ Exam Cram (book), 115, 181
AAL (ATM Adaption Layer), 108
Access control lists. *See* ACL.
Access rights, 228
ACL (access control lists), 121
ACU (Automatic Client Upgrade), 45
Add Printer Wizard (Windows NT Server), 39
Add User Accounts Wizard (Windows NT Server), 39
Add/Remove Programs Wizard (Windows NT Server), 39
Address Resolution Protocol. *See* ARP.
Administrative Wizard (Windows NT Server), 39
Administrator account, **232**
Administrator utility, 265
ANSI X3T9 committee, 189
Antivirus software, 126–128, **133–134**, 240
　　Dr. Solomon's Anti-Virus, 127
　　McAfee VirusScan, 127
　　Norton AntiVirus, 128
　　PC-cillin, 128
AppleShare server, 50
AppleTalk, **306**
Application layer (OSI), 152, **163**, **307**
ARP (Address Resolution Protocol), 69, 279, **283**, **303**
Asynchronous protocols, **298**
Asynchronous transfer mode. *See* ATM.
AT&T Bell Laboratories, 45
ATM (asynchronous transfer mode), 25, 107
ATM adaption layer. *See* AAL.
Attachment unit interface. *See* AUI.
Audit services, 122
AUI (attachment unit interface), 186
Authentication services, 122
Automatic Client Upgrade. *See* ACU.

B

B-ISDN (broadband ISDN), 107–108
Backbones
　　repeaters on, 141
　　topology, 25
BackOffice suite (Microsoft), 37
Backup domain controller. *See* BDC.
Backup techniques, 228–229, **233**, 239, 309. *See also* Tape backups.
Baseband networks, 27
Baselines, 224
Basic rate ISDN. *See* BRI.
Basic segments, 24
Bay Networks Optivity Network Management software, 246
Bayonet nut connector. *See* BNC.
BDC (backup domain controller), 37
Benchmark testing, 211
Berkeley Software Distribution. *See* BSD.
Bindery (Novell), 40
BNC (bayonet nut connector), 186
Boot sector viruses, 125, **134**, **284**, **311**

BRI (basic rate ISDN), 106–107, **112**, **114**
Bridges, 12, 143, 193, 270, **305**
Broadband ISDN. *See* B-ISDN.
Broadband transmissions, 27
Brouters (bridging router), **4**, 148, **158**, 193, **201**, **303**
BSD (Berkeley Software Distribution), 46
See also Unix.
Bus topology, 25, **304**

C

Cable
   10Base2, **29**
   10BaseFX, **30**
   10BaseT, 16–17
   100BaseT4, 17
   100BaseTX, 17
   100BaseX, 17
   100VGAnyLan, 17
   cabling plant design, 206
   CAT 3 UTP, 17
   CAT 5 UTP, 17
   category 5, 13
   coaxial, 14
   crossover cable, 19, **30–31**, **310**
   fiber-optic, 13, 171, **178**, 195
   multimode fiber-optic, 18, **218**, 206
   patch, 18–19
   RG58 A/U, 15
   single-mode fiber optic, 18
   testers, 245
   troubleshooting, **31–32**
   twisted-pair, 15–16
Cable testers, 13–14, **311**
Caller ID logs, 120
CAPTURE command, 229, **235**
Carrier sense multiple access/collision detection. *See* CSMA/CD.
CAT 3 UTP (Category 3 Unshielded Twisted Pair) cable, 17
CAT 5 UTP (Category 5 Unshielded Twisted Pair) cable, 12, 13, 17, 195, **300**
CCITT. *See* ITU.
CCITT X.200. *See* OSI reference model.
Centronics 50-pin connector, 188
Challenge Handshake Authentication Protocol. *See* CHAP.
Channel service unit/data service units. *See* CSU/DSUs.
CHAP (Challenge Handshake Authentication Protocol), 104

Checkboxes, 4
Clean Wizard, 128
Client configuration, 206–207
Client for NetWare Networks, **296**
Client/server network model, 22
Clustering, 86, 89
CM (corrective maintenance), 254
   follow-ups, 281
   maintenance histories, 281
Coaxial cable, 14–15
COM ports, **114**
Compatibility mode (NetWare 5), 43
Complex segments, 24
CompTIA certification exams, 2–3, 8, 290–291
   multiple-choice questions, 3
   Network+ home page, 8–9
Configuration Manager (NetWare 5), 44
Connection-oriented service, 151
Connectionless-oriented protocol, 149–151, **163**
Connectivity, 208
   communication cables, 172
   electrical lines, 172
Connectors
   50-pin high-density connector, **199**
   68-pin high-density connectors, **200**
   RJ-45 connectors, 195
ConsoleOne, 42
Contingency plans, **230**, **231**
Control system alterations, **233–234**
Corrective maintenance. *See* CM.
Cram Sheet, 2, 293
Crossover cables, 19, **30–31**, **310**
CSMA/CD (carrier sense multiple access/collision detection), 26, 148
CSU/DSUs (channel service unit/data service units), 13

D

Daily backups, 91
DARPA Internetwork Project. *See* Internet.
DAT (digital audio tape), 89
Data encryption, 123–124
Data Encryption Standard. *See* DES.
Data Link layer (OSI), 100, 142–148, 159–160, **303**
   brouters, **4**
   PPP, 101

Data recovery plans
　for workstations, 215
　Y2K, 215
DB-9 serial connector, 186
DB-25 SCSI connectors, 188, **200**, **302**
DB-25 serial connector, 186–187
DEC (Digital Equipment Corporation), 46
Default gateway, 68, **83**, 148–149
Department of Defense. *See* DoD.
DES (Data Encryption Standard), 123
Destructive viruses, 124
DHCP (Dynamic Host Configuration
　Protocol), 37, 68, **309**
　DHCP Server, 279
　NetWare services utility, 43
Diagnostics, 272–280
　cable testers, 273
　hardware loop-back, 272
　IPCONFIG utility, 278
　NETSTAT utility, 275–277, **286**
　Ping utility, 273
　software, 256, 272–273
　Telnet, 274–275
　Tracert utility, 277
　WINIPCFG utility, 278–279
Differential backups, 91
Digital audio tape. *See* DAT.
Digital Equipment Corporation. *See* DEC.
Digital linear tape. *See* DLT.
Directory services, 47–49
Disk duplexing, 87, **97**
Disk mirroring, 38, 87
Disk striping, 38
Disk striping with parity. *See* RAID Level 5.
DLT (digital linear tape), 89
DNS (domain name system), 21, 65–67, **74**
　Configuration tab, 66–67
　DNS Server, 37
　hierarchical structure, 65–66
　NetWare service utility, 43
　servers, 68
　troubleshooting, 267
DoD (Department of Defense), 153–154
　Host-to-Host layer, 154
　Internet layer, 153–154
　Network Access layer, 153
　Process layer, 154
Domain controllers, 39
Domain name system. *See* DNS.
Dr. Solomon's Anti-Virus, 127

Drive mapping, **234–235**
Duplexing, 26–27, 87, **97**
　full-duplex transmissions, 26, **31**
　half-duplex transmissions, 26
Dynamic Host Configuration Protocol.
　See DHCP.

E

Electromagnetic interference, 171, 244,
　285, **310**
Emergency response, 212–216
　disaster recovery plan, 214–215, **221**
　escalation procedures, 213–214, **220**
　for network equipment, 225
　response team, 213
　for servers, 225
　for workstations, 225
Encapsulation protocols, 100–103
Encryption services, 122
Encyclopedia of Networking, 136
*Encyclopedia of Networking, Electronic
　Edition*, 33, 54, 84, 98, 115, 136, 164,
　181, 204, 222, 252, 287
Enhanced small device interface. *See* ESDI.
Equipment documentation, 255
Equipment environment, monitoring,
　243–244
ESDI (enhanced small device interface),
　86, **96**
Ethernet, 27, **31**, 140, **312**
Ethernet frame types, 57
Event Log Service (Windows NT
　Server), 40
Event Viewer (Windows NT Server), 39–40
Events, 39–40
Exam
　answer-elimination skills, 290–291
　budgeting time for, 7
　exhibits, 4–5, 290
　guessing, 5, 7
　marking questions for later visit, 5
　memorization, 293
　notes, 292
　practice exam, 293
　question ambiguity, 6
　question-handling strategies, 6–7
　questions, 3–4, 290–291
　testing software, 292
Exhibits, 4–5, 290

F

Fail-safe plans, 227
Fast Ethernet, **31**, 140, **285**
Fault tolerance, 86
FDDI (fiber distributed data interface), 25
Fiber-channel connectors, 189
Fiber distributed data interface. *See* FDDI.
Fiber-optic cable, 13, 18, 171, **178**, 195.
  See also Multimode fiber-optic cable.
  multimode, 18
  single-mode, 18
File-infecting viruses, 125
File Transfer Protocol. *See* FTP.
Firewalls, 130, **132**, 299
  gateways, 21
  packet-filtering, 131
  proxy server firewalls, 131
  stateful inspection firewalls, 131
Fixes, **249–250**
Frame relay cloud, 13
FTP (File Transfer Protocol), 69, 76, **80**, 301
Full-duplex Ethernet, **312**
Full-duplex transmission, 26, **31**

G

Gateways, 20, **28–29**, 67, 193, **315**
  addresses, **297**
  default, 68, 148–149
  firewall, 21
  proxy server, 21
  standard router, 20
  troubleshooting, 270
Grandfather tape rotation method, 92
Group Management Wizard (Windows NT Server), 39

H

Half-duplex transmissions, 26
Hardware flash updates, 242
HDLC (High-Level Data Link Control), 102
High-Level Data Link Control. *See* HDLC.
HOSTS file, 69, **74**, 299
HP OpenView, 246
HP-UX (Hewlett-Packard Unix), 46
HTTP (Hypertext Transfer Protocol), 70
  port assignment, **77**, **308**
  proxy server, **79**
Hubs, 191, 270, **282**, 302
Hypertext Transfer Protocol. *See* HTTP.

I

I2O (Intelligent I/O), 42
IBM AIX (IBM Unix), 46
ICMP (Internet Control Message Protocol), 72, 273
IDE (integrated drive electronics), 86, **96**
IDF (intermediate distribution facility), 12, 170
IEEE (Institute for Electrical and Electronic Engineers), 145
  IEEE 802.1 Internetwork Definition, 145
  IEEE 802.2 Logical Link Control, 145, **308**
  IEEE 802.3 Ethernet, 146, **308**
  IEEE 802.4 Token Bus Networks, 146
  IEEE 802.5 Token Ring Networks, 146, **307**
  IEEE 802.6 Metropolitan Area Networks, 147
  IEEE 802.7 Broadband Technical Advisory Group, 147
  IEEE 802.8 Fiber-Optic Technical Advisory Group, 147
  IEEE 802.9 Integrated Data and Voice Networks, 147
  IEEE 802.10 Network Security Technical Advisory Group, 147
  IEEE 802.11 Wireless Networking, 147
  IEEE 802.12 Demand Priority, 147
  IEEE 802.14 Cable Modems, 147
IETF (Internet Engineering Task Force), 49
IGRATE utility (NetWare 5), 45
IIS (Internet Information Server)
Incremental tape backups, 91, **94**, **309**
Install New Modem Wizard (Windows NT Server), 39, 109
Installation plans, 170
Institute for Electrical and Electronic Engineers. *See* IEEE.
Integrated drive electronics. *See* IDE.
Integrated Services Digital Network. *See* ISDN.
Intelligent I/O. *See* I2O.
Intermediate distribution facility. *See* IDF.
International Telecommunications Union. *See* ITU.
Internet, 100
  as connectionless-oriented network, 150
  as DARPA Internetwork Project, 153

Internet Control Message Protocol.
   See ICMP.
Internet Engineering Task Force. *See* IETF.
Internet Information Server. *See* IIS
Internet Network Information Center.
   See InterNIC.
Internet Protocol. *See* IP.
Internetwork Packet Exchange. *See* IPX.
InterNIC (Internet Network Information
   Center), 66
Interrupt Requests. *See* IRQ.
IP (Internet Protocol), 59–63, **162**, **306**
   addresses, 60–61, 68, 267
   Class A addresses, 61
   Class B addresses, 61
   Class C addresses, 61
   default gateway, 60
   HOSTS file and, 69
   single address assignment to multiple
      workstations, **75–76**
   static address assignment, **75**
   troubleshooting, **282**
IPCONFIG utility, 278, **296**
IPCONFIG.EXE command, 71
IPX (Internetwork Packet Exchange),
   56–58, 104, **161**, **162**, **306**, **309**
IPX packet structure, 57
IRQ (Interrupt Requests), **114**, 267–268, **314**
ISDN (Integrated Services Digital
   Network), 106–108, **112**, **113**
ITU (International Telecommunications
   Union), 47, 52
ITU X.500 standard, **313**

J

Java (Sun Microsystems), 50
JVM (Java Virtual Machine), 42–43

L

LANs (local area networks), 12–13, 56, 100
   NOS security, 207
   Windows NT Server, 36–37
Laptop operating systems
   patching, 241
   upgrading, 241
LCP (Link Control Protocol), 102–103
LDAP (Lightweight Directory Access
   Protocol), 49
License Wizard (Windows NT Server), 39
Lightweight Directory Access Protocol.
   See LDAP.

Line conditioners, 171
Link Control Protocol. *See* LCP.
Linux, 46
LiveUpdate, 128
LLC (Logical Link Control), 142
LOAD command (NetWare 5), 41
Local area networks. *See* LANs.
Local Security Authorization. *See* LSA.
Logic bombs, 129
Logical Link Control. *See* LLC.
Login errors, 265
Loop-back connectors, **156**, 245
LSA (Local Security Authorization), 120

M

MAC (media access control), 58, 142,
   155, **297**
Macintosh, 50
Macro viruses, 125–126
Main distribution facility. *See* MDF.
Maintenance, 228–229
Managing File and Folder Access Wizard
   (Windows NT Server), 39
MANs (metropolitan area networks), 147
map command, 229
MAU (multistation access unit), 141, **303**, **315**
McAfee VirusScan, 127
MDF (main distribution facility), 12, 170
Media access control. *See* MAC.
Media filters, 142
Mesh network topology, 23, **29–30**, **303**
Meta viruses, 126
Metropolitan area networks. *See* MANs.
Microsoft BackOffice suite, 37
Microsoft Client for NetWare Networks,
   51–52
Migration Gateway (NetWare 5), 41
Migration plans
   one-time implementation, 173
   phased implementation, 173
Mirror sets, 87
Modems, **112**, 280
   16550 UART chip, 109, **112**
   configuration, 108–110, 108
   I/O addresses, 108–109
   interrupt address, 108
   serial port IRQ, 109
   shared pools, 209
   troubleshooting, 271–272, **284**

MPK (multiprocessor kernel), 41–42
Multimode fiber-optic cable, 18, 206, **218**.
    See also Fiber-optic cable.
Multipartite viruses, 126
Multiprocessor kernel. *See* MPK.
Multistation access unit. *See* MAU.

N

National Computer Security Association.
    See NCSA.
NBTSTAT tool, 72, 276–277, **314**
NCP (Network Control Protocol), 102
NCSA (National Computer Security
    Association), 125
NDPS (NetWare Distributed Print
    Services), 43
NDS (Novell Directory Services), 40, 48,
    52, 121, **296**
Near-line storage, 93
net use command, 229, **235**
NetBEUI (NetBIOS Extended User
    Interface), 59, 104, 148, **305**
NetBEUI Frame. *See* Windows NT NBF.
NetBIOS Extended User Interface.
    See NetBEUI.
NetPIPE utility, 211
Netscape Communicator for NetWare, 43
Netscape FastTrack Web server, 43
NETSTAT utility, 72, 275–276, **286**, **314**
NetWare (Novell), 40–45, **296**
    CAPTURE command, 229, **235**
    external network numbers, 267
    map command, 229
    NWAdmin utility, 228
    security attributes, 119, 121–122
NetWare Administrator. *See* NWAdmin.
NetWare Client32, **296**
NetWare Directory Services. *See* NDS.
NetWare Distributed Print Services.
    See NDPS.
NetWare Peripheral Architecture.
    See NWPA.
Network Client Administrator Wizard
    (Windows NT Server), 39
Network Control Protocol. *See* NCP.
Network hub, **157**
Network identifiers, 60–61
Network interface card. *See* NIC.
Network layer (OSI), **3**, 148–150
    brouters, **4**
    routing, **3**

Network medium, 13–15
Network Neighborhood, 38
Network News Transport Protocol.
    See NNTP.
Network operating system. *See* NOS.
Network termination device (NT1), 107
Network topology, 7, 22–26
    backbone, 25
    bus, 25
    mesh, 23, **29–30**
    peer-to-peer, **28**
    ring, 24
    segment, 24
    star, 22–23
Networks
    accessibility considerations, 172
    airborne debris, 170
    available equipment identification, **177**
    baselines, **219**, 224
    benchmark testing, 211
    bus topology, **304**
    business requirement evaluation,
        166, **175**
    cabling scenarios, 195
    capacity planning, 217
    climate tolerances, 170, **179–180**,
        244, 265
    component baseline, 210–211
    connectivity, 172
    data communications fees, **177**
    devices, 190–194
    diagnostic testing, 244–245
    direct costs, 168
    downtime, 280
    electromagnetic interference, 171
    emergency response plan for, 225
    equipment compatibility
        determination, 166–167
    equipment downtime scheduling,
        184–185
    equipment identification, 169, **176**,
        185–194
    growth planning, 217
    implementation checklist, 196
    installation plans, 170
    line conditioners, 171
    management consoles, 245
    mesh topology, **303**
    migration plan, 173
    monitoring, 243

one-time implementation, 173
partial implementation, **198**
peripheral placement, 207–208, **218**
phased implementation, 173, 184
physical security, 172–173, **178**
remote access setup, 208–210
ring topology, **304**
serial connectors, 186
site preparation, 185
staging area, 194–195
star topology, **304**
structure, 12
system stage, **202**
system upgrades, 216–217
TCO (total cost of ownership), 168, **176**
testing, 280
total implementation, 185, **198**
traffic flow considerations, 172
troubleshooting, 263–264
upgrade plan, 224–225, 246, **250**
vendor coordination, 173–174
NICs (network interface cards), 20, 139–140, 167, 190–191, **201**, 245, 280, **295**, **297**
   loop-back connectors, **156**
   troubleshooting, **155**
NNTP (Network News Transport Protocol), 76, **297**
Nodes, **82**
Nondestructive viruses, 124
Nonviral destructive programs, 128–129. *See also* viruses.
   logic bombs, 129
   trojan horses, 129
   worms, 128–129
Normal tape backup, **94**
Norton AntiVirus, 128
NOS (network operating system), 36, 86, 193–194, 224
   alterations to, 226
   LAN security, 207
   security measures for, 118
Novell Bindery, 40
Novell Directory Service. *See* NDS.
Novell NetWare 4.x, 40–45
Novell NetWare 5, 41–44
Novell NetWare Client, **51–52**
Novell Storage Services. *See* NSS.
NSS (Novell Storage Services), 42–43
NTDS (Windows NT Directory Services), 48
Nuisance viruses, 124
NWAdmin utility (NetWare Administrator), 45, 228
NWPA (NetWare Peripheral Architecture), 41

O

Offline storage. *See* Tape backup.
Open Shortest Path First. *See* OSPF.
Open Systems Interconnect. *See* OSI.
OS/2 Server, 47, **51**, **296**
OSI (Open Systems Interconnect), 56, 207
   Application layer, 152, **163**, **307**
   architecture, 138
   Data Link layer, 142–148, 159–160
   device layer identification, **197**
   IEEE 802 specifications, 145
   Network layer, 148–150
   Physical layer, 139–142, **156**
   Presentation layer, 152
   reference model, 138
   Session layer, 152
   Transport layer, 150–151, 161
OSPF (Open Shortest Path First), 149

P

Packet Internet Groper. *See* Ping.
Packet-filtering firewalls, 131
PAP (Password and Authentication Protocol), 104
Passwords, 120, **132**, **234**, **299**, **300**
   policies, 122–123
   as a security breach, 227
   security model, **132**
Patch cables, 18–19
Patch panels, 19
Patches, 240–241, **249–250**
PBX (private branch exchange), 108
PC-cillin, 128
PCI (Peripheral Component Interconnect) Hot Plug, 42
PDC (primary domain controller), 37
Peer-to-peer network topology, 22, **28**, **295**
Peripheral Component Interconnect. *See* PCI.
Physical address. *See* MAC address.
Physical layer (OSI), 139–142, **156**
Ping (Packet Internet Groper) utility, 72, **81**, 149, 273

PKIS (Public Key Infrastructure
   Services), 44
Plain old telephone service. *See* POTS.
Plug-and-Play. *See* PnP.
PM (preventative maintenance), 238, 254
   documenting, 238
   equipment rotation, 239
   maintenance schedule, 238
   rotation schedule, **248**
PnP (Plug-and-Play), 267
Point-to-Point Protocol. *See* PPP.
Point-to-Point Tunneling Protocol.
   See PPTP.
Policies and procedures manual, 225
Polymorphic viruses, 126
POP3 (Post Office Protocol 3), 70
POTS (plain old telephone service), 108
PPP (Point-to-Point Protocol), 101–103,
   111, **113**, 144, **219**, **298**, **313**
PPTP (Point-to-Point Tunneling Protocol),
   103–105, **111**, **299**
   control connection, 104–105
   TCP/IP and, 105
   tunneling, 105
Pre-emptive multitasking, 36
Presentation layer (OSI), 152
Preventative maintenance. *See* PM.
PRI (primary rate ISDN), 107
Primary domain controller. *See* PDC.
Primary rate ISDN. *See* PRI.
Print servers, 194, 271
Printer ports, **312**
Private branch exchange. *See* PBX.
Proxy servers, 78–79, 295, 298
   firewalls, 131
   gateways, 21
PSTN (public switched telephone
   network), 108, **113**
Public Key Infrastructure Services.
   See PKIS.
Public switched telephone network.
   See PSTN.
Public-key encryption, 123–124

R

Radio buttons, 4
RAID (Redundant Array of Inexpensive
   Disks), 36, 86
   controllers, 242
   Level 0, **96**, **297**

Level 1, 38, 87–88, **94**, **298**
Level 4, 88
Level 5, 38, 88–89, **97**, **315**
RAS (Remote Access Service), 37–38
rconsole utility (NetWare 5), 44–45
Redundant Array of Inexpensive Disks.
   See RAID.
Registry (Windows NT Server), 40
Remote access
   remote control, 209
   setup, 208–210
   shared modem pools, 209
   virtual PC sessions, 209
   VPN (virtual private networks), 209
Remote connectivity, 110
Removable hard drives, 93
Removable media storage, 93
Repeaters, 140–141, **157**
Resource ledger, 254
RG58 A/U cable, 15
Ring topology, 24, **304**
RIP (Routing Information Protocol), 149
RJ-11 connectors, **198**
RJ-45 connectors, 190, 195
Root servers, 66
Routers, **3**, 20, 58, 148–149, **160**, 194,
   203, **305**
   troubleshooting, 269
   upgrading, **231**
Routing Information Protocol. *See* RIP.

S

SAM (Security Account Manager), 37, 121
Santa Cruz Operation. *See* SCO.
SAS (secure authentication services), 44
"saving the state," 131
SCO (Santa Cruz Operation) Unix, 47
SCSI (small computer system interface),
   86, **96**, **302**
   50-pin high-density connectors,
      188–189
   68-pin high-density connector, 189
   80-pin single connector attachment,
      189, **197**, **199**, **200**
   Centronics 50-pin connector, 188
   connectors, 187–190
   DB-25 SCSI connector, 188
   fiber-channel connectors, 189
   hard drives, 242
   RJ-45 connector, 190

Tape backups **353**

type 1 connector and cable, 190
USB connectors, 190
UTP patch panel, 190
Secure authentication services. *See* SAS.
Security, 118
    audit services, 122
    authentication services, 122
    caller ID logs, 120
    data encryption, 123–124
    encryption services, 122
    equivalences, 122
    firewalls, 130–131, **132**
    Novell NetWare 5, 43
    passwords, 120, **132**, 227, **234**
    physical network security, **178**
    policies, 210
    public-key encryption, 123–124
    reference monitor, 121
    system changes, 226–227, **232**
    testing, 246
    user-level access control, **133**
    usernames, 120
    viruses, 124–128
Security Accounts Manager. *See* SAM.
Segment topology, 24
Sequenced Packet Exchange. *See* SPX.
Serial connectors, 186–187
    AUI (attachment unit interface), 186
    BNC (bayonet nut connector), 186
    DB-9 connector, 186
    DB-25 connectors, 186–187
    SCSI connectors, 187–190
Serial Line Internet Protocol. *See* SLIP.
Server Fault Tolerance. *See* SFT.
Server Manager (Windows NT Server), 39
Servers
    emergency response plan for, 225
    monitoring, 243
    troubleshooting, 269, **283**
    upgrades, 226
Session layer (OSI), 152
SFT (Server Fault Tolerance), 89
Share-level access control, **301**
Shared media protocols, 144–145
Shared modem pools, 209
Shared parity, 88
Simple Mail Transfer Protocol. *See* SMTP.
Single-mode fiber-optic cable, 18
SLIP (Serial Line Internet Protocol), 100, **313**

Small computer system interface. *See* SCSI.
SMTP (Simple Mail Transfer Protocol), 21, 63–64, 70
SNA (System Network Architecture), 21
SNMP, 70, 140, 243, 245, 263, **308**
Solaris (Sun Microsystems), 47
SONET (Synchronous Optical Network), 107
SOP (standard operating procedure), 206
Source route bridging, 143
Split seeks, 87
SPX (Sequenced Packet Exchange), 56, 151, **160–161**, **162**, **306**, **307**
Standard operating procedure. *See* SOP.
Standard router gateways, 20
Star topology, 22–23, **304**
Stateful inspection firewall, 131
Stealth viruses, 126
Stripe sets without parity, 86
Support Connection CD-ROM (Novell), 255
Switch-based networks, 143–144
Switches, 24, **157**, **159**, 192, 270, **302**, **305**
Synchronous Optical Network. *See* SONET.
System Monitor, 211
System Network Architecture. *See* SNA.
System Policy Editor (Windows NT Server), 40
System stage, **202**
System upgrades, 216–217
System V Unix, 45

T

Tape backups, 89–93, **95**, **96**, 208, 212, 220. *See also* Backup techniques.
    10-tape rotation method, 92
    archiving, 92–93
    copy backups, 90–91
    daily backups, 91
    differential backups, 91
    drive maintenance, **95**, **309**
    grandfather rotation method, 92
    incremental backups, 91, **94**
    normal backups, 90, **94**
    storage, 92–93, **310**
    tape drive maintenance, 90
    tape rotation, 91–92
    troubleshooting, 271

TCO (total cost of ownership), 168
    direct costs, 168
    indirect costs, 168–169
TCP (Transmission Control Protocol), 63,
    70–71, 151, **160–161**, **162**, **306**, **307**
    NNTP port, **76**
    Telnet port assignment, **77**
TCP/IP (Transmission Control Protocol/
    Internet Protocol), 49, 63,
    299, **306**, **309**, **314**
    nodes, **82**
    ports, 63–65
    utilities, 7
    Windows 95, 65
TDI (transport drive interface), 59
TechNet CD-ROM (Microsoft), 236, 255
Technical support, 256, **313**
*Telecommunications Engineer's Reference
    Book*, 33, 54, 84, 115, 164, 181, 204,
    222, 252, 287
Telnet, 72–72, **77**, **78**, 274–275, 304, **314**
Terminal Server (Microsoft), 50
Testing center, 2
TFTP (Trivial File Transfer Protocol), **83**,
    163, 225, 242
Thicknet, 14, 15
Thin-client (Citrix Corporation), 50
Thinnet, 14, 15, **29**, **300**
Token ring networks, 24, 27
    frame types, 57
    MAU ports, **158**
    network topology, **159**
Total cost of ownership. *See* TCO.
Tracert utility, 73, **79**, 277, **298**
Transceivers, 141–142
Transmission Control Protocol. *See* TCP.
Transparent bridging, 143
Transport drive interface. *See* TDI.
Transport layer (OSI), 150–151, 161
Trivial File Transfer Protocol. *See* TFTP.
Trojan horses, 129
Trouble calls, 256, 262
    error duplication, 259
    prioritizing, 258, **285**, **286**
    telephone responses, 257
    tracking system, 257
Troubleshooting, 259–264, **314**
    configuration errors, 266–268
    DNS (Domain Name Server), 267
    error duplication, 262
    hardware errors, 269

IP (Internet Protocol), 267, **282**
login errors, 265
modems, **284**
NetWare external network numbers, 267
persistent data errors, 265–266
philosophy, 260
point of error manifestation, 260–261
problem isolation, 261–264
servers, **283**
software errors, 268
tape backups, 271
user-caused errors, 262–265
WINS, 267
Twisted-pair cable, 15–16

U

UDP (User Datagram Protocol), 64, 71,
    150–151, **161**, **162**, **306**, **307**
UNC (universal mapping convention),
    229, **313**
Uninterruptable power source. *See* UPS.
Universal mapping convention. *See* UNC.
Universal serial bus. *See* USB.
Unix, 45–47, **51**, **296**.
Upgrades, 240, 242, 246, **249–250**
    hardware, 247, **251**
    software, 247, **250–251**
UPS (uninterruptable power source),
    171, **175**
USB (universal serial bus) connectors, 190
User Datagram Protocol. *See* UDP.
User Manager for Domains utility, 228
User-level access control, **133**, **301**
Usernames, 120, 210
Users
    access rights, 228
    account alterations, 227–228
    account naming conventions, 210
    profiles, 228, 265
    rights, 265
    software changes, 226
UTP cable, 16, 195–196
    cable runs, **311**
    category 5 cable, 195
    coaxial cable compared to, 15
    patch panels, 190

V

Vampire taps, 15
Virtual memory. *See* VM.
Virtual private networks. *See* VPNs.

Viruses, 124–128, 268. *See also* Nonviral destructive programs.
  boot sector, 125, **284**, **311**
  destructive, 124
  file-infecting, 125
  macro, 125–126
  meta, 126
  multipartite, 126
  nondestructive, 124
  nuisance, 124
  polymorphic, 126
  prevention strategies, 129–130
  signatures, 124, 240, **248**, **312**
  stealth, 126
  threat handling, **134–135**
VirusScan (McAfee), 127
VM (virtual memory), 41
VPNs (virtual private networks), 103, 209–210

W

WANs (wide area networks), 12–13, 36–37, 56
Web browsers, **78**, 100
Web sites
  CompTIA Network+ home page, 8–9
  Dr. Solomon's Anti-Virus, 127
  of equipment manufacturers, 255
  InterNIC, 66
  Microsoft, 54
  Novell, 54
  patch downloads, 240
  Symantec, 128
Wide area networks. *See* WANs.
Windows 95, 49
  net use command, 229, **235**
  NIC autodetect, 191
  System Monitor, 211
  TCP/IP, 65
Windows 98
  net use command, 229, **235**
  NIC autodetect, 191
Windows Internet Name Service. *See* WINS.
Windows NT Directory Services. *See* NTDS.

Windows NT Disk Administrator, 38
Windows NT NBF (NetBEUI Frame), 59
Windows NT Server, 36–38, 49, **51**, 296
  Administrative Wizard, 39
  Administrator account, **232**
  Entire Network icon, 38
  Event Log Service, 40
  Event Viewer, 39–40
  HOSTS file, **74**
  logon process, 120
  Network Neighborhood icon, 38
  PPTP support, 104
  pre-emptive multitasking, 36
  RAS (Remote Access Service), 37–38
  Registry, 40
  security attributes, 120–121
  Server Manager, 39
  System Policy Editor, 40
  User Manager for Domains utility, 228
  User Manager utility, 39
  user profiles, 40
Windows NT Workstation, 50, 104
WinGuard, 127
WINIPCFG utility, 71, **80–81**, 278–279
WINS (Windows Internet Name Service), 38, **53**, 67–68, **82**, **301**
  servers, 68
  troubleshooting, 267
  workstation configuration options, 67–68
Workgroup switches, 143
Workstation Manager (NetWare 5), 45
Workstations
  backups, 239
  emergency response plan for, 225
  troubleshooting, 258–259
Worms, 128–129

X

X.500 directory service, 47, 49, **52**, 313

Y

Y2K disaster recovery plan, 215

Z

Z.E.N.works (Zero Effort Networks), 42

Better, Faster, Louder!

Get certified on the go with EXAM CRAM™ AUDIO TAPES

A+ Exam Cram Audio Review
ISBN: 1-57610-541-5
$39.99 U.S. • $59.99 Canada
Four hours of audio instruction
Cassettes • Available Now

Network+ Exam Cram Audio Review
ISBN: 1-57610-534-2
$39.99 U.S. • $59.99 Canada
Four hours of audio instruction
Cassettes • Available Now

MCSE Core Four Exam Cram Audio Review
ISBN: 1-57610-631-4
$39.99 U.S. • $59.99 Canada
Four hours of audio instruction
Cassettes • Available Now

AUDIO TAPES

Hear what you've been missing with Exam Cram Audio Review tapes. Each set contains four cassettes jam-packed with the certification information you must have to pass your exams. Exam Cram Audio Review tapes can be used on their own or as a complement to our Exam Cram Study Guides, Flash Cards, and Practice Tests.

FLASH CARDS

Exam Cram Flash Cards are the pocket-sized study tool that provide key questions on one side of each card and in-depth answers on the other. Each card features a cross-reference to the appropriate chapter in the corresponding Exam Cram Study Guide or other valuable resource. Each pack includes 100 cards 100% focused on exam material, along with a CD-ROM featuring electronic versions of the flash cards and a complete practice exam.

PRACTICE TESTS

Each book contains several practice exams with electronic versions on the accompanying CD-ROM. Each practice question is followed by the corresponding answer (*why the right answers are right and the wrong answers are wrong*). References to the Exam Cram Study Guide and chapter or other valuable resource in which the topic is discussed in depth are included. The CD-ROM presents exams in an interactive format, enabling you to practice in an environment similar to that of the actual exam.

The Smartest Way to Get Certified Just Got Smarter™

The Coriolis Exam Cram Personal Trainer
An exciting new category in certification training products

The Exam Cram Personal trainer is the first certification-specific testing product that completely links learning with testing to:

- **Increase your comprehension**
- **Decrease the time it takes you to learn**

No system blends learning content with test questions as effectively as the Exam Cram Personal Trainer.

Only the Exam Cram Personal Trainer offers this much power at this price.

Its unique Personalized Test Engine provides a real-time test environment and an authentic representation of what you will encounter during your actual certification exams.

Much More Than Just Another CBT!
Most current CBT learning systems offer simple review questions at the end of a chapter with an overall test at the end of the course, with no links back to the lessons. But Exam Cram Personal Trainer takes learning to a higher level.

Its four main components are:
- The complete text of an Exam Cram study guide in an HTML format,
- A Personalized Practice Test Engine with multiple test methods

Adaptive:	25-35 questions
Fixed-length:	Four unique exams on critical areas
Random:	Each randomly generated test is unique
Test All:	Drawn from the complete database of questions
Topic:	Organized by Exam Cram chapters
Review:	Questions with answers are presented

Scenario-based questions: Just like the real thing

- A database of nearly 300 questions linked directly to an Exam Cram chapter
- Over two hours of Exam Cram Audio Review

Plus, additional features include:

- **Hint:** Not sure of your answer? Click Hint and the software goes to the text that covers that topic.
- **Lesson:** Still not enough detail? Click Lesson and the software goes to the beginning of the chapter.
- **Update feature:** Need even more questions? Click Update to download more questions from the Coriolis Web site.
- **Notes:** Create your own memory joggers.
- **Graphic analysis:** How did you do? View your score, the required score to pass, and other information.
- **Personalized Cram Sheet:** Print unique study information just for you.

MCSE Networking Essentials Exam Cram Personal Trainer
ISBN:1-57610-644-6

MCSE NT Server 4 Exam Cram Personal Trainer
ISBN: 1-57610-645-4

MCSE NT Server 4 in the Enterprise Exam Cram Personal Trainer
ISBN: 1-57610-646-2

MCSE NT Workstation 4 Exam Cram Personal Trainer
ISBN:1-57610-647-0

A+ Exam Cram Personal Trainer
ISBN: 1-57610-658-6

$69.99 U.S. • $104.99 Canada

Available: March 2000

Certification Insider Press

The <u>Smartest</u> Way to Get Certified Just Got Smarter™

Look for All of the Exam Cram Brand Certification Study Systems

ALL NEW! Exam Cram Personal Trainer Systems

The Exam Cram Personal Trainer systems are an exciting new category in certification training products. These CD-ROM based systems offer extensive capabilities at a moderate price and are the first certification-specific testing product to completely link learning with testing.

This Exam Cram Study Guide turned interactive course lets you customize the way you learn.

Each system includes:
- A Personalized Practice Test engine with multiple test methods,
- A database of nearly 300 questions linked directly to the subject matter within the Exam Cram on which that question is based.

Exam Cram Audio Review Systems

Written and read by certification instructors, each set contains four cassettes jam-packed with the certification exam information you must have. Designed to be used on their own or as a complement to our Exam Cram Study Guides, Flash Cards, and Practice Tests.

Each system includes:
- Study preparation tips with an essential last-minute review for the exam
- Hours of lessons highlighting key terms and techniques
- A comprehensive overview of all exam objectives
- 45 minutes of review questions complete with answers and explanations

Exam Cram Flash Cards

These pocket-sized study tools are 100% focused on exams. Key questions appear on side one of each card and in-depth answers on side two. Each card features either a cross-reference to the appropriate Exam Cram Study Guide chapter or to another valuable resource. Comes with a CD-ROM featuring electronic versions of the flash cards and a complete practice exam.

Exam Cram Practice Tests

Our readers told us that extra practice exams were vital to certification success, so we created the perfect companion book for certification study material.

Each book contains:
- Several practice exams
- Electronic versions of practice exams on the accompanying CD-ROM presented in an interactive format enabling practice in an environment similar to that of the actual exam
- Each practice question is followed by the corresponding answer (why the right answers are right and the wrong answers are wrong)
- References to the Exam Cram Study Guide chapter or other resource for that topic

The Smartest Way to Get Certified™